Rhetoric.

Today 9:01 AM

Morning bro. Quick idea for you that I don't think would be too difficult and you could get a Lil check.
Take all your most liked fb statuses, print them as a book and publish it.
I think it would sell ...what you think ?
*hits blunt 🙃

I'm already 2 books in

That's why I've been putting Rhetoric #ComingSoon

iMessage

Well I'm actually editing the first one and still working on the second one

Well got damn you gone slang them hoes or what nigga ? 👤😂😂

Oh ok

Hell yeah!!!!

#GreatMinds

Hell yeah lol best wishes of prosperity to ya homie !!!

      iMessage

WARNING: Alight, so boom. First of all, fix your face. This isn't the place for you to bring that imp in a hand-me-down, calcified lace-front from five years ago or hobgoblin with a beard full of Binge outlined in Dollar Tree eyeliner energy to your recreational activities. Whatever thoughts you arrived with in regard to how a book is supposed to be written, throw that shit in the trash because that's not what I'm offering to the people. I come bearing gifts of maddened comedic irreverence, salacious social commentary, and patchwork philosophies that more than likely fair far better in writing than in practical application. Nonetheless, I'm not extending an invitation for a seat at this table to any slack-jaw, trout-mouthed muthafuckas with cachectic dynamism due to a deteriorating handicapped sense of humor. Buckle up for the misadventures of a mind that I deem too much of a national treasure to go to waste. Yeah, I said it! Anyway, welcome to my stream of consciousness: My thoughts and sentient reactions to events, perceived as a continuous flow. I say that to say, this shit's all over the fucking place and I wouldn't have it any other way. Oh, and it pretty much starts off horribly because this did not start out as a book, but I promise you it gets better and more useful the further along you read. Enjoy! #NARF

Chapter 1: KARMA: kar·ma / ˈkärmə/noun: karma (in Hinduism and Buddhism) the sum of a person's actions in this and previous states of existence, viewed as deciding their fate in future existences.

15May2017

So, congratulations to me for nothing celebratory in the least. I woke up today with what can only be described as a fully-matured pimple constellation on my face. I know what you're thinking...wash your fucking pillow cases. Well, fuck you for assuming. I have washed them on a very consistent basis, but what I am faced with today...this landscape splattered with Satan's sizzling splooge is more than likely the result of the 90 Little Debbie's Honey Buns I consumed last week. Don't talk about me. Ok, you can talk about me, but just make sure you put it in prayer format. Are you a prayer warrior, prayer samurai or prayer yakuza? I ask because those are the only prayers I'll truly accept because the rest are merely Disney-powered wishful thinking. Whoa! On second thought, I'll just exfoliate and pray for myself because I don't trust that y'all's prayer knees aren't the same knees you kneel on while performing premarital mouth to genital shenanigans and shit thereby making your prayers no more powerful than Vick's Vaporub in a battle against plaque psoriasis. Just stared at Tasha Page-Lockhart's album cover art lace-front wig for longer than I should be admitting publically. It's not the kind that came with the baby hair attached, so her entire hairline looks like the weft of a track from a sew-in. Go look at it. It's from the "Here Right Now" single. Watch it turn out to be her natural hairline or some shit...egg on my face. I've been here 19 minutes and am already ready to go the fuck home, but I'm switching up my point of view. I've got a new attitude. If they want to pay me to sit here and do nothing, then gotdammit, I'll sit here and pretend to be the most industrious worker bee this hive has every spewed from its twat. Staring at this SnapChat notification knowing good and damn well it's from Team SnapChat on some Happy Mother's Day shit. Do I snatch the Band-Aid off like I'm angry and watch it now or do I let it sit, so I'll forget and get excited one drunken night thinking someone is having booty call thoughts of me? I'm a dreamer, so I'll let it sit.

If you listen to a person's music long enough and have a critical ear, you'll quickly pick up on their "thing". It's the sound or run around which their entire style is centered. You'll also detect their weaknesses. Surprisingly, they all lack something that would make them the perfect singing voice, but the genius of the singer is embracing their limitation and overcompensating in other areas. It's magical for a "sound nerd" like me. That was random, but that's what we're doing here, isn't it? If your entire fucking mood doesn't change when T-Pain's "I'm Sprung" comes on, then you need to scurry your lil ashy knees to the nearest restroom and self-satisfy that curmudgeon right on up out of your spirit because the shit is literally sonic dopamine. Teddy Pinned Her Ass Down really struggled to stick the landing on these notes without autotune, but that's neither here nor there. It's happy meal music and you will fix your face. Now playing "Fuck Up Some Commas" by Future and I imagine that his breath smells like panty stains in the morning. Don't ask. Don't tell.

Why do I feel so rebellious? Oh wait, let me stop right there. So, last night I think I had a nervous breakdown. But wait, I wasn't fucking nervous and I remained standing, so that doesn't apply here. Let's call it an emotional purge since it is extremely rare for me to be emotional. Anyway, I was all alone, so there was no one there to diagnose the gut-punch to my soul that I experienced, but it was probably just a meltdown...you know an adult temper tantrum of sorts. Either way, tears were shed. Ugly, face balled up into a fist to the point that I could no longer make use of my nostrils for fear of inhaling tears. I've been living an overall sloppy life and living it on autopilot. Imagine that. But that wakeup call though? Let's just say that sometimes you do indeed have to encourage yourself and I did just that. I destroyed some things. Threw some things away and put other things into perspective and I'm back in the fight. Mind you this meltdown lasted all of 15 seconds because I ain't no bitch, but it happened and I'm centered, focused and back in tune with my destiny. That's the thing about solitude addiction. There's never a shoulder to cry on or sweet ear in which to vomit my woes. Nonetheless, my aloneness is a weapon at this point and I'm wielding it like I'm flapping my flaccid phallus against my thighs in a high-powered interpretive dance with The Sprinkler as the hinge to it all. Catch that visual.

I think my gooch just had a mini seizure. Scared the shit out of me. Anyway, as a church kid, I would just like to say thank you to all of the entertainers who never spent their formative years in the Sunshine Band for their off-brand interpretations of what church is like. I love when I hear you try to infuse it into your music. I love it because that synthetic anointing is like excessive ice in a fountain drink. And don't get me started on your feigned catching of the spirit...because worshiping the God of the Bible should always look like the Double Dream Hands man going forth in an A – selection of praise dancing to the Macarena. ALWAYS.

Contrary to popular belief, it's the dudes who look like Lenny Kravitz during his "Romeo Blue I wanna be an R&B singer, but I have no vibrato" phase who have all the money. Study to show thyself approved ladies. I just put you up on some major free game. Now, you may have to endure S-curl stains on your pillow cases and jeans with bedazzled ass pockets and quite possibly a fanny pack, but your edges will be laid to rest like an Egyptian pharaoh and he'll only cheat on you with the time he spends stitching together your matching outfits for Comic Con, but you're now EA Sports. In the muthafuckin' game!!!!! You're welcome.

Everything is on my nerves right now...especially the sound of the people's voices surrounding me. How are you gonna be saddity with hog maws suctioned to the space below your eyes? Has this ever happened to you? You are not guilty of any crime other than sharing space and time. Your synthetic joy sponsored by an overpriced caffeinated beverage is an allergen to my peace because you are being braggadocios in your performance. There is little to no authenticity emitting from your showiness. You seek an audience to validate your mood and when none can be found, you go from place to place in search of applause. I want to punch you in the back of the throat.

I've been thinking things that lead to deeper thought. An exploration of my own emotional ineptitude you could say. I'm quite possibly perturbed, but who knows or even cares? Everyone is happily petty and disconnected. These disjointed interactions, made possible by inanimate objects, have us all spinning out of control in search of an unwavering foundation. It's that nagging innocence of bliss addiction. That wanderlust of affirmation that keeps us super glued to that 4.7 inches in size with a 16:9 resolution of 1334x750 (326 ppi, minus one row of pixels). I'm ambivalent most times.

I just cussed my shoulder out with my mouth scrunched up like an angry, Black mama who doesn't want people all in her business while she's filleting the flesh off of her kids with a gourmet cuss out. Why? Because it kept diddy bopping to Shining by Beyoncé x DJ Khaled and Jay Z. Sitcho friendly ass still up in this job!!!! Since shuffle brought Beyoncé up, I really want her to make a singing album doing all those backflips with her voice like she did on "Emotions". ALL SINGERS SHOULD SPEND TIME IN THE BLACK CHURCH, so they can learn how to emote the fuck outta some ad libs. Placement is cool, but passion is everything. And Dear Jay Z, if you want to be the Rolling Stones of HipHop, I'm going to need you to reconnect with clapping on 2 and 4, and infuse your lyrics with some deeply life-affirming and thought-provoking punchlines. That is all.

Post Script: I'm mad that the spell check on this computer's version of Microsoft Word picked up on the fact that I omitted the accent aigu from Beyoncé's name. I don't wanna fight. Alright?

The amount of thirst…are we still saying thirty to describe people desperate for attention or bussit? Eve was literally rapping about being thirsty last century. Has it been displaced and replaced? I'm not quite sure, so forgive me if I'm dated. But the amount of thirst on the internet is palpable. I read comments and imagine 95% of the people are typing with one hand and holding their genitalia up on a serving tray like that sassy emoji everyone used to convey feistiness before the emoji definition circulated. I love it though. VIVA LA WHORES!!!! They're your sexy bits and yours to smash or be smashed to smithereens at your leisure. DMs are the new Pornhub! My shit is dry though. God grant me the serenity to have a good enough attitude toward the world to receive unsolicited nudes on all of my social media platforms.

Everyone keeps trying to engage me about Cuarenta Y Cinco and I simply can't muster the interest. I know very well that he's playing Russian Roulette with the entire US Armed Forces and we could all very well be incinerated by some nuclear hanky panky at any moment, but I simply can't surrender my peace to the bullshit. I don't have it in me to wrestle against flesh and blood anymore, so I figure I might as well start practicing a sensationalized pop-culture caricature of voudon (an Afro-Caribbean religion that originated in Haiti, though followers can be found in Jamaica, the Dominican Republic, Brazil, the United States and elsewhere or a religion that began in West Africa and the Caribbean whose basis lies in a merging of Yoruba beliefs and practices with elements from Roman Catholic traditions). With my strong bone structure and shoddy painting skills, I'm sure I can at the very least summon an imp to ball in the mix like everythang this administration done stole, Lil KeKe done fixed.

Freedom of expression? Expression as the litmus test for liberty and justice for all. But why does expression have to look like it stinks? Why does it look like an infested crack whore reincarnated as a gender fluid street urchin? Why does it look like Holiday Heart in a waist trainer with frayed seams? Why does it have look like it sells expired, off-brand boy pussy?

Chapter 2: FATE: /fāt/ noun: fate; plural noun: Fates; plural noun: the Fates 1. The development of events beyond a person's control, regarded as determined by a supernatural power. "Fate decided his course for him"

16May2017: I feel like dried up cum in a dirty, discarded tube sock this morning, so if someone tells me this is the day that the Lord has made, I'm going to be side-eyeing Jesus' pregame festivities for when morning comes. But anyway, here goes...everything.

OMMFG I'm so tired of people telling me to STAY WOKE!! Like do you not know that I've been WOKE my entire life. I'm sleepy as fuck! But seriously, there is no going back once the veil has been lifted...unless you just make willful ignorance your modus operandi in all things. You can't unsee what lies beneath the thinly cloaked layer of fantasy that blots out reality. I'm forever policing this society for the many tricks it has up its sleeves whereas race is concerned. I'm not dozing off, but what I won't do is remain in a constant state of boundless, undirected anger. THAT shit is detrimental to all the healths. So while I'm peacefully minding my business and carving out my niche in this revolution, you stay woke and stand watch a little bit. I've earned the right to power nap from time to time.

I would sincerely appreciate people taking the time to consider how their mouths come across on camera. I shouldn't be ducking and dodging the gotdamn screen on my phone because your breath looks maliciously non-temperate and like it might chip away at my soul. Duck lips are not complimentary to every face. Everything below your eyebrows already looks like a cluster of war wounds and you actually think puckering is the key to attractiveness? Good luck with that. Let's just pray you don't wind up some overshared meme or Twitter hashtag.

Flavor is a right and not a privilege because God provided the seasons, so add some spice to your life. There is an upswing in individuals who can't tell the difference between existing and living. There are tons of catch phrases that urge us to take life by the horns, seize the day, go forth and be great, so if you're waking up each day with the mindset of just getting through the day, refocus your energy. Life is meant to be lived. I'm not suggesting that you have to ignore any circumstance that is weighing heavily on you. Just don't allow your present circumstances to transform your mind into believing that a shift in your perspective about the possibility of overcoming every obstacle that stands in the way of your happiness, progress and eventual success is not conceivable. Oh, and just say no to unseasoned poultry...and wash your fucking meat before you cook it you scallywags.

I learned to sing the hymns of a life spent kneeling in surrender to sin and the songs I sang prevented my vanishing. But when the coast had cleared and the Devil was busy smirking, my light was shining brighter then and I found myself ministering to madness. And if a river runs through it how can it ever be arid? And if the love is pursuant to lust, then what are we doing? So don't cry for time spent. And none of these walls would ever speak.

The message for today is loose lips sink ships...or in the case of Cuarenta Y Cinco, thin...thin flappy ass lips launch battleships. Oh the emails, the emails, the emails. That's all we ever hear from that wretched, decrepit mouth is "But what about the emails?"...oh wait...SQUIRREL!!!!!

17May2017

So this morning I'm discovering what the word BLOATED means on a personal level. I'm not even sure that I was aware that men could BE bloated. NONETHELESS, this disco inferno in my lower abdomen has my toes tucked under the balls of my feet like I'm at war with the nerve endings in my penis to prevent a minute man mishap.

Everyone is so caught up in a frenzy, not realizing that the lives we live are simply a struggle to exist within the imaginations of men who think their plans for this world supersede the plans set in motion by the omnipotent, divine spirit (cultures, societies, religion, government, etc.). I laugh because not even the "mother of all bombs" unsettled my spirit. They're playing chess with our lives and we're playing checkers according to their plans. How will that ever work in our favor? What would happen if we all took our pieces off the board? They'd have to play among themselves while we took our collective ball and went the fuck home. POWER TO THE PEOPLE!!!!!

Sometimes I get the feeling that a lot of people are suffering from undiagnosed fetal nicotine syndrome. Now I'm not quite sure if that's a real thing or not, but it deserves research because there has to be an underlying cause for the copious amounts of unmitigated fuckery I witness. And I surely see a number of pregnant bellies being polluted by the inhalation of cigarette carcinogens. You can't tell me that constantly being exposed to shit that contains more than four thousands fucking chemicals didn't fuck a whole lot of y'all up. Nigga, do you know what the fuck cyanide and lead are? BITCH, cyanide can cause you to have headaches, dizziness, an increased heart rate, shortness of breath, excessive vomiting, seizures, low blood pressure, loss of consciousness, and a muthafuckin' heart attack!!!!! This is the shit that happens to you after you've already been born, so imagine how it would fuck you up if you're still developing!!!!! And lead will fuck up a baby's bone and muscle growth. That shit will fuck up a developing infant's muscle coordination, nervous system, hearing, speech & language. It'll delay development and cause seizures and unconsciousness as well. That's only two fucking chemicals in cigarettes that can fuck a developing baby all the way up and them bitches contain at least SIXTY cancer-causing compounds. So the next time you have to hit somebody with a stern side-eye because it's apparent that something is wrong with their yang, ask that muthafucka if their momma smoked during her pregnancy with them...and if you were personally offended by this, there's a strong possibility you were huffing and puffing and blowing your womb down during pregnancy.

I loathe the politeness Double Dutch pedestrians sometimes try to play with motorists. Maybe it's a safety tactic to avoid being run over, but you have the fucking right of way for Pete's sake. While I appreciate your courtesy, I'm driving and you're scuffling along in some $1 Old Navy flip flops. Tuck that ass the rest of the way under, accelerate your gait, and get where you're going ma'am. I have no intention of running you over.

Your gift is how others experience the God in you. It may be something that society has not yet been able to put a barcode and price tag on, but it dwells within you. I fully understand the groupthink mentality. If you're unfamiliar, "Groupthink is a psychological phenomenon that occurs within a group of people in which the desire for harmony or conformity in the group results in an irrational or dysfunctional decision-making outcome." But check this out, fuck that group. It pains me when people become so obsessed with conformity that they eventually cripple themselves into photocopied versions of what marketing and advertising wizards deem the only acceptable way to function within society. People will literally stifle their brilliant self-expression (in whatever format) to blend. That has to be a rickety, Easy Bake Oven type of hell. Don't allow fear of standing out to force you into blending in to the point that you disappear entirely.

That awkward moment when you cyberfuck someone...by way of your phone...with gifs.

Why do I feel like my goddamn hands and arms are always full? Now I know why dudes always carry gym bags and backpacks and shit! But keep it rugged, rustic or athletic. My soul hasn't been anchored in the decorative man totes that look like distressed first cousins to throw pillows just yet.

People love throwing around phrases without scaling their underlying meaning? I LOVE YOU! Well, what the fuck do you about love me? Do you simply love that I am existing on the face of this Earth or is there something specific? I MISS YOU! Well, what the fuck do you miss? NO WE CANNOT FUCK! Well, why not?

I love manual labor. Who would've thought, right? Especially the part that lets me sit with my legs gaped open, donning sweat stains in salacious crevices, all mannish and shit.

I love everything about Mary J. Blige except her square-framed glasses, her Dumber & Dumber bowl cut...and her singing voice. Don't get me wrong, she makes good music, but it's the equivalent of five-star accoutrements and Spam as the primary cuisine.

I love lyrics that I can read like a narrative, but Eminem doesn't write raps. He writes essays that rhyme...graphic novels with Napoleon Complex, if you will. I love that Tupac cussed at least one muthafucka out on every one of his albums. He was such a Janice. Still posthumously cussing people out and shit.

One beef --> shit happens. Two beefs --> ok, ya name is hot. Three beefs --> watch out lil bih.

I pride myself on not telling people what they want to hear and when they expect the unexpected, I'm expected as hell. Keep 'em on their toes with their gooch at half-mast.

I was deep in the throes of you got me fucked up whereas these romphims (rompers for men) are concerned. The idea of grown men running around dressed like Oompa Loompa's was a no, but then a couple of pics surfaced that gave them more of a fashionable utilitarian aesthetic if your oxymoron will allow rather than a Coachella man-wedgy vibe and now visions of casually flaunting my dick print in public are dancing in my head!

I hate not being the best. HATE IT!!!! And it bothers me when those I give a fuck about are okay not being the best. I mean damn! Even if you know beyond a shadow of doubt that you'll never be the best, at least be the best at TRYING TO BE THE BLOODY BEST!!!!!!

Who did it? Who got the Vocal Bible out here lookin' like a Black Cynthia Doll from the Rugrats? Which fuckin' Janice loosed Satan?

Never underestimate the power of smelling good. This lady's body language is telling me that her clitoris is licking her pussy lips.

I'm hoarse and right now my voice sounds like winter-fresh Chapstick for vaginas.

Chapter 3: ATMOSPHERE: at·mos·phere /ˈatməsˌfir/ noun 2. The pervading tone or mood of a place, situation, or work of art. "The hotel is famous for its friendly, welcoming atmosphere"

18May2017

Soul-Snatching:

In this life, it's almost impossible to avoid the shit stains of people's insecurities, weak will, self-sabotaging timidity in matters of romance and all-around, lovesick fucktardedness. As such, ever-so-often you'll find yourself on the landing strip of the crosshairs of some dumb bastard who has chosen to interrogate you about a muthafucka who's been dragging them through the mud by their genitalia far before you became their love's object of affection. I don't write the rules. That's just the way muthafuckas act. You'll notice I have implicated you in entertaining the advances of their boo thang, but that doesn't mean that one day you might get a text message, an inbox, a DM or, God forbid, a phone call from this slack-jaw somebitch asking you, peep this, about what intentions the person they're so-called involved with has for you. Now, those of us with more than a Reading Rainbow/Your Baby Can Read education clearly understand that this is about the dumbest, most pathetic and misdirected course of action any self-respecting human being can take. Yet, in all the history of dumb shit people do in the name of love, good dick, or wet pussy it never ceases to rank at the top of the totem pole of nonviolent offenses. Therefore, just as you've been tasked to entertain the meanderings of this Bubba Gump dumb protagonist in the saddest love story to ever grace the pages of unwritten history, I hereby dub you with the unfettered permission to snatch every morsel of soul within this bastard's body! I want you to not only denigrate the unmitigated gall of this bitch-ass bitch or fuck boy, but I also want you to desecrate the swamp pussy from which he/she slithered! One would think that trying to check the tootsie of your so-called love interest's endearment would've been coat checked in middle school or some shit, but sadly there are still adults roaming the face of the earth who would rather confront the desired as opposed to the one with which he/she is supposed to be in a committed relationship. Bemoan her tattered edges. Belittle his hard-knock life, duckbilled platypus feet. Ridicule her jalopy booty and low-hanging outer labia. Massacre the barren wasteland that is his bank account. But most of all, make sure that every ounce of his/her self-respect is left balled up in the fetal position regretting the moment he/she made the unwise decision to ever come at you with that glorified bullshit! But don't get yourself killed. People are unhinged and eager these days. The end.

(The below is unrelated to the above)

A muthafucka just asked me if he knew me from city or county. I didn't press the issue because the muthafucka was on a bike and his shirt was on backwards, but apparently I need to comb my hair.

"Separation of church and state" is a phrase used by Thomas Jefferson and others expressing an understanding of the intent and function of the Establishment Clause and Free Exercise Clause of the First Amendment to the Constitution of the United States which reads: "Congress shall make no law respecting an establishment of religion, or prohibiting the free exercise thereof...". Romans 13 King James Version (KJV): "Let every soul be subject unto the higher powers. For there is no power but of God: the powers that be are ordained of God. 2 Whosoever therefore resisteth the power, resisteth the ordinance of God: and they that resist shall receive to themselves damnation." Am I the only one who sees the problem here? So the God places governmental officials in positions of power, but the church is supposed to be separate from the government that prints "in God we trust" on currency and forces people to swear on the Holy Bible before giving testimony in a court of law. Shit seems flawed. And yes, I'm aware that non-Christians are supposed to be offered a text suitable or proper in the circumstances to their faith, and for non-theists, they are supposed to have the option to assert strongly and publicly whatever solemn promise, often invoking a divine witness, regarding their future action or behavior to which they adhere. It still seems as though there are a few glitches in the design of the matrix that have long been overlooked.

Watchful eyes. What if storms are spirits? Burdens cascading down in nauseating droplets of melancholy. Salutations from the underbelly of depravity. Watchful eyes. Basking in the technicalities of erasure. Remnants. Faintness. Blotted crumbs. Open fire on dreams skipping in the atmosphere. Watchful eyes. Staring at the truth and refusing to see it is the sickness of delusion.

I LOOK LIKE SCAR FROM THE SIDE.

19May2017

Monogamy:

Shakira famously and gutturally sang the phrase "hips don't lie", but in the case of infidelity, neither do titanium erections and goopy pussy saliva! I don't know when, how, or why it happened, but sometime during the course of human history, we convinced ourselves that once we selected a mate for life our sexual attractions to others ceased and desisted. That's about the dumbest shit I've ever heard. Some will argue that monogamy is a choice and one of the greatest expressions of love. Well, bravo because I don't want to. I think it makes more sense than anything to cut the umbilical cord on that shit once you're no longer interested in a person. Why? Because if you're in a marriage that is anorexic of romance and lust, y'all are just two roommates going half on bills and shit. Thanks for the good times. Nice knowing you. Please stay in touch. You have my number, good day (or night, depending). I'm not about to sit up and look you in the face and neither my crotch nor my heart has a flutter. While I appreciate that love matures and transforms, the fear of being alone just isn't haunting me just yet.

It would seem to me that once you have chosen the person with which you are (hypothetically) going to spend the rest of your life with, due to the fact that your mind, body, and soul have developed a hankering for oneness with this person, you would no longer be aroused by others. However, we all know that couldn't be further from the truth. No, I've never been married. No, I'm not trying to tell you how marriage works. I'm telling you what's good with that creep life. Believe it or not, I'm not a cheater. I believe breaks are breaks and timeouts are timeouts and time apart is time apart and if we're taking any of those or their equivalents, then there's gonna be a whole lotta shakin' goin' on, but that doesn't mean I want you all in my business. Sorry for that tangent. Actually and personally, I don't believe in breaks and all that kiddie pool bullshit, but speaking in the first person and acting like I've been there was easier. A fuckin' break. I'm not interested. I hang up when someone asks me to hold on during a phone call. What I'm getting at, overall, is that I understand why people feel the urge to cheat. There are times when you crave the comfort of something familiar and there are times when you crave the excitement of something new.

Anyway, I have been in a few long-term relationships and just like with bread, when the shit gets stale no amount of butter, jelly, or Philadelphia Cream Cheese can reinvigorate it unless you're absolutely starving. At that point, you'd eat a kitchen sponge though. I've often heard married couples refer to their spouses as the love of their life and that may very well be true, but lust is a horse of an entirely different color. You see, lust is the poster child for reckless abandon. Lust stares karma in the face and laughs because the muthafucka is sociopathic. Lust was born barren of fucks to give. Try as you might to resist, but when someone arouses you, if the right thing is going wrong in your relationship, somebody is getting every ounce of it that you have to offer.

Monogamy is a mythical phenomenon created by ugly people anyway. I could be wrong, but I just don't believe anyone with options has been faithful in a marriage. Somebody got jacked off or their bean flicked like a cigarette butt a time or two. I don't think I could live with or wake up to the same face for the rest of my life someone for the rest of my life. The end.

Terrence Crutcher: I'm just at a place where I can't be more outraged than the family of the victim anymore. The energy investment sips my soul like soup. If what they are preaching is reform for the Tulsa Police Department instead of burning that bitch down and going on a witch-hunt for Betty Shelby and anyone else connected with the murder and cover-up, so they can beat the brakes off of them, then I'll support them in that. Apparently, that's what they need for their hearts and minds to heal and be at ease. I have fucking emotional PTSD from absorbing the flood of mixed emotions that come from account after account of videotaped, police murder of unarmed, Black people. My natural instinctive state has been left tattered. Don't call me to tear up the neighborhood YOU LIVE IN or any of that irky, ineffective, dumb, reactionary bullshit y'all like to do as "retaliation"! Holla at me when you're at your enough is enough. I'm just not here for the bitching about it on Facebook and impotent ass protests...not in 2017. Try me next year.

Dear Certain White Ladies,

Y'all have to stop with these conflicted ass hairstyles. What the fuck is up with this smashed and/or slicked in the front and this frazzled, fandangled, ratted ass tooted up nest of Aquanet in the back look? It's literally from 90s trailer parks. Stop it. They don't even want it back. How does this happen? What is the breaking point that drives you to mutilate your hair and wreak havoc on your overall appearance in this fashion? But this hairstyle pales in comparison to the old, white lady flat-top that makes them look like they've munched more carpet in their lives than a Dirt Devil. That cut combined with a robust fupa and a burgundy dye job convinces me their tongues are seasoned with convalescent vagina secretions, which is fine since their husbands are more than likely popping Viagara, so they can pay for happy endings at the massage parlor.

"Anything is possible when you sound Caucasian on the phone." – Savanna Tomlinson

Where is this girl? What is she doing with her life right now because I'm thoroughly impressed by her level of awareness? She is indeed a profoundly wise young woman; a true theoretician.

20May2017

While I may never be able to star in a low budget movie about my life when I'm 60, but if such a movie is ever made, don't y'all dare hire a 40-year old who has aged well to play me in my 20s.

I just feel like if people aren't talking about me centuries after I transmogrify from life to whatever's next, then I never existed and, no, I'm not changing my mind on that and, yes, this is a feeble attempt at forcing fate's hand to elevate me to fame and acclaim. A closed mouth...

People keep telling me that I'm a difficult person to be friends with, but I just don't feel like anything worth having comes easily.

A white girl on Netflix's "Unbreakable Kimmy Schmidt" just called a white boy woke. What the fuck we're not about to allow is the appropriation of the movement to the backdrop of kumbaya and yoga pants and shit.

I never thought legionnaires was a good name for a disease because it sounds to posh, elite and wealthy. Disease should sound poor...like Chlamydia, Gonorrhea, Hepatitis or Diarrhea. And not because only poor people get diseases, but because diseases leave you in poor health. This was a man-bun thought.

I was beginning to think I had become boring, but the reality of the situation is the conditions have to be right for me to be interested.

21May2017

Saturdays. He always had a deep, seething hatred for Saturdays. He hated their smell and the lower vibration activities in which people loved to engage both in the morning and during the night. He loathed being responsible for drafting his own agenda. He was the simplest of men...monochromatic in dress...linear in thought. He loved the scent of peppermint and fetish porn starring women of semi-average height. He lied about his age habitually, making himself older to be taken more seriously. He hated people who rode the motorized scooters at Walmart because they're fat and have knees suffering from debilitating angst and depression. He hated the smell of public restrooms...especially when they were freshly cleaned. Diluted lilac and bariatric surgery drainage were never a pleasant olfactory combination. He hated the art of the upsell. Did he ask for liability coverage on the filtration caps for whatever the fuck it is you're repairing? No, he did and will not. It is not his pedigree. He was a mechanic by trade, but sold weed out of his auto shop just to feed his adrenaline addiction. He was humbled by the lessons he learned from his friends; lessons that should've been taught by his father, but that lowlife fucker smoked his instructional video capabilities away in meth-laced binges as often as he could. He often bathed from the very same sink that he allowed sex workers to use once they'd finished singing lullabies to his genitalia. He was one of those people who recklessly added salt to prepackaged foods before tasting them because he really didn't give a fuck about his body as long as his soul was gardened. The end.

I "wish these people would shut the fuck up" far too often in life.

We could've been people's hashtag goals, but you kept using red in place of read and I'm scary of it.

So I just had an actual interview with myself because my sanity, like most people, is like socks with holes in them. In the interview, which had no questions and only a single answer because the greater portion of it took place in a nanosecond within my mind, I said this: I have always had a fascination with words and how I can put them together to create a proverbial solar system of possible images in people's minds. I will admit that it gives me a sense of control, so even if I'm not in control, the person who is has to bend to the will of my control based upon the words I use on them..."on them" is very significant. People often ask me to do videos and it's not that I don't like videos, but what I'm good at is selling you millions of options with my words, so if you see me do it, then you are robbed of that.

Why do I tweet when no one's looking? And if you're a part of those struggly 212 followers, you are indeed somebody...just not to me...on Twitter, but I dare you to unfollow me. Don't you think I deserve you even though I don't value you...on Twitter?

Triston for Dummies

@ApatheticKarma

ᔛ 423K Vine Loops

157 FOLLOWING   **212** FOLLOWERS

TWEETS   TWEETS & REPLIES   MEDIA   LIKES

 Triston for Dummies @Apa... · 11s ˅
This is me dropping her off to go
make bowls of cereal for her nine
kids by seven men. God sent me
an angel...with loose labia
minora.

Chapter 4: AURA: au·ra / ˈôrə/ noun: aura; plural noun: aurae; plural noun: auras; 1. The distinctive atmosphere or quality that seems to surround and be generated by a person, thing, or place. "The ceremony retains an aura of mystery"

I know I saw a video about this, but have you ever truly thought about how unsettling it is to get a knock on your door in 2017? Unannounced visitors in the 90s weren't that jarring unless you sold drugs or hung out with people who sold drugs and thereby knew how to cleanup an entire living room to showroom standards in under 30 seconds...or so I've heard, read and seen (on video, of course, because I used to take communion and am pure of mind, body, heart, soul and spirit). So yeah when someone knocks on my door without calling first (and it must be a phone call because you can't text me to ask or tell me you're coming to my house), I bet I won't come outside either. See what I did there? Anyway, my neighbor knocked on my door after the sun had set, which is already fuckin' offensive and instantly makes me angry to the level of Satan... SURPRISE!!!!! There is no rest of the story. It was just somewhat of a commercial break, if you will.

I've been trying to figure out why people still talk to me since I was five years old. #MySeauxCalledLife

(1) Her: Stop that! You went to church this morning lmao

Me: I didn't even watch church in tweets.

(2) Her: PayPal? MoneyGram? Walmart to Walmart? I need to send a Green Dot card... How we doin' this?
Me: You can send money via Facebook Messenger at no cost whatsoever.
Her: Don't do it... real talk... they jacked my friend for $2500 for a whole week...
Explanation: he was trying to send me $300 and they put a hold on his account (which had $2500 in it). The hold prohibited him from using the account for 7 days...
Me: Sounds like your friends account was irky shenanigans to begin with. I've had no problems whatsoever. Post Script: A hold and jacked aren't even distant cousins.

Her2: Bamm, I'm sick of you! HAHAHAHAHAHA

Me: I don't know why I am the way that I am, but I could tell your scent from a rose on the grain...or whatever Seal mumbled through those facial scars he acquired during his time as a member of a Compton street gang.

(3) Her; Hemlock Valley, British Columbia send them my way lol

Him: Lol you say that now

Me: *Slaps hands against thighs in juvenile fashion* You sound like a murder mystery waiting to happen.

(4) Her: What is wrong with you?

Me: The government won't legalize marijuana and prostitution for the criminally insane among us.

My battery percentage is rarely low in the morning when I'm not ugly.

22May2017

I didn't watch the Billboard Music Awards last night because I haven't had any type of cable transmission coming to my home since they found out I'd been receiving it for free ninety-nine for the past five years, but anyway. What I do know is that all of the Drake haters, detractors and self-made enemies are somewhere pouting like a toddler who can't seem to bully their parent into buying each useless thing they pick up and present for purchase in the grocery store. I get it. It sucks to see someone you think (keyword) you're better than, but others don't agree, achieving all of the successes you think (keyword) you deserve instead of them, but guess what... TOUGH TITTY, so SUCKLE HARDER! Let that man be great in his own lane because unless y'all are conjoined musical twins, you should have your own fuckin lane and you should be filling that lane with fans that'll buy your music and help the rest of us understand why you're so great and deserving. Now get in the studio and make some hate music with your pants saggin'. Warning, if you get in that bitch and just mumble or repeat the same line over and over again with ad libs shouted in the background at full volume, be prepared for a life of rented jewelry and video vixens with malignant belly fat orbiting their navel.

I have never been a Dave Chappelle fan EVER. Conversely, I have never been one to speak ill of him unless my opinion of his comedy was requested by one of the folks I know who swear by it. I have just never been able to get into his acting and sketch comedy because it was always too corny and predictable for me. I don't like it. But last night I watched his comedy special on Netflix and I legitimately laughed more than once. So I wanna thank God for his nervous breakdown and voyage to Zamunda because perhaps it was the great awakening he needed to let what I would classy as some Laffy Taffy wrapper shit go. Comedy Central and Adult Swim out here gassing people up and shit because they'll give a raw chicken puppet a show & drug abusers will watch it and think it's the greatest thing since Harlem Nights, but no. While it may be something to watch while you eat your feelings and ingest manmade inebriants, and you may genuinely laugh during the episodes, the shit is mad goofy in my personal opinion. Anyway, I liked it, the comedy show, but that other shit can stay locked away in the Illuminati vaults.

I hate when eye sores feel good about themselves, go on a selfie posting spree, and each image just gets more heinous and decrepit than the one before. Holup bitch. Sit down. Be humble.

9:34 AM: A lady at my job loves to stir up unnecessary drama, so I'm currently torturing her by staring at her feet every time she walks by because they look like locust exoskeletons on rotting tree bark. She's wearing sandals.

Chapter 5: FEELING: feel·ing: /ˈfēliNG/: noun: feeling; plural noun: feelings: 1. An emotional state or reaction. "A feeling of joy". 2. A belief, especially a vague or irrational one. "He had the feeling that he was being watched"

23May2017

Relationships between Black Women and Men:

It's simply impossible to discuss the modern framework of relationships between Black women and men without examining the historical framework by which they've been fortified. The relational dynamic between Black men and women dates back to the Slavery Era without question. Slave masters were intelligent enough to realize that the Black nuclear family was a source of strength and had potential for disruption to the programming of Africans to view themselves as chattel, so in order to reinforce a mentality of subservience, they would often sequester the genders from one another. This engendered a sense of division and disconnectedness. Initially Black/African men were held to be the primary labor force until 1794, when the United States Congress began to regulate the international slave trade, thusly Black/African women did not have a very significant role. That is until in March of 1794, Congress put a halt to the fitting out or building of any ship to be used for the introduction of slaves. The law further put the kibosh on ships sailing from U.S. ports for the purpose of trafficking in foreign countries, therefore ships sailing from the United States to Africa, even if of foreign registry, were required to "give bond with sufficient sureties, to the treasurer of the United States, that none of the natives of Africa, or any other foreign country or place, shall be taken on board... to be transported, or sold as slaves in any other foreign place, within nine months thereafter." Congress also went so far as to impose penalties under the new law that included fines ranging from $2,000 for outfitting a ship to $200 for an individual working on such a vessel. Were a ship found to be in violation of this law, it ran the risk of confiscation. Being the wily and shrewd "businessmen" they were, slave masters thusly found a way to weasel around the encumbrances of the new law and started "breeding" their own slaves. Slave breeding in the United States was inclusive of any application or use of an idea, belief, or method of slave ownership that aimed to systematically capacity to have an effect on the character, development, or behavior of slaves with regard to the production of offspring by a sexual process of in order to increase the abundance of valuable possessions or money of slaveholders. Slave breeding was inclusive of compliance with sexual relations between male and female slaves as the result of force or threat, actively encouraged interest or activity in pregnancies of slaves, and publicly showed preference for female slaves who could birth a relatively large number of children. The reason for which slave breeding was so aggressively advocated for was to achieve ownership of new slaves without becoming subject to the cost of purchase, and to rectify situations in which free labor could not be obtained in sufficient amounts caused by the termination of the aforementioned Atlantic slave trade. Suddenly, the role of the Black/African woman increased in importance exponentially as she would be needed to mate with the Black/African man (I could go into the introduction of the Black/African woman into the fiery pits of the slave labor force, but this request didn't beg that question). However, these men, women and their children weren't allowed to operate as families. To make an incessantly long story short, this severely impacted the mentality of all three. The Black man grew fearful of trying to be the priest, provider and protector of his family due to the threat of brutal, barbaric and damn near (and sometimes actual) fatal punishment he would receive for the attempt at doing so. This is why Black men began to cling to one another while developing a natural aversion to being in the company of Black women for fear of death or severe bodily injury. This disinclination became instinctive/second nature and thusly we see it in practice today. Generally, dudes spend the majority of their time with their homeboys, less time with their woman and even less time with their children. It's hardwired into the mentality. Don't take that as an excuse, but more of a shedding of light upon. The Black woman was left to be the head of household, yearning for both the love and touch of her man, but fearful of the lives of herself, him and her children. What a heavy burden to be both longing for the companionship of the one who gifted you with children while traversing the torrential waters of serving in the capacity of both parents in addition to trying to avoid being raped, pillaged and sexually dehumanized by some muthafucka who'd staked claim to your personage. Lastly, the child was left to function as an incomplete jigsaw puzzle; a fragmented portrait of what he/she could be had he/she been granted to be a part of a family unit. This impeded all aspects of the child's development in most instances back then and continues to do so now (a lot, but not always). It has also been said and widely believed that the continued decline in Black two-parent homes was reinforced under the administration of Lyndon B. Johnson. I mean, when you have programs like WIC (Women, Infant and Children) that make no mention of men nor give attention to the importance in the household, it's easy to draw that conclusion about intentions. While I'm not sure that there are actual policies in place that make the acquisition of benefits more difficult if there is a man living in the home, you'd be hard-pressed to convince me that the agency doesn't have practices that reinforce this belief, practices that have been handed down from years upon years of disenfranchisement. The saddest reality of today is that we are equipped with the knowledge of these centuries-old transgressions and have yet made it our timely preparation for future eventualities to find remedies for them. I'm confident that things are gradually improving, but as race relations soften on the dating front, we continue to see a breach in the bond between Black men and women as we venture into relationships with persons of different races, often leaving the scabs of our own inability to connect to fester. The end.

24May2017

Didn't realize I'd run out of coffee creamer, so I thought it was a good idea to use a little pancake batter as a substitute. Shit tastes like abominable queef blowback!

I don't like things I don't understand. Right now my mind is grappling with death. I don't understand its purpose. I am both vexed by and enamored with its ravages. It hurts. Its silence is shrill. My whole train of thought just got fucked up by watching this older, White lady try to sip soup sans lips.

I literally just sat through my coworker's going away lunch on the phone with headphones on for over an hour.

I only like the word "yo" when it's used as a possessive pronoun.

People who say "I miss the old you" are stuck in the very same way place from which you've grown and want desperately to lasso you back to that place with their passive-aggressive, nostalgic guilt trip. Fuck em.

25May2017

BooPac? Oh no the fuck he didn't! HAHAHAHAHAHA

I dance like Mary J. Blige at work all damn day!

I just successfully parallel parked on the first attempt. You can't tell me SHIT for the rest of the day!!!!

LISTEN! The day I have hair growing from my back out of the collar of my shirt is the day I throw all of my underwear away and let my balls just dangle.

Black lips head ass. Forever working out and still built like a middle finger.

"I remember skimming pond scum off the surface of water to quench my thirst." <-- I'm sure this was about to be good, but the 211s kicked in lol

26May2017

Well, I promised the lord that I would hold out...but I lied.

I'm so fuckin mad at Post Malone for being built like Rodney Dangerfield and Nacho Libre! And what kind of demonic mullet double braided bullshit has he allowed to adorn his crown? The Heavens are telling. (My reaction to a picture of Post Malone with Allen Iverson)

Chapter 6: KISMET: kis·met: /ˈkizmit,-ˌmet/: noun: kismet: destiny; fate. "What chance did I stand against kismet?"

27May2017

<u>The Dangers of Consuming Copious Amounts of Dairy Products:</u>

First of all I'm just gonna talk about milk because I feel like it's the Beyoncé of dairy products.

Okay? So ever since we were weaned off of our momma's titty (if we were ever given the option because some momma's titties have cotton mouth), Similac or one of its derivatives, we've been pumped full of cow titty juice...that is if we aren't lactose intolerant or allergic. For the most part, we've been taught that suckling the nectar of udders was healthy, but some argue that this might be a nappy-headed hoe ass lie. For as long as I can remember, we've been psychologically pimp-slapped into believing milk is to our bones what spinach was to Popeye, but a quick scavenger hunt for receipts that verify this claim will leave you befuddled by their scarcity. Just look at Asia. They barely sip cow's milk and their bone fracture rates ain't poppin'. But that doesn't finger-fuck the overconsumption question. So here it goes. Yes, milk is a great source of potassium. Too great as a matter of memes and we all know memes are the lost commandments of Christ in the contiguous United States. Anyway, the amount of potassium used in USDA recommendations are way more than a hop, skip and a jump higher than what we should be consuming to ward off fucking up our kidneys. That's right! Too much milk can give you raisin kidneys or some shit like that. Also, if you're trying to get your bouncy house built ass in shape, be aware that too much milk can literally upsize the lard in that ass as it's lowkey high in calories. Add bloating, flatulence, nausea, cramps, gas, and diarrhea equivalent to warfare to the mix and the dangers should become even more apparent.

28May2017

Minding Your Own Business:

This is a tricky one. On second thought, no it's not. It's rather simple. If your involvement in a situation purely serves to create or fuel drama and bullshit, then zip the fuck up and go sit down somewhere. However, if your involvement serves to aide someone in danger, peril or a sticky situation that they themselves haven't the faculty to traverse independent of assistance, then by all means, put a little love in your heart and lend a helping hand. This whole turn a blind eye, or even worse, "let me grab my smart phone while this poor, unfortunate soul is being victimized" mentality is a societal outbreak of emotional scabies. People have become so cold, disenchanted, disengaged and jaded that they'd rather try to go viral by capturing the suffering of others than to try to intervene on their behalf. Neither Jesus nor Mufasa died for that shit, but to you messy bitches, grab you a fuckin' steno pad and jot down a business plan for the humdrum tomfuckery you seek to immerse yourself in rather than kicking the hornet's nest in someone else's life. Life is too short and too complicated enough already for instigators and agitators to be drumming up unnecessary, unscripted dramatis personae in my or anyone else's life story. Thusly, you should drink a healthy dose of Bitch Be Gone...expeditiously!

29May2017

Why Black Women Hate on Other Black Women:

Let's keep it funky, misogyny and a patriarchal, social modus operandi pit women against one another. Hating on one another really isn't unique to Black women. The shorter lifespan of men, incarceration and social engineering are responsible as well. Just listen to Chimimanda Ngozi Adichie's verse, I suppose you'd call it, on Beyoncé's "Flawless". "We teach girls to shrink themselves... To make themselves smaller. We say to girls, "You can have ambition, but not too much. You should aim to be successful, but not too successful, otherwise you will threaten the man". Because I am female, I am expected to aspire to marriage. I am expected to make my life choices. Always keeping in mind that marriage is the most important. Now marriage can be a source of joy and love and mutual support, but why do we teach girls to aspire to marriage. And we don't teach boys the same? We raise girls to each other as competitors, not for jobs or for accomplishments, which I think can be a good thing, but for the attention of men. We teach girls that they cannot be sexual beings in the way that boys are. Feminist: the person who believes in the social, political, and economic equality of the sexes." She hit the nail on the head with the heel of a stiletto! Little girls are raised to crave marriage and to be "chosen" by a man as his lifetime living trophy. The very nature of choosing indicates a sense of competition. Thusly, you have to be the embodiment of what the patriarchal society deems most appealing about women within the era in which you live, be that beautiful, voluptuous, Skeletorish, career-driven, borderline prostitute, et cetera. And to win often means not only being more resplendent than the competition, but also dulling the shine of the competition, thereby making her look ashy, crusty, off-brand and undesirable in the eyes of a potential suitor. Shit sucks, but until the entirety of women withdraw from the game and establish their own set of rules, the shit will continue. The problem with that proposal is that a great many women like the competitiveness of pussy poppin' on a headstand for the adoration of men. They enjoy the psychological warfare of cattiness. So then it becomes about a majority of women who see the fuckery for what it is banding together and flipping the script rather than continually sauntering around in ignorance wondering who in the hell left the mufuckin' gate open. In a nutshell...

30May2017

The Persecution of the Black Man:

One of the most profound explanations I've read, heard or whatever the fuck for the unyielding desire to suppress and eventually eradicate the Black man from the face of the Earth by all races, and chiefly White supremacists, is the potency of his nut. Ironically, it was White supremacy, in an attempt to dissuade a person from procreating with Blacks that animated, no that's giving too much fuckin' credit, reinforced the dominance of Black DNA by way of the One-Drop Rule. Now I pray, though I'm doubtful, that in 2016 all people have knowledge of exactly what this rule indicated, but in the off chance that you were educated by either apathetic, rose colored glasses wearers or blatantly prejudiced nincompoops, I will give you a brief rundown of it. Let us turn to the Book of Wikipedia: Chapter Google: Verse Search: The one-drop rule is a social and legal fundamental truth or proposition that serves as the foundation for a system of belief or behavior or for a chain of reasoning for racial classification that was historically prominent in the United States asserting that any person with even one ancestor of sub-Saharan-African ancestry ("one drop" of Black blood) is considered to be black (Negro in historical terms). Capisce? You see the prowess of the Black man's semen is so on fleek (allow me to resurrect that slang tragedy for a moment) that a mere handshake with the DNA of another race results in a submission hold and the Black DNA's eventual absorption of that DNA...leaving trace amounts of the subordinate DNA's characteristics of course. If you're White, of course that's some fuckin' frightening and unsettling ass shit. In my ratchet White person voice because it's going to amuse me, you mean to tell me a Black man's nut has the sovereignty to wipe us off the face of the Earth...like for good and for real? BITCH SWERVE! WHITE POWER!!!! WHITE POWER!!!! HOODS WITH HOLES IN THEM!!!! BURN CROSSES!!!! SET UP SOCIETY TO PRODUCE OUR ADVANCEMENT AND THEIR ABYSMAL FAILURE...or whatever. Which is wholeheartedly dumb as fuck because White people and every other race CLEARLY descended from Black people. Combine every color there is and you'll only get one result...BLACK! Only through the diminution of Black do you get other colors. So, fear is essentially at the core of the incessant persecution and murder of the Black man...fear of fading from existence. NARF!!!!!

31 May 2017

Everybody's out here trying to establish something real and I'm still just trying to get my dick sucked or an old-fashioned hand job on the low with no strings attached.

Raising Black Children in Today's Society:

It is the feeling of walking over egg shells sprinkled on a tight rope woven out of permed edges. As a Black man, or caramel if we're being technical with no difficulties, the idea of raising a son or daughter in the world today is a perpetual state of fright night, morning, afternoon and evening. I mean shit. At first, it was Black men being shot down in broad daylight on city streets with the shooter being exonerated of any wrongdoing even though the whole shit was captured on film. Then it spread to Black women. Now Black children are on the menu. I literally almost had an Antoine Dodson moment, but the Holy Ghost is a keeper and bound my tongue or whatever. Anyway, it's like we, as parents, are robbed of the opportunity of focusing on teaching our kids how to be happy, well-adjusted adults because we have to focus on teaching them how not to dress like a suspect; how to recognize when you are being discriminated against in your classroom and other aspects of your daily life; how to act when approached by authority figures who have a license to take your life; how you have to be 80% better than everyone else just to be considered on equal footing with everyone else; how slavery ended hundreds of years ago, but we aren't really extended the same liberties as everyone else because when this country was founded, we weren't even viewed as fully human, so many of the rights and privileges extended to others still don't apply to us; and I'm guessing you can see where I'm going with this because the list could go on and on and on in perpetuity. I, at one point, thought teaching my own offspring to become so important that the world valued you and thusly wouldn't stand for you being senselessly snuffed out, but now I can't even stand by that as I've seen far too many prominent Black people have their character torn to shreds and their legacies dissipated into nothingness. So in essence, in order to raise a Black child in today's society, you simply have to teach them what it means to be Black, how to effectively be Black and how to survive being Black because you are undoubtedly issued both a birth and death certificate on your day of delivery.

Chapter 7: Protection from creditors granted to individuals or companies who legally file for bankruptcy, providing for liquidation of certain assets to pay debts

Seventeenth of All

Artwork by Anthony Rosas

Pussy for Sale: 24 Sep 2016 0729 PM

Regardless of the scenario captured on film and dispensed for the visual consumption of the masses, there is always a vomit-inducing attempt at blame-shifting to the now deceased for some measure of non-compliance. These words are the venom that drips from the forked tongues of muthafuckas who actually believe that a police officer armed with a Taser, mace, a baton, a firearm, and God knows what else, AND who just so happens to be flanked by five other officers who are equipped with the same tools, can somehow fear for his or her life while standing before someone who is only wielding the color of his or her skin. I call bullshit and I pray that it echoes within every valley and bounces its way through both suburbia and rural America. You took a job that requires you to enforce, so when you suit yourself in your uniform and adorn yourself with the trinkets of enforcement assigned to you, you do so with the full knowledge that you are expected to compel observance of or compliance with the law. You do not get the privilege of cowardice. You are supposed to esteem yourself with bravery and courage each and every time you represent your particular division of law enforcement and if you aren't able to do so, you have chosen the wrong fucking profession.

While I am well aware that many of the recent shootings that resulted in the deaths of Black people were predicated by some measure of racial hatred or apprehension, what I am beginning to realize is that we are also witnessing the manifestation of cowardly lions operating under the guise of a license to kill. These muthafuckas are slaves to the very itch in their trigger fingers and the sugar water coursing through their veins.

So Sayeth the...Soothsayer?

Do you know why you should always check a vehicle's Carfax? It's because your eyes can't accurately drudge up historical data. The same shit applies when these bitches start grasping at straws trying to identify some justification for the most recent addition to their body count. Eyes can't Google criminal history or conduct meticulous background checks, so unless a person was caught in the act of committing a crime that warrants lethal force, LIKE EATING A MUTHAFUCKA'S FACE OFF [pause for the dramatic side-eye], what bearing does what he or she did over a decade ago have on what's happening in real time? No sooner than the last drop of blood has sauntered its way from the exit wound, the spin doctors are hovered over their desktops and laptops trying to fact check everything from jaywalking citations to questionable social media posts, so the demonizing of the dead can begin. But what in the corncob pipe fuck does any of that have to do with the split second decision that was made. As far as I know, the fictitious character of Professor Xavier bore no children, so it stands that the decision to take a life was made based upon factors from the killer's life, not the victim's. And yes, badge or no badge, if you pull that trigger with no clear justification other than what you claim to have felt and a heart never beats again you are forever branded with the moniker of murderer, assassin, slaughterer, killer, executioner, and homicidal maniac.

Bitch Better Have My Peace

Do you ever leave your chakras dripping with sweat after successive bouts of pseudo-intellectual debates with marginally evolved troglodytes about being Black in America, systemic racism and the tentacles of oppression? I'm sitting here typing with my right hand while my left hand is fully extended because I've not only done so, I'm a repeat offender. For so long, I felt that it was my melanated duty to go toe-to-toe with anyone who offered what I perceived to be an adverse and underhanded opinion on issues that had encapsulated my heart. I wanted to both educate them and cuss them down to the cellular level, but then one day something that was either the ever-elusive Holy Ghost or my subconscious whispered to me "So you're just gonna sprain your peace having mental fisticuffs with people who have no vested interest in these issues?" In that moment, I was branded with the scarlet letters of "you sho is right"! There is absolutely no reason for me to be depleting my life force for the purpose of futile battles of wit. I was allowing myself to be Rick rolled and trolled AT THE SAME DAMN TIME!!!!! My energy, your energy, OUR ENERGY is much too valuable to be expended in inconsequential tête-à-têtes. The Principle of Least Interest is one of the indicators of power in interpersonal relationships. It suggests that the power lies in the hands of the person who cares the least about the relationship. I apply this theory to many an interaction, whether fleeting or deeply personal, so as to avoid giving more of myself than will be respected or reciprocated. In these jiffies, when we find ourselves at the precipice of foaming at the mouth with passion in regard to our fallen brothers and sisters, our slackjaw adversaries are reeling with delight fostered by a nest egg of apathy with regard to the very same cataclysms. In that the truth requires no cheerleader, speak yours and unhitch your wagon from these entanglements, so as to exert that energy where it can better serve the progression of equity and peace.

In my closing, as pastors love to say seventeen times before actually concluding, always remind yourselves that bullies know who to pick on and right now we are the unimposing, abstract children with high-water pants, pocket protectors and hand-me-down clothing trying our very best to find our way in the cafeteria of this planet without having to return home to our parents and explain yet another shiner. But survival cannot come without standing up. So when courage is flirtatious and we see that our antagonist's brawn is fortified with weaponry that has been stockpiled well in advance of our being sick and tired of being sick and tired, we must be wily. We must be covert and we must be strategic, but most of all, we must be steadfast and resolute. I've been Triston for Dummies and you've been reading The Seventeenth of It All. Be good to yourself and those who share your struggles. Until next time...

A Brief Audit of Solange's "A Seat at the Table"

3Oct2016 1211AM

Solange has truly found her voice and it is bellowing FUCK THAT BEYONCÉ'S LITTLE SISTER moniker! Her latest offering, ♪♩A Seat at the Table♪♩, is such a demure toure de force. It is a lilting witch's brew of rhythm and introspection; a whispered protest of staccato hand claps between every melodied audit of the Black experience in America.

Sugar has been described as the most destructive force in the universe #MenInBlack3 and if that's truly the case, Solange's voice oozes sugary sweetness as she waxes philosophical on the sable lacquered elephant in the room that we are talking about, but everybody else is avoiding discussion of by critiquing our conversation instead. There's power in poetry.

This isn't your _To Pimp a Butterfly_. There is no frenzy or browbeating, which most certainly serve a purpose. This is a nuanced, retrospective gallery opening and Solange serves as the curator. It's not as simple as HipHop versus R&B. It's rebellion versus being seated upon your grandmother's lap and having her school you in the ways of the world while she brushes your hair. This is Hennessey and Coke versus Mint Julep. This is brown gel versus water and grease.

There is a very patient & deliberate attentiveness & sensitivity to each and every note and lyric. A feat made perfect by the very fact that Solange served as both a writer and producer on every song. And kudos to both of the Knowles sisters for becoming a part of the conversation in their own unique ways. Whereas Beyoncé offered us a glass of "Lemonade" (imagery), Solange provided us "A Seat at the Table" at which to enjoy it (commentary).

I've been Triston for Dummies and this has been The 17th of It All.

The Abortion of a Nation

9Oct2016 1050AM

Expectation breeds disappointment. Learning of Nat Turner was a pivotal moment in my youth. I credit his legend with unearthing the spirits of activism and rebellion within me, so when I learned that there would be a movie about him, my excitement began to coil itself around my imagination. Every day leading up to its release found me at the proverbial edge of my seat. I was eager to compare and contrast the many years I'd spent conceptualizing how it all unfolded to what would be presented cinematically. While it was coated in an artistic tapestry to rival the unfettered beauty of a tulips, it was supremely deficient of the unmitigated savagery for which I had hoped.

It was like a kaleidoscope of sybaritic lovemaking without an orgasm or your favorite beverage after over half the ice has melted or an oral happy-ending from the girl of your dreams when she's battling chapped lips and cottonmouth. The cinematography was exquisite. The acting was the cat's pajamas, but rather than breathing new life into the complexities of what transpired, it orbited the allegorical escarpment.

I don't want to give the impression that the film was a complete flop. Nate Parker should be applauded for serving as this stories herald. However, I anticipated greater attentiveness to the actual rebellion than the events leading up to it. The brevity of Turner's bloodied clapback left me wanting.

I transgressed against my assertion that I would forever abstain from watching anymore movies about slavery for this one and I'm toggling between regret & disappointment for that decision. Nonetheless, I do not wish to dissuade anyone from endorsing this project. I'm by no means a critic. I'm just giving you the 17th of it all.

Chapter 8 of the Traffic Signs Manual: The training teaches how to place signs to create a safe environment for workers and highway users.

The Miseducation of the Modern Day Coon

9Oct2016 0615PM

You poor, unfortunate clusterfucks. What a wasteland of muffled melanin you are.

Clawing and scratching, or should I say shucking and jiving, your way through the sanctity of your Blackness only to turn Judas for the chance at adorning yourself in a dilapidated leash that is transfixed to some good 'ol boy's serving tray of a belt buckle. I find it comedic that you fashion yourselves as the ambassadors of some seemingly befuddled "new Blackness", when in all actuality, you're nothing more than the paramours of White delusions of grandeur. The volunteer brigade for a centuries' old God complex dressed in sandwich boards that read "Will betray my people for social acceptance". Double-stuffed Oreos who'd rather see us pledge allegiance to some tongue-in-cheek rhetoric that proffers liberty and justice for all than to stand with us as the veil is ripped in twain and the dawn's early light casts a shadow on this harlot dissimulating herself as a democratic debutante.

America, the land that I'm supposed to love without condition. I, the child abused and neglected, running back into her arms after she has she beat me into a pulp so bloody that I now have an ocean's tide of pain that splashes upon the shores of my cantankerous heart. A nation that affords me certain freedoms while granting others the uninhibited ability flourish in the lap of privilege with little to no oppressive restrictions imposed by authority on one's way of life, behavior, or political views. But you muthafuckas drape your yoke of oppression around your neck as though it were a gold chain. And dance because it catches the light just right and makes your selfie pop. And you spew those soundbites that gut-punch the rest of us in our souls. And you smile with bleached teeth as the nemesis puppeteers your buffoonery. And that jangle of your chains make mocking melodies because we see the leash to which they are attached.

You curtsy at the beckon of their God complex. You willingly offer up your genitalia to be the Isaac in the trek up this societal Moriah, but there will never be a ram in the bush because the Abraham you silently and secretly worship is not operating off of Christian Faith. He has appointed himself God of this world and you're simply another eraser helping to wipe away the truth and history of a people that would still welcome you back, castrated and all, if only you could see yourself for the Judas you truly are. But you can't, because in your quest to be accepted and sceptered with the full breadth of assimilation, you now foolishly claim to see the world through "color blind" glasses...as though the color blind can't distinguish light from darkness.

I used to feel so offended and personally betrayed, but then I had to remind myself that the path you walk doesn't blister my feet. You are more than welcome to be the mascot for the people of color who consider themselves unscathed by the modus operandi of racism. You are free to dance your ignorance jig on a cloud of delusion if that's what helps you sleep at night. O.J. Simpson did it. That is until he found himself driving down the interstate in his white Bronco flipping through his mental Rolodex trying to phone a friend for some solace. He was sobered. He was forced to realize that his blackness was not a limb that he could sever and continue to function as normal. Instead, it ended up being the altar upon which he could cast his sins and find comfort. So too will your day of reckoning come and when it does, I pray that you are reminded of every bridge you burned with the acidity of your hate speech against those who look like you. There are no refunds when you sell out your race.

Binge Watching Marvel's Luke Cage

10Oct2016 0346PM

Warning: This will be disjointed.

"It's easy to underestimate a nigga. They never see you comin'." Rafael Sadiq, all up in the Kool-aid, I'm the connect, Dante, Black Lives Matter, making it rain, a towering Biggie portrait, it's all about the Benjamins, Fox News slams...Netflix's Marvel's Luke Cage is 21st century blaxploitation done...right? After completing the very first episode, I'm not certain if the sounds of blackness radiating from my flat screen are complimentary or mocking. Is this an effort to pay homage or cliche? And was that a jack move from Denzel's Equalizer danger assessment I just peeped? I'm torn. And adding a guest appearance by Faith Evans to episode two left my opinion all the more scatterbrained and ramshackled.

I'm struggling to decipher whether the writers are actually Black or some band of stumble bums who've come to think they understand Black culture by way of Word Up Magazine and Madea movies. It's the difference between cheesecake out of the box and cheesecake made from scratch. And I truly had...have (since I'm now about to watch episode three) such high hopes, but the Hollywood Shuffle of it all is leaving much to be desired.

It's like they're trying to balance themselves somewhere between Empire and Power, but they've been stricken with vertigo. Episode 3 is starting to feel a little less like Miley Cyrus twerking and more like the Rachel Dolezal Effect. But where the fuck are the New Yorker accents? Everyone sounds so phonetically ambiguous.

I must applaud the fact that the staple of the Black barbershop is central to the plot of this series, however.

"Slavery was always a good offer...to a master." Now they're speaking my logarithm. Then they ruin it with these Velcro lookin' ass wigs they've strapped to this man's face and sideburns. Is this some kind of homage to Kimbo Slice tho?

Episode 5... Jidenna as the opening scene...sold. Benign neglect got you shot in the face and just like that, shit just got real. Dapper Dan cameo. Ok, I see y'all.

RECORD SCRATCH!!!!!

I had to abruptly end my criticism of this show because of complaints from Twhite Tweople on Twitter about the show being so Black. Deep sigh. I'm so fuckin' annoyed. Drape up and drip out this tang in every ounce of Blackness y'all can muster...for the CULTURE!!

13Oct2016 0132PM

I'm tired of egg shells. I don't like their smell or the way they crunch beneath my feet. And it may come as a surprise to many that someone as verbally outspoken and reckless as I am has at any point been...cautious. Sure I talk SHIT, but I'm no fool.

GIRL POWER FOR PRESIDENT!

13Oct2016 1109PM

This election has confirmed every suspicion I've ever had about the preselection of presidents. I'd like to say it was well-orchestrated, but I can't...because it wasn't.

Barack Obama set a precedent for breaking barriers in the position of Commander in Chief. What message would we be sending as a nation were we to return to the same old dilapidated record of long-toothed, White men serving as leader of the freed world? And so it had to be a woman. And it had to be a White woman because the process is always slow and deliberate, so it could be no other type of minority. And it had to be a flagrantly imperfect and polarizing woman to counterbalance the seemingly pristine "character" of President Obama. A woman who quietly allowed the victimization she suffered at the hands of her husband's lechery to sharpen her incisors and talons.

Beyoncé, the reigning Pop Queen of Girl Power Feminism, making bold and controversial artistic communiqués about both Blackness and cuckoldry. The perfect bridge over troubled waters to satiate our obsession with entertainment.

The irony of Donald Trump finding favor with the poor, White trash sect of undereducated nationalists. A buffoon of a celebrity with a gregarious amount of moxie. A caricatured kazoo, so rancorous that all Hillary Clinton has to do was heed Snoop Dogg's caveat to lay low.

And I wouldn't be so resolute in my position were it not for the tide that has turn on the heels of "grab 'em in the pussy"-gate. As I sat here watching First Lady Michelle Obama teaspoon her heart out in front of a New Hampshire assembly, thereby transitioning this from a political campaign to a women's issue, a lightbulb shattered in my brain. And all of the threads were drawn together and I could clearly see the plan laced up neatly right before my very eyes.

Outrage over 6-month sentence for Brock Turner in Stanford rape case. No prison for Colorado college student, Austin Wilkerson, who 'raped a helpless young woman'. Former Indiana University student, John Enochs, charged with two rapes gets one day in jail.

These are White men who were transgressing against White women...and getting away with it with slaps on the dick. And I know it's all conspiracy theory-ish, but we scream where there's smoke there's fire for everything else and I hear detectors going the fuck off! Mind-programming works best when the superficially unrelated are in fact surfing on blurred lines. Get it?

Pompous vs. Dowdy. Ostentatious vs. Awkward. Lewd vs. Pneumonia. Donald Trump Is the Epitome of Everything the World Detests — and Admires — About America! #HuffingtonPost Donald Trump, national embarrassment: The rest of the world is gawking at his campaign — and us! #Salon Think America's terrified of Donald Trump? Check out how the rest of the world's reacting! #VoxExplainsTheNews Hillary Clinton: "I'm Really Not Even a Human Being" #VanityFair WATCH: Here's Your Proof That Hillary Is Actually A Robot! #ThePoliticalInsider Hillary Clinton 'is a robot' because she didn't flinch when a fly landed on her face during TV debate #Mirror Playboy vs. Stepford Wife.

NOT TO FUCKIN' MENTION

Is 'The Purge: Election Year' About Donald Trump? The Horror Flick Has Some Eerie Similarities To Real Life! #Bustle Donald Trump, Hillary Clinton influenced The Purge: Election Year #EntertainmentWeekly The Purge 3 Was Inspired by Donald Trump & Hillary Clinton #MovieWeb

Look Sway, I don't have all the answers, but my spidey senses just took the shackles off their feet, so they can dance! This was all the perfect storm to ensure that it looked as though Hillary Clinton would park her purse in the Oval Office. They've put GIRL POWER on

Skid Row in nothing more than a waste trainer, some fishnets and some Asics and told her to pop that pussy for a real nigga! But we all know the good 'ol boys aren't about to let that happen.

Donald Trump folks? Really? That guy? The one with the puckered face, cocaine drip sniffles, Vienna sausage fingers and a sordid past that includes accusations of raping his own wife? He's potbellied misogyny personified. There's no way that someone who stands for so much that we're ashamed of and abhor would ever beat someone who mechanically scoured the earth seeking whom she may devour in the name of liberty and justice for all...allegedly. Is there?

Donald's ship is sinking and the ink is drying on his check. Win or lose, it's still good business for his brand folks. Hillary's lining up her kitten heels, eager to send The Donald a thank you email. Prematurely, no doubt, but I can envision it.

So now that I'm pretty damn sure that Bill Clinton's side wife was chosen, I'm not chomping at the bit that know...why.

[THE GAPS IN THIS TRAIN OF THOUGHT WERE INTENTIONAL]

I've been Triston for Dummies and this has been the 17th of It All.

Chapter 9: A bankruptcy proceeding that provides financially distressed municipalities with protection from creditors by creating a plan between the municipality and its creditors to resolve the outstanding debt. Municipalities include cities, counties, townships and school districts.

Status Updates

Black males are being imprisoned to halt procreation because of the dominance of the Black genetic code. This is to ensure the survival of the White genetic code.

22Oct2016 8:36 AM: Started my morning off with a freebie...so fuckin' American. Correction, so fuckin' First World...not everyone is able.

1:15 PM: Shout out to all of the people who took a hoe bath, but didn't get no good lovin' body rockin' knockin' boots all night long last night.

1:29 PM: NO WEAKNESS.

7:28 PM: #DenasiaLawrence bolding kneeling in the face of white supremacy while singing its' anthem is the very definition of #BlackGirlMagic.

24Oct2016 9:14 AM: "No" is a reality. You will deal.

2:48 PM: I'm lookin' fuckin' factionless as hell today.

3:37 PM: I was called both "Hitler af" and "satanic af" today. Are the Heavens telling on me?

3:43 PM: A truly supreme being doesn't have to trick anyone into believing its supremacy.

7:43 PM: I hate when I post about a missing person and ask people to share the post to spread the word, and I end up with twice more likes than shares ☹

25Oct2016 4:35 PM: The concept of convenience has the average American mind fucked up beyond repair.

26Oct2016 12:49 PM: Y'all are really lettin' Trick Daddy's bloated smoker face ass get y'all's outer labia in a bowtie knot when clearly that nigga needs to tighten up on his lip exfoliation and a loofa for the rest of his face?

5Jul2017 2:51 PM: Do I want people to know now, like on a daily basis via social media, so much so that it becomes vapid and forgettable or do I want to starve them throughout the remainder of my life now that I've wetted their appetites? (A thought I had while watching Inside the Mind of a Serial Killer: Season 1: Episode 3: Anders Behring Breivik)

Insecurity and cowardice combine in a sloshing, lethal cocktail within the hearts and minds of pampered, white boys who haven't been told no and therefore are incapable of fielding the flood of emotions that come with rejection, whether real or perceived, and so their only recourse is to destroy. Then and only then does their world again return to spinning on the axis they've been bred to believe responds only to their contentment. Fucking loose leaf pussies. Don't force your feet into shoes they don't fit.

I know few beasts that walk on two feet, but standing atop the heap is the devil cloaked in a pale, unassuming and seemingly sheepish face.

When peace becomes an insult to a sense of powerlessness, destroy the weapons, stand in the sun and watch the magnificence of natural selection manifest.

What does malice feed upon? Fear and helplessness? I believe it feeds upon the desires of its host. Its pleasure is to produce an abundance of whatever brings the host joy...and a unique brand of comfort in many respects.

The genius of self-righteousness finger fucking delusions of grandeur...lethal weaponry right there, folks. Deadly. The sobering reality of realizing you're standing alone on a breaking branch, splendid.

Where was I in 2011 when all of Nobel's peace was being violently ripped out of Norway's vagina? I was here in Oklahoma and more than likely loathing the bastion of racial bullshit this tart land of slavery proffers.

You think of America as the serial killer's playground, but I've been humbled by this docuseries. Surender Koli ate children in Noida, India because he had a sad dick that couldn't lift its head up for women his age? Something is missing and then the classism angle of the caste system emerges. When will we learn? Culture shock by way of decorated deviance as a gateway to a sociopathic soul. It's always the unremarkable ones that crack and try to absorb remarkableness from the world around them by killing their triggers.

On this day, The Shade Room presented the world with the latest installment of the script chronicling the lives of Tyga, Blacc Chyna, Kylie Jenner and Rob Kardashian written and directed by Amber Rose, I'm presuming.

4:26 PM: Mark Rust, the sex pest. I've never heard of a sex pest before. And what about the 70s produced so many sexual deviants who would go on to become serial killers? Wasn't everyone free sexing and snorting poppy's and shit like that? Guess all of the Hug Johnson's who couldn't date rape drug themselves a piece of pussy turned all sadistic and murderous from aggravated blue balls.

One Night Stands When the Woman Gets Up and Leaves:

Boy oh boy! That's what dreams are made of! Let me talk to my SINGLE fellas for a second...not you committed man-whores who make declarations to support her, push her, inspire her, and, above all, love her, for better or worse, in sickness and health, for richer or poorer, as long as y'all both shall live, til death do y'all part before God and man (or some watered down fuck boy version via private text message conversations as a response to "What are we?")! How many times have you been at the tail end of a chance, yet phenomenal bussit session and immediately started calculating just how in the fuck you're gonna "coyote she ain't ugly, but she's gotta go" yourself out of those awkward moments of afterglow in which she wants to cuddle and get to know you better amidst a fog of post-coitus breath. Wouldn't it be Heaven-sent if she just slipped back into her clothes, kissed YOU on the forehead and said she was going home? That would be like the Rolaids of post-non-committal sex stress, right? I say all of that to say this, Nike slogan that shit. Give that nigga (of any race) a gentlemen's handshake or a gentle pat on his twig & giggleberries, stuff your boy shorts in your pocket book, and chunk that nigga the sexiest deuce you can muster. I promise you all will be right in the world if y'all practiced safe sex. None of "that awkward moment when" bullshit. No fruitless small talk. No forearms and hands falling asleep because you want to lay up under him for a minute or forty-five while the wet spot evaporates. Just a seamless transition from nut to exit stage left. I'm sure we can all agree that we're here for it...well, at least those of us who have not been stricken with some malignant form of serial monogamy. We're both grown. We both wanted to treat our undercarriages to a fantastic voyage...no need for the knick knack paddy wack bullshit immediately thereafter!

What Different Types of Men Want:

This is about to be a big game of Guesstures or some shit because I'm just one dude and I've never ran to heavily with a pack per se and I've limited myself to a working knowledge of how these niggas think and operate, so as not to fuck up friendships. But since it was asked, I'm going to reach down into the depths of my knowledge and paint a picture. Trifling niggas want to trifle. They want to put you through as much shit as they possibly can to see if you'll break or if you'll remain committed to proving your love for them. They'll steal money out of your purse. They'll try to fuck your cousins, close friends, sisters, aunties, your mom and even your seventh grade teacher who still calls to check up on you to see how you are progressing in life. They'll show up at your job and take your car without notifying you; get a flat tire within the first five minutes; drive around for hours without stopping to have it repaired; and then return it without ever saying anything to you. Chances are the shit is on E as well. They'll pick a fight with you then send their homeboy to comfort and be sweet to you on the low to see if you're going to give up that pussy or keeps its lips sealed. And some more shit. Moving on. So wow #FauxShockAndSurprise, women really asked me about "keepers" knowing good and gotdamn well y'all generally keep us as long as the dick has the breath of life in it on a consistent basis. A nigga can legitimately collect cans for a living, but if he knows how to dutty wine in that pussy, some woman somewhere will sign a blood oath with her menstrual cycle drool as ink to keep that nigga in her life. I mean I can literally sit here and write a honey-do list of bullshit niggas do ranging from being caught freestyling to Lady Gaga instrumentals in his chick's g-string to getting some random bitch pregnant while telling his main chick he doesn't want kids and I guarantee there's a whole pom squad's worth of chicks ready to absolve these types of dudes from guilt with a "but he [INSERT ANY

RANDOM, BULLSHIT ASS EXCUSE THAT ESSENTIALLY TRANSLATES TO SHE'S ADDICTED TO HIS DICK GAME]", but y'all in love and stuff or whatever. The next inquiry was about the men who want a mama. I mean shit. That should be self-explanatory. This nigga is a Toy-R-Us kid and chances are he's got a whole Trapper Keeper full of enablers that have done little to help his balls drop through the portal of adolescence to manhood. Let's hopscotch on over to the polygamy niggas. Come on now. Clearly these dudes want a smorgasbord of pussy. Let me try to make sense of this because I kind of oversimplified it with the smorgasbord reference. No one wants to listen to one CD for the rest of his life no matter how mind-blowing it is. The fact of the matter is, once you've become common with all of its nuances, it's hard to reclaim that initial excitement and no amount of acrobatics, bells, whistles or sex toys can make familiar pussy as exciting as uncharted territory pussy. These niggas live for and feed off of that excitement. Paradoxically, many polygamy niggas like the constancy of a relationship, so to avoid losing interest in you they introduce other women to offset the impending boredom and lack of joie de vive that is to come. Juggling women is an adrenaline rush. It's also like relationship sudoku...a brain teaser. It keeps them on their toes. That adrenaline rush of a non-secret love affair is an aphrodisiac in many instances. And sometimes it's less about balancing more than one relationship than it is the thrill of the hunt...like the Hunger Games for pussy. Racking up an impressive, sexual body count and shit! Lastly, inquiring minds wanted to know about the men who want a wife. I find that most dudes see this as both a status symbol and completion. They've either grown up with or in the absence of an example and yearn to either continue or trailblaze the marital tradition within their family. I actually know niggas who just can't stomach the thought of being alone and marriage to them eliminates the threat of loneliness and solitude. Then there are those who just get married because they've been taught that it's just what you do...as in, it's the natural progression of life. It's like marriage is just another accomplishment on a checklist of things they were supposed to complete in order to measure up to the idealism of Americana. "Achieve the American dream" probably fits better there, but I just like the word Americana. WHEW! I'm really glad that's over or whatever. Felt like I was breaking some kind of guy code that I never really knew existed or gave a fuck about until I was asked this convoluted ass question. Egats!

Chapter 10: Bankruptcy, management is displaced, and a court-appointed manager or trustee oversees the reorganization or restructuring process.

Why This New Generation Doesn't Respect Their Elders: Why Are They So Ignorant and Rude?

Because parents ain't shit themselves. You've got people out here prostituting their kid's paedomorphosis in the hope of going viral. Babies twerking in pull-ups. Little boys bucking up to adults like Deebo. I'm mufuckin' tyde and the like. I mean when you've been allowed...skurt...rewind...when you've been encouraged and praised for being an uncouth hellion since before you cut teeth, you don't automatically become dainty or chivalrous during puberty. People always cite the lack of ass whooping in child's life, but I think it's more the lack of the practice of training people to obey rules or a code of behavior, using punishment to correct disobedience, coupled with a fuckin' lack of training in the customary code of polite behavior in society that's got these kids all fucked up. Kids are running amuck chiefly because parents view them as byproducts of a fuck session and not the future of the world. When parents don't have their shit together and don't give a fuck about getting it together, chances are you'll end up with little domestic terrorists. They aren't being loved. They don't receive true affection. The only set of rules they have to follow is not fuckin' up whatever their momma, daddy or both got going on. Their inundated with violence and disrespect in all forms of art and media. Their diets are all fucked up. They aren't getting proper sleep and so on and so forth. Then on the other hand you have these other muthafuckas who treat their kids like an accessory. Oh, they're dressed up really nice and probably more fashionable than most adults, but they aren't bonding and being nurtured. And no, not all of them, so fix ya rabbit ass mouth, but a lot of them. And to you muthafuckas out their reading this shit asking yourself who the fuck I am to tell you that you're fuckin' your kid(s) up with your piss poor parenting or why the fuck I give fuck...it's because I have to send my offspring out as sheep among the wolves y'all are creating. Let me drop yo bootsy ass off in the middle of a fuckin' ISIS training camp and see how the fuck your sphincter puckers. And as far as not respecting their elders, shit these elders ain't shit either. They're still thottin', tootin' powder, in the club with stockings on or the dudes with their sternum tucked into their britches. Now I'm not saying all kids are hellfire heathens, all parents suck ashy balls or all old people ain't shit, but the number is growing exponentially by the day. Standards are trash from the oldest to the youngest of these in this day and time. If you don't sit yo forearm-length titty havin' ass down somewhere and be a granny. And take yo strange fruit hangin' from a poplar tree Stretch Armstrong do ya balls hang low do the wobble to and fro can you tie them in a knot can you tie them in a bow can you throw them over your shoulder like a continental soldier long testicle sheath havin' ass down somewhere and be a paw paw! I mean you've gotta at least GIVE these kids something worthy of respect in order to be demanded that it's reciprocated. Ya dig? The shit works both ways.

Being a Single Dad in Today's Society:

Is fucking awesome and an American terror story. You know what's funny? I'm like a fucking Chimera or some shit. Mythological and what not in case your knowledge is limited to Tweets and reality television reaction videos on YouTube. Fathers are kind of treated like benchwarmers or the minor league when you think about it. It's funny how single mothers get praised for doing it all, but a father who is at the helm all by his lonesome is told he deserves no pats on the back for doing what he should be doing. Eat my ass with marshmallow puff! The world has a deadbeat dad problem. That's not debatable. Now I'm not requesting a parade or no shit like that, but give me my propers for holdin' it down. Anyway, chicks dig it, as do some of the bros applaud it. Couple niggas look at you sideways like staking claim to ya seed is a deterrent to hoes, but see I'm goin' for broke and I don't mean dollars and cents. See I'm owning up to my strokes that led to new life beginning. Times get hard, but I'm purposefully living. I'm not trying to impress anybody, so I limit my spending. My offspring is my passion, so I'm comfortable with rations as long as I remain capable of being the priest, provider and protector until such time that wings sprout and he takes flight into that good night as the captain of his own ship. And really I extend that same covering to his best friend and his sisters in that I view them as my children as well. I've always said that my son is my guardian angel because prior to his birth, my self-destructiveness was set to cruise control and I was really headed down an abysmal path. So, for me, single fatherhood has been such a tremendous blessing and I count it an honor.

Being a Unique Artist That Dares to Go Against the Norm of Today's Music:
I'm glad someone asked this question. You know, at the end of the day, I have to be true to myself. I feel as though I'm musically adaptive, so I can incorporate components from the

current of music into my signature sound, but only if I feel it's poppin'. If it's a bunch of bullshit, I'm cool on it. As a singer, my goal is to preserve the art of singing. A lot of singers are dumbing their gift down and making this fucking karaoke ass music because people wanna sing along. I'm sorry, though I absolutely love when people learn the lyrics to my songs and sing them; I make music for music lovers who like to LISTEN to music. Stop raking people over coal because they have a gift. It's the equivalent of asking Van Gogh to simplify his paintings, so that you can trace them. GET THE FUCK OUTTA HERE WITH THAT BULLSHIT!!!!! Music is art. It is an individual expression of the artist's life experiences, emotional responses and cognitive reactions to the immensity of life. When it becomes about remuneration, it tends to take on an assembly line type of vibe. I'm not interested. I think what motivates and inspires me most is simply the end product resulting from the process of creation. I love approaching a blank canvas (the beat) and layering textures upon it (verses, choruses, melodies and harmonies) and sitting back in awe of the finished product.

Taking Back a Cheating Spouse:

YEESH!!!!! As a man who has never once re-dated an ex, I simply can't fathom why in the fuck someone would set themselves up for the okie doke, but that's just me. I'm not one of these opinionated narcissists who can't entertain the perspective of others, so I'll lay my personal bias aside and speak to the heart of the matter. It has been said for as long as I can remember that the heart wants what the heart wants and sometimes your heart simply wants a muthafucka who has no qualms about spreading his/her ass cheeks above your face and shitting in your mouth while you're asleep. I'll be the first to admit that the only person I've ever loved more than myself is my child, so I can't posture myself as an expert on the side effects of a love jones. I've also never been married and quite possibly may never be, but this I do know. The best predictor of future behavior is past behavior. People should be very clear when making their wedding vows because lechery is NOT included in for better or for worse. Even the Catholic Church frowns upon infidelity and they treat divorce like aborting Jesus in Mary's womb at the very moment the Holy Ghost caused him to leap. Or was that John the Baptist? Anyway hell, they even count beating your meat or flicking your bean as infidelity. I mean ultimately it's your decision whether or not you trust your partner enough to commit themselves to rehabilitation of their whorish ways, but the odds on that gamble are skewed and you're putting yourself at risk for a rerun of heartache. My best advice would be to save yourself, but if you choose to weather the storm, don't be scared to rock the boat. That means task that muthafucka to prove their renewed commitment to your nuptials. Be explicit, but realistic, with your expectations and demands. And please, for the love of God, don't make excuses for someone who made you a parishioner of community dick or pussy. And I totally get that it can be difficult to just walk away from someone you've invested years of your life into, but man look, they left the gate open for you to throw up your church finger and tiptoe the fuck away when they went to rub their genitals on the grass they presumed to be greener on the other side.

Men and Women Who Have Multiple Biological Parents for Their Children:

Look here, to those of you who manage to make these situations work without ripping one another's throats out, I'm bruising my palms with the round of applause I'm giving y'all because co-parenting is no easy feat...and my son's mother and I get along like friends. For the rest of y'all, ain't no fuckin' way!!!!! The amount of stress you must endure with varying opinions and beliefs as to how children should be raised, not to mention moods, personalities, and vindictiveness...might make ya head blow off!!!!! Mind you this all hinges on whether or not all parties involved are actually involved and haven't just bred. I wouldn't wish the potential for drama and bullshit on my worst non-existent enemies (there's a few people out there silently seething, but they ain't hittin' on nothin', so fuck em! They don't count!) But as far as how I personally feel about people having multiple baby daddies and baby mamas, I personally don't give a shit. I mean it's their pussy and their dick and thusly, their right to do with them as they please as long as it's with consenting adults. People have the right to procreate...abundantly if they so choose. I just hope the kids don't get caught up in a shit-storm of exacerbated fuckery because the parents are swept up in self-centeredness or some shit. I also hope that people aren't biting off more with their genitalia than they can chew with their finances. Kids are not inexpensive. Let's do some two plus two is four minus one is three quick math. The estimated amount of money expected, required, or given in payment to raise a child has become greater in size, amount, intensity and degree in the last year, according to a report from the Department of Agriculture and for a middle-income family the process of promoting and supporting the physical, emotional, social, and intellectual development of a child from infancy to adulthood in 2017 costs $233,610. That one fucking kid! That means raising two kids costs $467,220, which means raising three kids costs $700,830 and four kids costs $934,440. EVERYBODY AIN'T ABLE!!!!! And, yeah, that's really all I have to say about that. Handle your scandal!

Men on the Down Low:

Let's just keep it funky, it's still very taboo to be a gay man (especially in Black and Hispanic communities). People say shit like it's 2016. Live your truth. Be who you are. Blasé whoopty pop. But the fact of the matter is, who you have sex with still either increases or decreases the value of your masculinity. I'm sure folks just fear the weight of that burden. I think it's probably getting easier for like the millennials because they are seeing all of these explosions of acceptance, not to mention an upswing in persons who are not limited in sexual choice with regard to biological sex, gender, or gender identity, unfold before their very eyes or whatever, but even many of them still commit suicide due to bullying and rejection, so there's that. Referring back to the aforementioned comment I made about Black and Hispanic communities, the constraints for men are very stringent. Self-expression is picked apart and categorized to the point that if you aren't either out here thuggin' or adhering to the letter of an unwritten man code, you're gay. Wear fur, you're gay. Color your hair, you're gay. Wear tight pants, you're gay. Dance fluidly, you're gay. Listen to female artists, you're gay. Abstain from bashing gay men, you're gay. Take one too many selfies in a day, you're gay. Eat bananas or ice cream, you're gay. Use a straw, you're gay. Groom yourself more than just a little bit, you're gay. Show affection toward your male, blood relative, you're gay. And so on and so forth. Well, if you're painting dudes who are truly heterosexual into that corner and leaving them very little room to move around and be true to themselves, what makes you think some nigga who likes booty and dick is gonna let you peer into his closet. And don't get me started on religious guilt. The idea of burning in hell for eternity keeps many a secret tucked neatly away out of many a finger-waggers line of sight. That being said, you niggas ain't off the hook. REMINDER: I'm speaking of every race of male when I say niggas. Stop dragging these women through the trenches of your lube-stained covert operations. They don't deserve that. I mean if you're bisexual that's one thing, but if you're bearded up just to save face, that shit is trifling. You're truly a whole bitch and a half if you've been married for 20 years and have been sneaking out to sword fight with other hard legs in ya birthday suit for 19.7 of those years. What the fuck are you doing? Just don't even walk that aisle and have you some secret rendezvous or discreet encounters or whatever the fuck until you're ready to live out in the open or until arthritis robs you of your ability to tap your foot beneath an accompanying bathroom stall and you're forced to cruise fuck buddy apps. And if that time never comes, just do you behind closed doors or in densely foliaged public parks if ya nasty.

Police Brutality

Pro·tect prə'tekt/ verb

1. Keep safe from harm or injury. "He tried to protect Alaysia from the attack"

Synonyms: keep safe, keep from harm, save, safeguard, preserve, defend, shield, cushion, insulate, hedge, shelter, screen, secure, fortify, guard, watch over, look after, take care of, keep; inoculate"they fought to protect their homes and families".

Serve sərv/ verb

1. Perform duties or services for (another person or an organization)."Malcolm has served the church very faithfully"

Synonyms: Work for, be in the service of, be employed by; obey"they served their masters faithfully"

2. Be of service to, be of use to, help, assist, aid, make a contribution to, do one's bit for, do something for, benefit "this job serves the community"

3. Be a member of, work on, be on, sit on, have a place on "she served on the committee for years"

The Police officers Oath

I DO SWEAR,, THAT - I WILL WELL AND TRULY SERVE - OUR SOVEREIGN COUNTRY AND STATE - AS A POLICE OFFICER WITHOUT FAVOR OR AFFECTION - MALICE OR ILL-WILL - UNTIL I AM LEGALLY DISCHARGED, THAT I WILL SEE AND CAUSE - OUR COMMUNITY'S PEACE TO BE KEPT AND PRESERVED - AND THAT - I WILL PREVENT TO THE BEST OF MY POWER - ALL OFFENSES AGAINST THAT PEACE - AND THAT - WHILE I CONTINUE TO BE A POLICE OFFICER - I WILL - TO THE BEST OF MY SKILL AND KNOWLEDGE - DISCHARGE ALL THE DUTIES THEREOF - FAITHFULLY - ACCORDING TO LAW. SO HELP ME GOD.

I wanted to begin this little pop off in that way because this is how we've been taught to think of police officers, but more and more the fabric of that perception is becoming increasingly rugose as an increasing number of law enforcement officers seem to be more committed to bogarting than keeping us safe. Now I'm not saying all officers are bad. That's just plain stupid. But justice can't just be a shibboleth. What hope does that promise us? Yes, criminals should pay for their crimes (all criminals, not just those without badges) and yes, some do resist arrest, fight officers and make policing a royal pain in the ass, but old people, scrawny teenagers and unarmed, cooperative citizens deserve better than near fatal injuries or death! I can't recall the last time it's been an annus mirabilis for law enforcement. It's as though the bad apples are actively trying to quash our faith in the entirety of officers of the law. It seems this savage behavior has begun to reticulate. These sadists are instantly petulant upon arrival to both the possible and certain scenes of crimes. But you know, this has been said, studied and published...it is bordering on favonian...whispy...vaporish. The more we cry out and protest, the more our pleas are likened to an act of cavil. But fuck that!

The actions of these men and women who bastardize the law are undoubtedly invidious. Only the hidebound defend this fuckery because rarely are they its victims. With all of that being said, I cannot conclude this narrative without encouraging you to do your Googles. Here are some titles you should look up and from which you should ingest knowledge: The History of Policing in the United States, Part 1 Written by Dr. Gary Potter; A Brief History of Slavery and the Origins of American Policing Written by Victor E. Kappeler, Ph.D.; How the U.S. Got Its Police Force by Olivia B. Waxman; The Early Days of American Law Enforcement by David R. Johnson; Slave Patrols, "Packs of Negro Dogs" and Policing Black Communities by Larry H. Spruill; Policing and Oppression Have a Long History by Stephen L. Carter; and Slavery and Police Abuse: The Continuum of History by Joyce A. Joyce. These writings should give you a clear understanding of the current climate between Black people and the police.

Transgenders:

Someone asked how we can accept transgenders when they aren't able to accept themselves. Someone else said perhaps them seek to change their physical to match identifying with or expressing a gender identity that differs from the one which corresponds to their sex at birth is the greatest expression of acceptance they can offer. Still others ask why we should care either way if it doesn't affect us personally. I've never really formulated an opinion on transgenders because I've never actually participated in a conversation on the subject of them, but I'll try my best to limn a clear thought. I'm just on some let people do them type shit. If they like it, I couldn't care less as long as they're not out here deceiving people...fine by me #MissSophiaVoice. There are bigger fish to fry in this crazy ass world than what gender a person identifies as. I mean unless you're feeding, financing, or fucking said person, why are you so invested in their life choices? I know this affects bathrooms and sports and shit, but in the grand scheme of things does it really fuck up YOUR life in a significant way when someone chooses to gender swap?

Having Sex with Coworkers:

I mean, read your employee handbook I guess. Y'all know good and damn well they frown upon that shit for the simple fact that people get all in their feelings and bring their dick slingin'/pussy poppin' drama to the workplace and make shit stressful for everybody. In between frying chicken, you're out in the parking lot slashing Carol's tires because you felt that she lingered a little too long when she gave Brennan a hug this morning. Now everybody's in Deandre's office looking dumbfounded because you had a pussy tantrum. And we all know shit like this happens all the time. Somebody at your job is toting an abortion secret right now because they got bills and a lil after hours dick from Daniel in the next cubicle ain't about to fuck up their coins! Handle your fucking scandal like adults, people. Leave all these middle school theatrics at Booker T. Washington or wherever the fuck. If you know you're prone to get pussywhipped or dickmatized, don't shit where you sleep or eat or whatever the saying says. Find you some non-company bussit and sit down somewhere!

Chapter 11: Protection from creditors given to a company in financial difficulties for a limited period to allow it to reorganize.

Where Has All the Good/Real Music Gone:

That's quite the subjective question. My best advice would be, if you aren't getting what you like from the mainstream music industry, you might wanna look underground for some independent artists. Explore! There is an abundance of music sharing sights that host a plethora of music for you to peruse. If you're so bent out of shape about the music you're being fed, go on a hunt. Find something, someone or a group of folks who create the music that speaks to your soul. It's definitely out there. You just have to get out there and look for it. Then again, you might just be getting old. Think about it. Your parents probably thought the music you loved was trash just as their parents probably thought the music they loved was trash. Perhaps you should create a playlist from the era of music that up jumped your boogie. I, for one, am able to enjoy the progression of music. Furthermore, no style or genre of music has ever truly left the scene. Sure it may not be on the Billboard Hot 100, but somewhere there is someone making it and making it well. The question then becomes, how much do you want to hear it?

[Before I get into the next topic, shout out to all of the people who have the courage to write their need for help on a cardboard sign! It can't be easy to swallow your pride and stand out in traffic asking complete strangers for assistance. And I'm talking about all of the people who genuinely need the help! Fuck all of the pretenders who are out there scamming people when they don't really have a need! And fuck all the people who ask dumb shit like, "Well, where did they get the marker from to write on the cardboard sign?" It might seem like a legitimate question in some instances, but most of the time you're just looking for an excuse not to be of help!]

Why Is Everyone Trying to Keep Up with the Joneses/Who Are the Joneses:

"Goals are like magnets. They'll attract the things that make them come true." - Tony Robbins

The good 'ol Joneses are just that…a goal. Who they are is different to every individual who aspires to be like them. To some, the Joneses are flashy jewelry, expansive estates, luxury vehicles, gourmet cuisine and shit like that. To others, they're white picket fences, soccer mom vans, two parent households, three kids, a couple of pets, upper middle class wages, a cul-de-sac, trust falls, camp fires and shit like that. To others, they're tantric sex, sex swings, blowup dolls, anal beads, nipple clamps, wife swapping, orgies and deep dish pelvic thrusts six days a week. On the seventh day, they rested and shit like that. The Joneses are simply the greener grass on the other side; the carrot dangling from a stick above the donkey's head. And to others still, they are a trap god and his queen, the bando, put that on the set, automatic assault rifles, minion little niggas at their beck and call, police in their pocket, roundtable meetings like Nino Brown or King Arthur and shit like that. They are what motivate people to get up each morning and face the day with their definition of optimism. Everybody has a fuckin' Jones of some sort.

But What Was the Question and Who Asked It?

#580: I find that when people have complaints about relationships of any kind, those complaints are usually rooted in that person expecting others to view and operate in relationships as THEY do! That's rarely going to happen. Sadly, when you dive in head first without thoroughly examining your surroundings, you run the risk of head trauma. I'm not suggesting that you allow people to change you. I'm suggesting that you require people to earn you. Unrequited love depletes us mentally, physically, emotionally and spiritually. Don't allow people to drain you. Operate on the system of cravings. Give people a taste of the magnificence of you then withdraw yourself and allow them to seek you out. But more important than anything, at the first sign that your love is being taken for granted, unplug them from it.

#8769: So I'm about to give you the best advice, not opinion, for your music that I can offer. The first thing you must identify is who your audience is. There is a specific population of people whose taste in music will be satiated perfectly by what you're creating. FIND THOSE PEOPLE! That's your mission!!!!! Also, when you've created a song that you know is a banger, promote that hoe within an inch of its life. As artists, songs get old to us way sooner than they do to other people. Don't be in a rush to put out new material without properly putting your full weight behind something good. Maroon 5 promoted their first album for something like FIVE YEARS before they blew up. Can you imagine how sick of that shit they must've been? But they believed in it enough to keep introducing it to new people until it popped. Always be professional in all aspects of the game. Remember that you are your brand, so whenever people see you they associate you with your music and if you don't have your shit together, both your brand and your music will suffer. Also, as a woman, LEARN THE BUSINESS FOR YOURSELF, so that you're not at the mercy of men to get shit done for you.

#2: I'm really not a fan of being the bigger person when it comes to someone disrespecting me, so I'm not going pretend that this advice is at all objective...and it will be short. Ma'am, cuss that bitch out down to the cellular level and tell her to put some respect on your name. I know you want to be a role model for your kids, but what better role can you model than that of someone who stands up for herself? Try to do it privately and if she continues to avoid you, blast that ass. You might be saving her from the ass whooping she'd receive from someone who isn't her family. I feel you need to address it because it's bothering you. If it wasn't, I'd suggest you leave it alone.

Say your peace and leave it there.

#3990: Oh cry me a fuckin' river! Who doesn't hate their job? Plus, you said it pays well and you don't have any better options, so suck it up. Your problem is you have nothing to stimulate or entertain you beyond work. And no I don't mean TV or social media. You have no passion. Sure you have your kids, but what are you doing for you exclusively? What are you doing that adds value and sustenance to your life? What are you doing that excites and interests you? If nothing, then you'll likely always be miserable unless you create or stumble upon work that fulfills you and affords you the same pay. Until that happens, you're going to have to do SOMETHING besides home and work to make sure you don't go off the deep end.

#27: To keep it all the way <u>100</u> with you, if you aren't 100% confident in your mental health right now, then leave your son exactly where he is. The mere fact that you're fearful of assuming responsibility for him again communicates to me that you're lacking confidence in your ability to both be effective and survive. I'd say it's much too soon. You need to spend more time focusing on you, so that when the time comes that he is placed back within your care, you are operating at full capacity. Mental health isn't like the common cold, especially when suicidal ideations are on the table. Just because you feel better at the moment that doesn't mean you're out of the fire. Seek professional help and make reunification with your son the end goal of your treatment plan. But please don't assume this is just something that will pass. Depression and the stress of parenting, not to mention all of the random stressors that can pop up in our lives at any given moment, can be a lethal cocktail. I say all of that to say, get you right so you can do right by your kids. Hope this helps, love.

#38: Are you crippled by the responsibility itself or the expectation of you having to handle the responsibility in a particular amount of time or in a particular fashion? Often we allow the expectations of others to become barnacles in our lives and if that's the case, tell said persons to either share in the responsibility or shut the fuck up. If it is indeed the responsibility itself, you cannot destroy yourself because of your limitations. I'm not suggesting making excuses or shirking your responsibility, but the fact of the matter is you can only do what you CAN do. Focus on what's most important, prioritize and what not. God grant her the state of being calm, peaceful, and untroubled, so that she can accept the things she cannot change; the bravery to change the things she can; and the experience, knowledge, understanding, common sense, and good judgment to know the difference. Live one day at a time. Enjoy one moment at a time. Accept hardships as the pathway to peace.

#553: The number one problem I have with people who petition me for relationship advice is that they are always looking outwardly rather than looking inwardly. You're the only constant. Everything that you are attracting is a reflection of everything that you are emitting. If you've been attracting disingenuous people, then chances are you haven't been genuine in some aspect of your life. It can be something as simple as telling "little white lies" habitually. It could be lies by omission. It could be smiling in her face then rolling your eyes when she turns her back. Maybe I'm different, but I've just never been the type to obsess about what the other person brings to the table. I've always been more focused on being so on my shit that she can't stand to sit across from me because my energy causes her discomfort. So maximize YOU and watch the fakers start being repelled by your energy. The unwanted can't creep in if there are no cracks.

#2695: The first red flag for me is when people quote the number of times they've been cheated on in conjunction with the number of years they've been with someone. The second red flag for me is someone who has endured, and thereby condoned multiple acts of cheating, actually having a crisis of conscience when they start to get that tingle. You can't kill the problem unless you kill its root and the root of the problem is not that he cheated or that you're contemplating cheating. The root of the problem is WHY YOU STAYED!!!!!! I'm going to go out on a limb and say you stayed under the veil of your vows. You stayed to show him that you could be for him what he couldn't be for you. You stayed to show him that you were the superior spouse. You stayed because you wanted him to regret his mistakes. You stayed because you wanted him to make it up to you. You stayed because of advice you either rejected or listened to in favor of your own choice. You may have even stayed for children. But you never healed. You never healed because cheating was in fact a deal breaker for you, but you stayed. And now you're tempted. And you feel justified in your temptation because you stayed. But the root has ensnared you. See, if you go through with it, you become the antithesis of every reason you stayed and if you don't go through with it, you remain a prisoner of the root. But you've already gone through with it in your mind and you're not sure you'll recover if you go through with it with your body. Now I could either tell you to cheat on your husband or not and be done with this, but I'm not. I'm going to challenge you not to cheat on yourself...because you stayed. I'm also not going to tell you to just abandon your new object of interest...because you stayed. I'm going to challenge you to stand at this crossroads and decide whether you're done staying or whether you want to move forward. If you're still truly a prisoner of the root and don't foresee yourself ending your marriage, then don't soil your legacy of staying and complicate that other man's life. But if you're done staying, then just leave and see what the future holds beyond the root.

#777: First of all, don't tell me what type of fuckin' advice to give you! Second of all, you're acting an ass and being evil to people because you don't want to accept that you may die in 2-5 years, but are there not better ways to not give a fuck? I'm not going to tickle your pussy and tell you that everything is going to be okay because that may not be the case. I will, however, challenge you to cram as much life into that 2-5 years as you possibly can. Live in defiance of death's advancement upon you. You can either live beyond your highest expectations for 2-5 years or you can have a long, drawn out 2-5 year death. The latter sounds like fucking trash. Oh, and the surest way for you to die alone is isolating your loved ones by being a chapped asshole and by keeping your illness a secret. Make life your bitch. Be a bitch to death. I always like those characters better in movies.

#811: You say you're single by choice and have high standards, so the only way you'll be single forever is if you choose to be. No? And do you live up to the standards you have for others?

#39: My advice is to put that shit on the table from the jump. It'll scare away the ones who can't handle it and save you from developing interest only to be disappointed when you find out it's a deal breaker for them. Ask them to share something personal then you share (no matter what they say). Be prepared for either a positive or negative reaction. I was a case manager at Regional AIDS Intercommunity Network for five years, so I'm very familiar with stories like yours. The fear of rejection after your health has been hijacked by someone you trusted with your body. You're older (not old), so unfortunately you're dealing with a generation of people who still view HIV/AIDS as a death sentence and who view those LIVING with HIV/AIDS as the disease rather than a PERSON who has it. Shit sucks, but it's the reality of the situation. They've got images of the early days stuck in their minds. This new PREP generation isn't as imprisoned by that fear. Were I still at the job, I could've directed you to dating sites and events in your area where everyone in attendance is either positive or positive-friendly, but I left. The first time is always the scariest and most uncomfortable, but don't cross that threshold until you're ready. And don't deny someone the choice you were denied. Hope this helps!

#1000 The advice I give to the entrepreneur who knows that he or she can do it, but doesn't is please give your idea to me and watch me do it. One of two things will happen: 1. If they give it to me, they were never serious about it in the first place. 2. They get scared by the thought of me becoming successful from their idea and that causes them to get active. As such, inbox me your ideas so I can get started.

#62270 You're so focused on finding someone that you've become a maze. Like I told #26, maybe you need to be found. I don't even talk to you regularly and I can feel the energy of your longing. Sometimes it's hard to see when you're looking. Sometimes you have to look away and allow your eyes to focus before you can see clearly. Invest all of your energy elsewhere, like ensuring that you're whole and ready for love, so that when love arrives on the scene you have the energy to invest in the love!

#22 Trust issues don't just spring up without a genesis. Your problem is easily solved by explaining to your love that you have these issues and asking for patience. Your true challenge for yourself is not overcoming your trust issues, but rather not using them as excuses to deny yourself love. The right love will dissolve those issues. The right love will be patient with those issues. The right love will be the doctor to those issues. Love covers many a fault and what not. When you're someone who has been hurt and who has become calloused, the encumbrances you present aren't decorative. They are armor. The right love will patiently caress your fears and undress you from them until you stand naked before love ready to be made...love.

#100 You have one of two options. You can turn the other cheek or you can shake the table. I eliminate disrupters to my peace to make it all the more easy for me to focus on my blessings. I'm not a fan of fucking with people who get under my skin to the point that I wanna cuss them out, so I erase them from memory. You can love them...from a distance.

#91 What people think of you is not your problem...it's theirs. Your responsibility is to live the life that makes you happy; then and only then will the universe surround you with people who truly celebrate your uniqueness. Right now all of your energy is focused on judgment, so you're being rewarded with judgmental people. Cut that dead weight, find you then run off into the sunset with yourself!!!!!

#26 Have you ever thought that maybe it's not about you finding someone, but maybe you should be found? I find that with attractive people it kind of makes you feel inadequate to be alone...like something must be wrong with you. Then you bump and scrape through situationships trying to find someone who will see beyond your looks and accept you for who you are. Then when they find out you're feisty or quirky or crazy, you haven't even prepared for that hurdle. Just chill. Date without the hope or expectation of a relationship. Enjoy YOURSELF and allow the romance to unfold when you are in alignment for it. Sometimes the desire to be in a relationship is a pungent smell that keeps people at bay. And trust me, there's someone whose crazy fits neatly into the crevices of your crazy to make a smooth masterpiece.

#16 Don't allow fear and contentment to rob you of an amazing opportunity. Chances are the reasons you want to leave are the very reasons you want to stay, but where will you be better able to flourish? You never want to have to ask yourself "What if?" And considering that this move is for a job that means you're starting out with somewhat of a foundation. You can move and remain connected, but you'll never know all you can be or what possibilities lay ahead if you allow yourself to be anchored when you truly want to soar.

#5 Use your cell phone to call the bank and ask them to have the janitor to bring you some tissue so you can wipe your ass or cup your shit, hobble over to the paper towels, wet a couple and voila you in the game.

I, Too, Am Oppressed

Regarding the "Pro-White" Rally in Stone Mountain, GA on 23 Apr 2016 I believe it was: Oppression leads to people feeling the need to express appreciation for their race. Yes, you can be Pro-Black even when you're not oppressed personally because you see how the tentacles of oppression are choking the life out of those who look like you, but haven't been able to seemingly rise out of the oppression. White people have no need to be Pro-White because everything in this country that isn't labeled with a non-White racial identifier serves the interests of White people. Notice I said need. Rallies and protests are meant to challenge a certain stigma attached to being something (rallying for Black lives, for example, because blackness is perpetually stigmatized). Why are White people rallying for Pro-Whiteness when Whiteness is promoted daily on media outlets and within virtually every facet of this society? There's no need for it to be broadcasted during a rally. The fact that Pro-White has meant anti-Non-White throughout the annals of American history does not necessitate that Pro-Black or any other minority means Anti-White. So when I read statements by White people such as "Why can't there be a White Women Expo" or "Think of all the hell that would break loose if there was a Miss White CU Pageant", my soul vomits because there has never been a need to label something as White when those who have maintained control are White. You see, anything that was created for Blacks, Latinos or Asians, etc. was created to offset exclusion from institutions that were intrinsically understood to be for White people ONLY. We can't even take credit for the idea because it was given to us by White people with drinking fountains and bathrooms. Lastly, when you fix your mouth or fingertips to propose why we just don't get over something that happened "so long ago", ask yourself why you can't in that you're either willingly or unknowingly contributing to the symptoms and ramifications of something that happened "so long ago". I understand that this may be difficult, but boohoo. You're being asked to consider. We're being asked to ignore and endure. Racism was created by the White Supremacist initiative. White Supremacy is what caused so many of your ancestors to abandon identifying themselves as Irish, Scottish, Norwegian, Scandinavian, etc. to reap the benefits of marching beneath the banner of Whiteness. The sooner that White people get past this stage of denial and start dealing in truth, the better this nation will be and America can truly be great for the first time in her history. I do not hold you accountable for the sins of your fathers. I hold you accountable for these tantrums you throw publicly, which serve to undermine the plight of people in this country who are fighting to survive despite the fact that we were never intended to be citizens of this country. I love America because it is my home, but I won't pretend that she has not been ill for centuries just because it makes you uncomfortable. I would never ask you not to be proud to be White. I would ask why you only feel the need to brandish your Whiteness when other races are finding the courage to dignify their pride with a demand for true change...change that will ensure equity, rather than equality. Because how can there be equality when an entire race of people is struggling to get on equal footing after centuries old deficits? Asé

Chapter 12: Lap-dancing with Shadows

"I like Migos a lot. I fuck wit em heavy. You know? It's just somethin' about that energy that I connect with. I done seen a lotta crazy shit, but I done been through even more crazy shit. I done been cut a few times. A bitch tried to throw bleach on me one time...over a nigga. I beat that bitches ass every time I seen her for three weeks straight. I think the bitch moved to Dallas or some shit. I don't know. I just know I don't see the bitch no more. When I talk to crows, they hear my heartache. I've been down so long, up look like make believe...but God got me. He always do. It seem like no matter how much I fuck up, he be like Lay, you know betta than that shit HAHAHAHAHAHA! My God. My god.

I done had some good ass jobs over the years. I used to drives buses. I worked at Ft. Sill National Bank. I can't even tell you why I started smokin' crack. Well, yes I can. This ol part-time job havin' ass nigga I used to fuck wit talked me into tryin' it. Now I know you like BITCH that's some dumb ass shit, but I was bored and playin' imaginary in-love just tryin' to distract myself from that gotdamn hamster wheel. Had I been thinkin', I woulda maxed out my boring ass life and got the fuck up outta here, but I got trapped chasin' that high.

My nigga you don't even realize you lookin' different to people and the world is burnin' around you when you floatin' all day. And I'm a relentless ass crackhead. Bitch, I'm a muthafuckin' rocket scientist when it comes to scheming' up on some crack. By the time I realized I wanted to reboot my life, I was buried underneath a shopliftin' habit outta this world, sellin' my body to anybody wit a couple of dollars who could get hard and fuck me, and absolutely no fuckin' sense of self.

Lawton is the perfect breeding ground for a muthafucka like me. I was too afraid to leave and I convinced myself that I could rise above the curse, not realizin' the town itself is a livin', breathin' sorcerer. Shit, I'm 43 muthafuckin years old and all I can honestly put on a résumé for the past ten years is suckin' dick and buildin' crack pipes outta random shit you find around the house or in alleys.

Nigga do you know how long I been out here lap-dancin' wit shadows? I dance to the bombs burstin' on Ft. Sill. And I had to learn to be okay with being either invisible or the butt of a joke that nobody says out loud. I'm a life without memories. I'm a story without a plot. I happen without expectations. I am a carcass that's been left to rot. If I should die before I wake, I pray the Lord my soul to take, but he ain't listenin'. I'm a call forwarded to Voice Mail. Nigga I died today and I am standin' at the pearly gates tryin' to explain how my pursuit of Heaven became my personal hell.

They'll find my body in about three days. It'll be by accident because no one is actually lookin' for a bitch. There are park benches sittin' on top of the ashes of the bridges I burned. It makes sense that you will be able to sprinkle my body in about 45 minutes." #LawtonViews

Chapter 13: Sometimes You've Gotta Say Bless Their Hearts to Keep from Cussing

"Beyoncé all day. I don't know. She just makes me wanna fuck shit up in a glamorous, yet still connected to the hood type of way. I don't know why people hate her so much. She works hard as hell. I really just respect her strength. No, I'm not a member of the beehive.

I've been managing this property for three years. It's sad and it's hard. You know, some of the people who live here are here by no fault of their own. They literally inherited the poverty spirit like a generational curse. I just look at them sometimes and it feels like their outlook on life is spitting in my face. How do you get through to someone who truly believes that welfare is a come-up? I've held groups and lectures and workshops and I swear to God attendance is due to the free food. But this is what I signed up for. I think of it this way, maybe I won't get through to the parents, but there's a chance that I might get through to one young man or one young woman.

There's this girl. She's such a beautiful young woman. Her mom is Black and her dad is Comanche. She comes to talk to me just about every day and there's such eagerness in her eyes that I just wanna give her hope. I've heard about the inordinate amount of undo stress millennials are under, but I've always taken it with a grain of sea salt. She carries herself in a manner that would suggest she's been taking care of herself, and possibly some younger siblings, for a long time. This wasn't just some latchkey kid story. This child was fending for her own survival and it was only a matter of time before an older man with a little bit of money and a bloodlust for young pussy came along and smeared the last remnant of her youthful innocence in a puddle of sexual fluids. I did not want to see her become another pile of dry bones lying in the wet spot after giving her flesh to some undeserving bastard whose value for her was equivalent to Happy Meal.

I'm quite sure I could venture out and find a job at a more reputable complex, but I feel as though young girls like her are my ministry, so I stay and I suffer right along with them so to speak.

Then there are the ones who have committed themselves to a life of, pardon my ratchet, no fucks given. They lend a very particular brand of lack of interest, enthusiasm, or concern to our little community. If I'm being honest, I don't really manage these folks. I mostly pray that they don't show up at my office talking loud, smelling loud, and expecting mountains out of molehills even louder.

I don't want to feel as though I need SWAT gear every time you come to report some minor issue. And I knew what I was signing up for when I took the job, but Jesus has to be tired of being a fence all around me. I say that at least 15 times a day.

Oh, and I never get tired of people assuming that I'm working with the police to catch them in some type of criminal activity. You just can't keep your business inside your home because you feel like it. I'm involved by virtue of my job title.

Anyway, I think I'm ready to be done with this shit. They can have it." #LawtonViews

Chapter 14: Thug Passion

"I just needed for there to be blood. I wanted there to be sacrifice on a loop to add meaning and value to my voids. I just needed for there to be endings because my life never stopped starting. I was always rebooting. My eyes were thirsty. They needed drink. They were tired of being dry day in and out. How the fuck would a life such as this be able to make space for genuine smiles?

I've dreamt of good times. I've lost myself in wonderings of what my body would look like dancing, but the kind of dancing that spoke to the fucking and sucking of freedom. I was often touched in ways that rolled over and stared deeply into the eyes of orgasm. And I would blink to a rhythm of portraits. Perhaps I should've been more cautious with the blood.

The bullets run too fast to check for smears of hemoglobin above a doorframe. And I was wildly lecherous with my heart, but infidelity was bred into the culture. And I liked having the name that was a key to any entrance, but breaking and entering allowed me to feast upon a constant diet of cardio. And you see these things made manifest right before your eyes, but you know there was no trigger because you are the space between their life and death.

And if her pussy became wet because she was fearful, I was a master surfer. And I would stomp a hole in her tide. And people often speak of going numb, but you had to have some sense of what feeling was like in order to have something with which to compare it. And these Pitbulls became an emblem, so I learned to sleep with both eyes suspiciously resistant to closure. And these are the times when I would forget who I was completely, so what I would do is begin to reenact fragments of stolen glances at programming I wasn't allowed to be interested in.

And the rules were genetically encoded into your understanding of the world, so no one ever spoke or wrote him. And when you flip a coin and both sides are death, you begin to see the gift and the curse of it all. And there are no hauntings that nag at your subconscious because the blood was sent to purify the redundancy of your inability to go beyond. And so they blur into a pulp of fiction because snitches get stitches, so even your recollection fears the witness stand and suicides itself.

And you wonder about the good times, but there was only one. Survival. And I could write the great American novel, but I would become a stagecoach and it the revolver that would rob me of my good time.

You know I only write like that after I've been listenin' to Tupac on repeat. I used to be a Pimp C ass nigga off top, feel me? But after a nigga done lived thru and seen so much, you don't wanna keep force-feedin' yaself the same drugs. Nigga, I got four whole daughters out this mufucka, feel me? Four beautiful lil thangs that will one day grow up and have a nigga call em all kinds a bitches or try to force em to betray the love I taught em to have for they self. That's my legion demons." #LawtonViews

Chapter 15: Continually Continued

"Okay, so don't laugh cuz I'll fuck you up, but I really be lettin' my inner white girl to that Firework song by Katy Perry. HAHAHAHAHAHAHA I told you not to laugh, shit. But, you know, my inner white girl is just my escape route. I have to sit in these people's faces every day to assess if they're really capable of not being a safety threat to their kids. Nothing prepares you for the day when you're no longer able to be shocked. They warn you, but that's not really preparation. And even worse than losing the ability to be stocked is discovering that all the problems and issues your loved ones are having are inconsequential as shit. This puts the heaviest of strains on relationships.

The eyes of children speak an entirely new language to me now. It's a shouting tongue-twister of inexplicable emotions and minimal word selection. Their crumbled spirits like wads of discarded scratch paper with the secret exploits of abuse and neglect written on them. The shit that makes little old ladies clutch their pearls or borderline ain't-shit parents sit up straight and pray to the gods of do better.

All of the storm clouds that paparazzi stalk me bear the erasure marks from silver linings that once were. I've rehearsed this porcelain smile to the point of perfection because with THIS BITCH ping-ponging in my brain on a loop, I have to pad my professionalism with a little rehearsed sincerity.

Piles of animal feces. Malodor. Dirty diapers. Food waste. Exposed wiring. Soiled laundry. Closets serving as makeshift nurseries. Chained. Bound. Bruised. Beaten. Bleeding. The new normal they've been melted and poured into for the chance at a future is just as traumatic as the skeletons from which they emerged.

Real shit though. I used to feel as though I was draped in an invisible cape...for like the first six months. I felt like I was changing lives and it was lowkey inebriating. But like all good Wizards of Oz, there are intricately woven curtains shielding the truth of the matter.

I'll never forget the very first photographs I had to take of a severely malnourished little girl. She was honey blonde. Her eyes were aquamarine. The flavor of meth vapors had tattooed her taste-buds. It was as though her rib cage was some archaic instrument. Her bed sores were like busted, puckering lips. Her smile muscles needed exercise, so she looked somewhat like she'd suffered a stroke. The simple taste of applesauce changed her world. We sang harmonies with our silent stares. She was four and fifteen foster homes later, the taste of applesauce still quenches her chaos." #LawtonViews

Chapter 16: Sticks, Stones, and Broken Bones

"This here is my nineteenth year. I got that wrist shit...carpel tunnels or however the fuck you say it. My knees fucked up. My neck fucked up. My back fucked up. My feet bad. But my mortgage don't give a good goddamn? If it wasn't for DMX, I probably woulda walked out this bitch a long ass time ago.

Shit, I'm pretty smart and I can't write when I want to, but I wasn't ever no good in school and shit because I hated it, so I ain't really have no choice, but to get hired on out here. Tossin' tires done almost took me up outta here, but a nigga built Ford tough and shit. But I can't really complain too much. This job has kept me and my family afloat. I've been able to send my kids to college, buy a nice house and cars, take vacations, and just live more comfortably than a lot of folks I know.

I told my kids to get the fuck up outta here and never look back. I mean they're always welcome to come back home, but it better be on some last resort type shit. The world has so much more to offer and I just want them to get out there and get it how they live. I don't want them on social media lookin' up to people and wishin' they could have those experiences. Get the fuck out there and have them yourselves. Mama and Daddy gon be alright, you feel me.

I think back to when I was their age and I really wasn't shit. I was out here doin' ignorant shit and fuckin' up, but thankfully my mama knew a preacher and he sat me down and helped me put some shit into perspective.

Have you ever seen that documentary 13th? That's some real ass shit. That could be me. A victim of systematic racism; Just another black man further stripped of his identity and heard it into a steel labyrinth of inhumanity. There are no truly meaningful tokens of appreciation when you're a menace to society. People masquerade their fear and pretend to really rock with you, But all that superficial shit is really just a hi and bye glorified to look like loyalty.

Boredom will get you in a hurry to become a burial plot and tombstone. The memory of you becomes an obituary on a T-shirt. You become the architect of your own phantom. You design a version of yourself that exists outside of your loved ones' ability to sense you.

They want more than anything to keep you alive, but as with all dead things you become something that must be removed from view. If they are to ever suffocate the pain, then they must remove its air supply. So they pick out a few stellar moments and really do nothing with the others. Eventually the others become fugues, never finding their way back.

Things once taken for granted rip through as they wrestle with your nonexistence. And your greatest roar is, but a whisper to the mortal ear." #LawtonViews

Chapter 17: Even Diamonds Need to Be Polished from Time to Time

"It's hard out here, bruh. That's why I worship at the altar of UGK. When you say you wanna be a rapper, you instantly become a clown to a lot of people. And the constant uphill battle is proficient in tearin' you down. You report firsthand how your mind interprets the world with the hope the something so relatable is made manifest as you unfurl. Braggadocios tenacity serving as your ember of hope. It lies dormant beneath layers of fuck bitches, get money, sell dope. You find yourself in competition with not the lyrics of a peer, but the beats upon which you share your gift become the adversary you must commandeer.

These are weeping sentiments for some whorish addiction to attention. This is the blood of my blood; the sweat of my sweat; essentially my soul's crucifixion. But a round of applause is like nourishment, so I feed upon it voraciously. What a gift that someone carved out a space to wine and dine me. Yet, I tumble still as the slope remains slippery at every given turn. And the heat I know my mixtape emits is sadly perceived as a slow burn.

So my rhyme scheme gets thrown off and my cadence becomes the prisoner of a stutter. This ghoulish doubt that circumvents my progression muffles every metaphor I mutter. No recklessness powers my folly, but rather apathy cloaked in feigned interest. So my punchlines scramble to escape the land of mental midgets because my hyperbole confounds stupidity as it's given. Oh, this fucking prison.

I'm not some autocorrected, ghostwritten product. I'm not some fly by night nursery rhyme spewer. I'm not some forgettable wonder that ain't the shit because his counterfeit is manure. I maneuver through these tapestries like a thief hopping fences evading hot pursuit. The only problem is I'm supposed to be chasing down my dreams not trying to add a proverbial brain fart to my commute. And I'm so resolute in my thinking; thinking that my resolution is so astute." #LawtonViews

Chapter 18: Happily Pissing on Flowers

"I am not invisible. I cannot be. I cannot. Simple things really, but who are we to quantify majesty, right? This guy knows what I'm talking about.

You think that bravery means painting your fingernails and smearing your penis against surfaces cool to the touch. Phlegm. Phlegm and masturbation. That's what you are.

I wrote, but mostly I screamed...into pillows or open fields...at whomever or in whatever would hear me. I body roll on creaky corridors of the mind. I'm heavily into symbols, Peter Pan and Lois Lane...leather, chains, whips, ships and muskets. I feel I'm rather iridescent; a sparkling mess of emotional waste. You'll find me riveted by perspiration and Latter Day Saints.

Cycling widens my vocabulary. I'm a mechanical breeze of sorts. Just imagine my melodies. They tremble for no other reason than to stand apart from the vanilla of it all. Biting my nails. Biting my nails. Biting my nails for the fun of it. Do you know that I used to fuck teachers and imagine they were Presidents and Captains of Industry? That was a rip-roaring good time. I should've been bored enough to expose them, but life was such a wanderlust then.

Most of these ungrateful cunts don't appreciate the upper echelon chemistry we get to ingest. They can call it psychotropic, but I know it is all mind-altering, little lambs...little lambs. Someone should've noticed that I liked to lollipop crayons while solving Sudoku and Rubick's Cubes. But people will never reveal that they're intentionally negligibly homicidal to children's brains.

The greatest compliment I ever received was that my singing voice was a hysterectomy for the ears. People don't bathe in cow's milk enough. My hobbies include calculus and knitting bikinis for the elderly. I would wear a choir robe daily if weather permitted, but I don't want to walk around smelling like a cheeseburger with horse radish like I did the summer of 2013.

I'd like to fistfight Bjork one Sunday per month for shits and giggles. I wouldn't mind if I ate a side order of Church's Chicken and beef fried rice with every meal. I want to swim in seltzer water. I dream of Jin with a proclivity toward date rape.

Am I being filmed or tape recorded? You've stopped writing. You're built like a gourd up top and a clubbed foot down bottom.

I would literally dance naked at a klan rally if I was guarded by at least 15 top ranked UFC fighters. I once faked Tourette's Syndrome for an entire year. I told my doctors I was cured by consensual anal sex. Hi, Barb. Hi, Claude. Last names and credentials and shit. I wrote over five thousand letters to the Department of Defense begging for my pussy to be declared a weapon of mass destruction. Still waiting.

I once lived off a strict diet of oyster crackers and backwash. No, seriously. I collected all of my friends last few sips in 2-liter bottles and froze them, thawed them and drank them with frozen grapes as ice cubes. My immune system is a filthy whore.

I once set a goal of fitting a cue ball in my mouth. The attempts served as the catalyst for my fear of getting stretch marks around my mouth. I film myself every night to catch myself sleepwalking. Don't ask me to view the videos. I'm a sickeningly free spirit.

CAN WE GET A CUP OF TADPOLES OVER HERE FOR CRYING OUT LOUD? I had to register as a sex offender because I blessed the vestibule of City Hall with diarrhea. If you laugh, I'll run into you at full speed. I contend that it was a twerking accident. I love being followed. There aren't enough stalkers in this town. I could literally flick my bean at one of our many adult virgins and they'd sooner call the cops on me than let their dicks sneeze in my hair. Are you any good at hypnosis? My bowels need a cheerleading coach.

Droplets of rain on an ashen tongue. I am not a worry wart. Leveled playing fields left sunken and inverted. This is my testimony and I purchased every syllable of it at a hefty price. I am forever manifesting and unpacking, you know? Because people are really just irrepressible globs of irritation that I just can't seem to soothe by soaking in ice cubes.

I'd suck an entire foot for a lap dance right now. I'm sorry. What was the question again?"
#LawtonViews

Chapter 19: The Void Beyond the Whispers

"I'm a perfect storm...and I mean that in whatever way you just interpreted it. I was raised in what most would consider dysfunction and I was ostentatiously the living embodiment of it. I began with lighting fires. The rush of adrenaline has the uncanny ability to transport me between realms. I would sneak with the hope of being caught. With every ember of mischief, I grew braver. Getting yoked up was the most attention I received in months. My tears intoxicated me because I was feeling. You don't realize these things when you are a small child, but as you grow older the rush becomes addictive." #LawtonViews

Chapter 20: GTFOHWTBS

ONYX and OSIRIS

Onyx: I'm so sick of us. I'm sick of us and marching. I'm sick of us protesting. I'm sick of us begging for the approval of people who have never given a big fat rat's ass about us. The Munchhausen syndrome is out of control. What happened to us?

Osiris: Because of your intelligence and education, I know that you know exactly what has and is happening to us. Since the before Civil Rights Movement, there has been an imbalance of influence on our way of thinking. After the Civil Rights Movement, the government murdered all of our leaders (unbeknownst to us at the time), which left us in the vulnerable position of having no stratagem or guidance for digging our way out of the hole in which forced residency in this country tried to bury us. All of our attempts to unite and progress were forcibly thwarted by violence, ex. The Bombing of Black Wall Street in Tulsa. We've collectively had a broken spirit as a people. It's hard and quite possibly impossible to swim to shore when a shark has you by the ankles and is trying to swim in the opposite direction.

Onyx: Bro, I really need you to go and do some research on those organizations from the 60s and get back with me on how our efforts to progress have been thwarted.

Osiris: I'm VERY familiar with Black Wall Street. I'm an Oklahoman originally and my mom is from Tulsa. It was never rebuilt. It was swept under the rug and erased from history. The fact of the matter is, there is not a "what has happened to us". There's a "what IS happening to us". We have always been under attack. How can a people truly build when they are constantly being targeted for all manner of egregious assault?

Onyx: We have to stop making excuses and spring into action. This shit is beyond out-of-control.

Osiris: What we have to stop doing is thinking that we can undo centuries and I literally mean centuries of disenfranchisement at the hands of this country within a couple of years. Everyone's always trying to rush ahead of survival to get to prosperity. Liberty is still the order of the day. There can be no other agenda.

Onyx: Aye, do you think Taylor Swift dates Black guys?

Osiris: Slit your wrist and don't call 911.

#ConversationsOfTheBlackBourgeoisie

Chapter 21: Switching Gears

26Nov2017 - 2Dec2017

What sticks is phenomenal. Scraps and pieces of bullshit memories to make sense of the fleeting. Interrupted abruptly, but not perturbed. The feeling of falling is the only thing that keeps me from gritting my teeth. I'm trying to be impressed by mediocrity, but there are no refunds for those fucks.

Those aren't whispers in the wind. The voices are just smaller and thusly occupy less material space. And if acidic tears don't mangle faces then the pH balance of the sorrow is skewed.

Guts splattered over the expressway like decorative art pieces in protest of decency. Our views on body consciousness forever skewed as we evolve toward the normalcy of multiple births. Oh, to be mesmerizing in a world full of interesting. Better yet, to be breathtakingly peculiar. Slavery in Libya. This is 2017. Cheap labor for lazy stumblebums who fuel their physical ineptitude with synthetic evil. And the council of the United Nations sits twiddling its thumbs with fidget spinners. Such a farcical assemblage of figureheads. Imagine an eye roll emoji as punctuation. But why am I perspiring? Exasperation is not a cardiac event to which I'm accustomed. Everything is accelerating, yet the collective consciousness of the world is at a standstill. I want to escape this form, so I can play interplanetary hopscotch among the stars. Feet singed...marred, but the merriment will be well worth the disfigurement. The non-pigmented hands that rock the cradle of life. Dear Africa. Will you ever receive royalties for ghostwriting civilization? The audience is rarely the same when the student's splendor of the last laugh is afforded.

Far too many become that which their talents have been characterized as. Thots with the vibrato of Jazz vocalists try to emulate the ethereal when their souls truly cry out for pussy popping on a headstand. So to be the chameleon, she must suicide her truth in order to appease expectations and understanding. She trades in twerking for Zills, Turkish finger cymbals. On beat, but inauthentic.

It's 4:23 AM and there is this image of me in my head. It is as though I am trapped behind paned glass and screaming at the top of my lungs to the point that the veins in my neck are pulsating and my eyes are bloodshot and bulging, but I have no reaction to it. It's as though I'm watching myself have a psychotic break coupled with a temper tantrum and I'm just allowing it to run its course. I won't let me sleep.

Fast forward. This ass backwards fascination with bullshit that profits less than the pruning of much needed brain cells. Your whole personality is a gaggle of synaptic misfires. You pride yourself on being taken out of context in such glorified fashion that you couldn't pick yourself out of a stack of descriptions. This encrypted nonfeasance you've emblazoned upon your mind's eye makes a cyclical mockery of your imagined buffoon. You're chafed and raw to the point that dew is acidic. Septic sensationalism causes a bloodlust for salaciousness. Schemes encoded within schemes and buried beneath revisions of dreams you once had.

I think about quitting. It's a passing thought. It never lingers or meanders for any amount of time greater than I spend searching for personifications of it. The proverbial what-if. Doubt should only be galvanized when the evidence is a middle finger poking you between the eyes. It never lies unless you back it into a corner with threats of violence.

Exercises in patience aren't supposed to cause perspiration, but when the vibrational energy is in frenzy, it's somewhat difficult to be contained. In a constant state of observation, but hoping to never intrusively disrupt the natural order that has been so carefully crafted. Retracing steps like a hand on paper. Stealing tiny moments of time and sifting through them to find meaning. Wandering beyond corridors that require very specific access.

Crooked halos look kind of creepy and cryptic when their resplendence melds with the whirring of siren lights. In any scenario, some befuddled innocence was unsheathed and placed on exhibit before the eyes of would-be judges, jurors and executioners. Spin doctors don't really fascinate me. Their escapism is just a gussied up ruse intended to quell and further indoctrinate their already captivate audience into a depose hypnosis. Fools love to be fooled by the fool-hearted woggle. It makes them feel like kindred spirits with matching low intelligence quotients. Poetry is never keeping it real, raw and uncut for it is a well-dressed truth intended to attract admirers more than it is designed to liberate. And that's not to suggest that it isn't honest, but the scenic route is typically more of a luxury than a necessity.

You can't pour out your heart when you're siphoning the fluids from someone else's reservoir. I marvel at the insincere weeping of attention-whores wielding camera angles in the place of Kleenex. The evening has come and gone, yet the weeping has had no sunrise. It's like recycling the question "Who wants to be found?"

It's a dog eat dog world. You can be Fido or Alpo.

When you get to this part in the book, go to Facebook, answer these questions, and TAG ME.

A.   Are you in a state of feeling or showing pleasure or contentment?

B.   What makes you feel or show pleasure or contentment?

C   Why does this make you feel or show pleasure or contentment?

D.   What would make you happier?

E.   Are you trying to be happier or is happy the glass ceiling before eternity?

F.   Has anyone ever called you ugly?

G.   How did that make you feel?

H.   Have you ever felt ugly?

I.   Why?

J.   Don't tell me what you want me to read. Tell me the real why.

K.   Are you ugly?

L.   Who are you?

M.   Who are you to your friends?

N.   Who are you to your parents?

O.   Who are you to people you try to impress?

P.   Who are you to people you fuck?

Q.   Who are you at work?

R.   Who are you when no one is looking?

S.   What motivates you to lie when you lie?

T.   What music are you listening to currently? List as much of it as you feel comfortable listing.

U.   Have we met?

V.   If we haven't met, would you like to meet?

W.   What would we do when we met either again or for the first time?

X.   Where are you reading this?

Y.   Where will you go when you die?

Z.   What makes you feel powerful?

AA. What makes you feel powerless?

BB. Who do you love?

CC. Are you for sure?

DD. What is the best place you've ever lived?

EE. What was special about it?

FF. What brings you fulfillment?

I think I'm done here. #BreakingThe4thWall

Chapter 23: | STUCK |

3Dec2017 - 9Dec2017

I'm bored with the thought of doing better because it requires me to be better, which requires me to finely tune my "I am". Some days I'd rather just pass out drunk than contemplate the customs of proper behavior in a given society. With a growing addiction to notifications and a distancing of myself from any and everything except that which depends on me to live, my "I statements" have become cursed by brevity. I could go in search of inspiration, but I like to think I'm better than that, so I lay in waiting to be struck by awe.

Once the world gets a taste of you, it tends to overindulge until it can no longer even tolerate the scent or sight of you. Up at 3:09 AM, fighting the urge to pace the floor in deep thought; envisioning silly things like speaking words set to percussion and a bouncing ball. Cloaked in a cheap robe and all its comforts. I've never needed to mingle. I've always preferred to be my own gravitational pull. There's a sense of control in that. And are love and sex really so distant? And how does the magic go unnoticed at dusk and dawn? We style ourselves in complacency mounted upon envy. Right now I'm explaining myself, so you can understand that there's no pressure to fly. We are the sky to smaller things, so we're soaring. When I look up into the sky, I wonder if I'm staring at an intricately woven back pocket of some celestial thing that views me as a mitochondrion. I grin and bear it. I could wrap myself in bullshit and pretend the stench was fashionable. I could play peekaboo with emotions and label it a work of art. I'm not that boring though; bathing in peach soda and such. That's not rooted. It's performance; a parasitic fugue state. All of the greats will tell you that the dance became redundant. They'll deepen their explanations in order to better clarify the sublimation. Fiction surely has its place, but never in the spiritual. I'm having fun at others' expense because I was taught that is the American Way, but no way was ever made for me because brown has always had a footnote of offense here. I'm brown, but I'm Black and I'm

Black, but I'm translucent unless a scapegoat because traumatically retarded fear needs a fall guy.

True magic costs in the millions. Many find its pursuit worth low levels of servitude. Souls suffering from spinal fractures. Classy is much more interesting when it's ratchet cleaned up. I didn't know bones could moan. Never has permanently lost sight of forever and we wonder why it remains in a constant state of envy and fury. There are really no blurred lines because they are all fictitious. I feel you tugging at me as though I'm pulling away when, in fact, I've remained steadfast and resolute. You don't feel securely attached.

People are crippled by their fear of questioning what they've been taught. Standing upon creaking comprehension is a house of startling horrors in and of itself. Having the proverbial rug of your entire life's meaning snatched from beneath you is a free fall that jerks one's heart into one's throat. So you're not only uncertain, but you're also ridiculed by shortness of breath when suspecting deception is all that's really being asked of you in the grand scheme of it all. For what can we truly know besides the unfounded beliefs that have been force-fed to us if we're afraid to challenge them by way of research? I suppose it's simply easier to go along just to get along.

Falling in love with silence is a beautiful choice for fate carves out a space for wisdom to dance. Tangled up with in interpretations of what we should be doing is that pearl of absolution. Though we struggle to consciously trust our instincts, we never question our breathing.

I've never been entertained by the moving picture show of other's tears, so I fail to grasp how love can be used as a weapon to add emotional injury to cognitive insult. Even without the soundtrack of screaming each droplet of saline dew belies an agony that rips through my resolve and knocks the wind out of my sympathy. Your hurt causes me physical pain and I'm not even the catalyst. So I listen; speaking only to fill the gaps of silence that are peppered by sniffles. You deserve much better than what you've allowed. Embrace yourself and hold on so tight that you squeeze sight into the blind eye you've turned. You are a lesson to those who depend on you.

The mirror awakens each morning anxiously awaiting the opportunity to speak a prophecy over your life. We slaughter the passions of youth and supplant our own fiendish will upon their lives, never truly lending the much needed support that will inspire them to greatness. We steadily drive their dreams into an early grave. We try to predict their futures from our failures; slowly assassinating their uniqueness...their individuality, with our refusal to allow them to blossom and flourish in their own soil...their own souls. We covertly categorize our efforts as protection without ever giving audience to the fact that smothering forced their fire into an eternal coma.

I am disgusted by my inability to sleep. It isn't sexy or enigmatic. It's a mocking torture that doubles as a conversation starter.

Do people talk to themselves because they feel that no one else will listen? Or are they simply responding to the unseen forces that communicate with them telepathically? When someone is ranting and raving at the air, I always wonder who they are cussing out...or are their words directed at the world at large. Will their shouting cause a butterfly effect that ripples through the cosmos and impacts someone hundreds of miles away?

I love allowing people to believe that they understand and connect with me because it comforts them and amuses me. Most people are a bundle of emotions, but I am a labyrinth of personality traits.

Mumble rap en Español es loco decente.

Chapter 24: | THE | CRISPENING |

18Dec2017 - 16Dec2017

It's quite the labored effort to fly under the radar while being hypnotized by the symphonic calls of mockingbirds. This ain't no "Singing in the Rain" moment, but there's a groove. Trying to force an idea into existence against its will. Who really calls for everyone to dance in public places? What type of need is that masking? Judge me then or judge me not. Just make it a statement piece; a subtle kindling that beckons the exhibitionists into the light.

Disconnected from customs. Traditions feel like trinkets of a make-believe I had no hand in imagining. Distrustful of the dealer's shuffling due to card tricks that misappropriate the tarot's intentions. Palms facing upward toward a petty sunburst seeking to blister. Read by beams of ultraviolet light with foggy recollections of exactly how the incantation is intended to be recited. Theories can also be unrequited manifestations of miseducated guessing games, so we toss around the idea of gambling our value. Luck be a lady before the brunch degrades to lukewarm.

Anger should not be orgasmic. It shouldn't coat the body in rapturous convulsions. It shouldn't melt discomfort and enshroud within cuddles. It shouldn't comfort, but it does...and well.

Stopping abruptly in random places to breathe deeply and center yourself because characteristics that are not indicative of your essence are trying to cross over to the forefront of your existence.

18Dec2017 - 23Dec2017

Intercepting mixed messages from highly decorated hypocrites. There's nothing clever about crying for your supper, but crawling is impressive. People often wonder why I'm in love with solitude. Let them wonder. Sometimes I stare into the eye of the surveillance camera's lens hoping to catch the eye of whoever's surveilling. It is a blank, ominous and transient gaze into nothingness impregnated by the possibility of connecting from the safety of my solitude. Let them wonder.

Send me a love letter to the last known address you have for me. A heart in need of tenderness could be residing there within an end zone of insufferable losses life has hurled at it.

I'm glad I don't wake up in some mess every day. Drastic measures pepper the taste buds of salivating shit-talkers. When you're really good at what you do, everything you do is a performance. And yet another mystery weasels its way into the world. There are whispers and within them morsels of white lies commingle with declarations of independence.

At 3;07 PM on 22Dec2017, I wrote the sentence "Drastic measures pepper the taste buds of salivating shit-talkers" while watching Episode One: Star Wars of "The Toys That Made Us". At 3:10 PM, I wrote "When you're really good at what you do, everything you do is a performance" while watching the same thing.

On 22Dec2017 at 4:01 PM, I was looking at the latest post by jillisblack on Instagram when I wrote "And yet another mystery weasels its way into the world."

It was 8:12 PM on 22Dec2017 and I was watching a man that was built like a pile of soggy hemlines walk on the treadmill at the Lawton Family YMCA when I wrote "There are whispers and within them morsels of white lies commingle with declarations of independence."

Chapter 25: Desperately Seeking Azealia Banks

24Dec2017 - 30Dec2017

How to make a monster of the "strong, Black woman". There's even a degree of disrespect in the quantifying of both gender and race. Tropes and tight ropes and shit you're expected to tiptoe across in bloody shoes, right? The greatest victim of news media editing becomes a hot button whip for social programming and shit. We create dragons out of gossip and selective coverage only to slay them with shares and retweets when they start breathing fire. The one thing that speaks louder than truth is frenzy, but the dust always settles and that low hum never grows faint. Never cast spells with emotion. Stop trying to compete in spaces that weren't designed to accommodate your gifts. Sometimes they laugh because they are embarrassed by their own intelligence and level of understanding. They secretly question their hidden agendas, so that when they stand face-to-face with the devil, the mirror, they feel prepared by way of their studying. Is the goal really to be accepted by those who credit dancing with monsters in the moonlight among their accolades? Everyone knows that puppets have hands up their asses. There are times when a divine appointment can double as a dangerous liaison.

I'd much rather see you nosedive into a blaze of glory than to goldfish into a puddle of your own tears. There are two types of people: those who perfect the audition and those who perfect the connection. Have you ever stopped to listen to see if the man standing on the street corner makes any sense at all? It's kind of hard not to commentate on the tales of the pathetic and distracted. Sometimes motivation serves as a curse. Using one's face to break through a wall is still considered perseverance.

The shackles shimmer as sunbeams waltz across their skin. High-frequency meditation and yet there is no exit wound for the tempo. The cracks are filled with slithering drool. To be hidden and silenced. To dine with lust with unblinking eye contact. To hide screams one degree behind laughter. To steal the hinges and bury them in the ground unmarked by x. To daydream until nightfall dumps its ashes all over the mind's eye.

People who jump on the bandwagon simply to align themselves with what is perceived as cool and popular don't deserve to have tailgate parties. There will be no celebration for the conformist mob mentality. She attacks. Your whole body is a bum knee. You look like you can eject your makeup. You're built like a bundle of yoga poses draped with sweater material. I've seen better bodies on a pulled pork sandwich. You look like a hangover came to life and threw up. You look like you have a degenerative disease concentrated in your face muscles. You look like your face got stuck mid-yawn. You look like labor pains and menopause had a catfight on your face.

Dancing within hypnosis, imperfect synchronization captured as picturesque. The feeling of being encapsulated by a world created within an icy gaze.

Chapter 26: | RECONFIGURED |

31 Dec 2017 - 6 Jan 2017

Internal dialogue that worms its way into the ethos for shits and giggles. Recitation of protocol 17...slow clap. My heartbeat is speaking Morse Code. Beholden to a sense of anxious delay. The perturbed state of my gut is a reminder of the moment.

All the saints and sinners convened for an orgy of their auras. Analog hand-jobs muster digital orgasms. The Holy Ghost paces the circumference of the assemblage making note of who willingly surrenders to the salaciousness.

I had nothing else beautiful to say, so I'll leave you wondering what I was thinking. And then I was overwhelmed by so much to say. And then I couldn't connect the dots.

Chapter 27: Ramen Noodles

7 Jan 2017 - 13 Jan 2017

My mind has been largely empty. I mean...there have been things present, but nothing of merit. Jerry Seinfeld should really get some filler in his top lip. I'm surprised it doesn't have stretch-marks from his lifetime of smiling. He's keeping the blazer and jeans combo alive and kicking, so there's that.

Do you know that there are people who actually believe there were votes cast for the most beautiful or sexiest woman/man in the world? They comprise Donald Trump's voter base, of that I'm sure. And for a man with such moxie and self-importance, you'd think he'd want people who can at least succeed at Word Finds supporting him. But if his complexion and hairstyle were a group of people...#KanyeShrug.

Name Me: A story about a guy who let every person he built an association with give him a name because Dontavious was just what his parents wanted to call him. He started this practice at age five. He liked Calypso music.

I think I've mastered the art of eating healthy from Dollar General. Label reading and calculating have never made my hodgepodge, public school education more valuable.

There are some instances when I enjoy people being unaware that they're being made fun of and other instances when I laugh at people being unaware that they're being made fun of.

I currently can't afford the type of cool that I aspire to be, so I hardly try to recreate it on my income because I'm lazy about coolness and don't want to be creative. If your cool requires a lot of effort, it's basically oxymoronic.

I'm really not into comedy because I like to be caught off-guard by laughter, so if I know it's your intention to make me laugh...well, fuck you. Isn't that just pissy? Don't you just love it?

Okay, maybe I haven't mastered the art of eating healthy from Dollar General, but I tell myself that I have and that comforts me more than I'm willing to say.

I'm obsessive about my picture being taken because I'm afraid of being unflattering in a slideshow.

I've become far too comfortable simply hearing the television and catching tidbits of content every now and then, but I love comfort, so suck it.

I think it should be illegal to sell any product to the public that doesn't produce results after just one use. Bitch, I'm not trying to develop a relationship with your brand.

I'm not in a relationship or traditional friendship because I don't think people who claim to love me should have fun without me even if I don't feel like having fun, but I'm unwilling to reciprocate.

I only get mad when people talk about me behind my back because I didn't get to laugh before anybody else did. I'm selfish like that.

I get mad at people for posting videos of teenagers fighting, but find myself spending time watching videos of teenagers fighting.

My hair hasn't grown in a year. It has erectile dysfunction.

I've never said this publicly, so why not get it off my chest now. I've always thought the lead vocal performance on "Silver and Gold" by Kirk Franklin Nem was abysmal.

Live your life like you'll become famous after you die.

I like to go in the opposite direction that my emotions are leading me except when it comes to anger. Anger has me on a choke-chain.

Nothing makes me thirstier than a road trip in which I see the sunrise for some reason.

I think I might remove "falling out with someone to the point that they recruit people to spy on my social media accounts on their behalf" from my bucket list this year.

I've never been married yet I have the same apprehension about dating that newly divorced people do.

Shitting spells relief. Clearly, I'm shitting right now. 7 Jan 2017, 2:09 PM.

The saddest funerals are those in which attendees say the same three things about the recently deceased and they aren't even a trifecta of excellence. Make connections, B.

Where were you when you watched "One Priest One Nun"? How one derives sexual pleasure from having someone shit in his/her face is beyond me.

If water was sold in shots for like a quarter, I would drink far more of it.

Sometimes I randomly laugh at the memory of Chris Rock's original teeth because it's the best thing for my mental health in the moment.

It frightens me to not have the right words. Sometimes there is a ticking like my thought process is on the precipice of implosion. It is a grandiose staccato. The reverberation seems to giggle. Passersby shimmy to its rhythm longing for a tock that will never come. It is so very coy that it adorns itself with mystery. It warms itself with the kindling ire of craving.

Naturally impressive. Be that. It's a pity that the extravaganza has become so trite. My plight is not a song for the lonely. Why surf on vibrations when you can float on a vibe, right?

Chapter 28: | DOCUMENTARY |

14 Jan 2017 - 20 Jan 2017

The feeling of being stuck in a displaced state while trying to make connections with muthafuckas whose thought processes are so one dimensional that they fancy themselves deep when in all actuality they're just a scratch on the surface. But I suppose a scratch has depth if you're on the surface yourself. We look in the direction the magician tells us because that's the show for which we paid and shit.

Word of Mouth: The story of a modern-day human rights leader who hypnotically sermonizes his beliefs to every person he encountered, thereby sparking a movement that changes the world without a single rally. Sometimes it's not what you say, but how you say it.

Connect Four: The story of an island girl who moves to America to use her beauty as currency, not as a model, but as a habitual dater. She accepts money for gifts, her appearance, parties, vacations, etc. She becomes a master couponer. She builds up an impressive bank account by masterfully DIY-ing the affluence in which the men she dates live. #Whew

Comic Book & Clayton: The story of two friends, one always drunk and the other one always high, who always have great discussions from completely different contexts, but they always flow.

Remembering Jigga: A dark comedy that proposes a post-racial America in which the word "racist" has replaced the word "nigger" as the most offensive slur in American English. It is the story of a biracial (Black & White) teen named Omani who hates everything about both of her cultures and wants nothing more than to be Korean because she's obsessed with K-Pop and wants to start a group with holograms of the multiple personalities her psychoanalyst has identified.

Oxtails in the Morning: The love story about an Indigenous American artist and a Jamaican chef who, after meeting at a spoken word event, fall in lust and build a small fortune together over the course of seven years by selling their homemade, visual art pornography, only to lose interest in one another when Vivid Video begins to court them for a contractual agreement.

Dysmorphia In Crimson: The story of a world filled with manufactured geniuses and the social engineers who quietly hate and envy them from the assembly lines. Then in 2087, a set of twins named Parker & Townsend disrupt the entire system through a series of scientific experiments aimed at perfecting The Phillips code, a method for activating increased brain capacity.

Two in the Stink: The story of a city sanitation worker/rodeo star with dreams of becoming a Hollywood fashion stylist, but his ultra-conservative, WASP, Bible Belt family sees men in the fashion as Brokeback Mountaineers and they control his trust fund.

LOTION

Lotion wears a cat-suit everywhere she went. She has an assorted collection of them to rival Mr. Rogers' old man sweaters. She is not a carefree spirit, but her wanderlust for adventure will lead you to believe her caution was a kite. When most people dance naked, they present the act as homage to footlooseness and fanciful freedom. Lotion doesn't dance naked. She performs in her flesh. "I used to pop pussy in clubs, but then I decided to stop pimping my pussy pop to become an art piece. Pay yo fare. Comb yo hair. Head ass." They call her Lotion because of her natural glisten. She is a vixen without conviction. She is the antithesis of contrition. She is a bitter child of divorce with a whiplashed soul. She is addicted to spades and cigarettes. She likes to flirt with the postman even though he is built like a disfigured piece of bacon. Protesting causes championed by unattractive underdogs is her hobby. She likes to soak her feet in peppermint. She likes vodka and lemonade with a shot of peach Fanta. She likes coffee before bed. Dancing to 90s booty music from Miami each morning and doing 100 cart wheels a day is what she calls exercise. She never leaves home without the artistic accoutrement of intricately swirled baby hair framing her doll-like face. She is an atheist who attends a Pentecostal church regularly for the rebel yell. She is an open book with page after page of encrypted text.

Chapter 29: | HEADLINES |

21 Jan2017 - 27 Jan2017

There comes a point when people stop adding you to their collection. At this point, you settle into the comforts of your minuscule. You feel the pull of another hoorah, but they just aren't dripping from the sky as they once did.

The Frankenstein spirit is squatting in the world's collective consciousness. People, quick to butcher themselves to maintain a head-start on the hands of time, are walking around covered from head to toe in scar tissue that I wish they saw as reprobate self-esteem.

28 Jan2017 - 3 Feb2017

Imagination dries up. It cracks and bleeds all over our souls. Sometimes the mood is Uncle Luke music chopped and screwed. They gladly snort line after line of radioactive isotopes as though they can't distinguish between dawn and morning.

4 Feb2017 - 10 Feb2017

Bouts of inconsistent passion leave me floating atop the abyss of the shoulda, woulda, couldas. Tonight, I met tears as though it were the first time, not for the aforementioned, however.

11 Feb2017 - 17 Feb2017

• Dancing among wolves while dressed in death by a thousand cuts.

• When predictability is the protagonist, even sorcery is home drunk.

• There's nothing like being humbled by your price range on a Sunday evening.

• Her vagina was like a week's worth of Monday mornings.

• Life just feels better when your dick's in a mouth.

• Slitting my wrists to lick the wounds because I like the taste of life leaving my body is supposed to relieve me of emotional pain, but I would have to be emotionally retarded to think that physically pain is loud enough to reverberate well into the depths of my emotional clusterfuck.

• "Smiling Through Acne" would be a great name for a Netflix comedy special.

• I feel very human this morning. I feel every ounce of my humanity this morning. I do not feel like the idea of myself this morning. I'm about ready to be a tornado in some unsuspecting hopeless romantic's life.

Chapter 30: | ZINGERS |

18Feb2017 - 24Feb2017

I would gladly strip my imagination naked and present it on the auctioning block to be gangbanged by the highest bidders if the final asking price proffered me a year of existence above the fray. Believing in all things invisible because the distance between proof and disproof from the starting point of uncertainty is identical. And life begins not with mystery, but with the pulsating rhythm of lust.

26Feb2018 - 3Mar2018

When her vagina belongs on a faces of meth poster, let the power of Christ compel you to prayer and fasting for research purposes.

Hotep Pussy: The story of a woman who tries to fuck the woke back into a Black man who only dates white women.

8Mar2018: There is a bitterness that skis within the veins of the bitter and betrayed. Broken hearts have become internment camps for the wounded warrior project. Auras stepping away from personhood to stand on street corners and shouts obscenities at an unseen God. Tears of sorrow are set to the rhythm of the wind's percussion and lightning's tympanic whimpering.

13Mar2018: When I start getting close to someone, which is rare because I'm sufficiently walled, I always wonder which of us will become more like the other. Or will it simply be a case of one filling in the blank spaces of the other and vice versa.

14Mar2018: Sometimes I want to destroy myself with self-indulgence. A gentle suicide seasoned by sugary confections.

Religion is a pedophile.

19Mar2018: I am ensnared by the slippery slope. I am a VIP for the masquerade. My moral compass is a parody of snippets of religious text and witty quips from memes that I've plagiarized into an amalgamation of self. I tiptoe on land and krump on cracking ice. I don't flirt with danger. I finger fuck it then stir the poison I've selected to amuse my synaptic misfires with the same finger.

She was the type of classy that has a special pillow made to rest her knees upon while she's sucking dick.

20Mar2018: Pussy Patrol: The story of a group of feminist prayer warriors on a mission to exorcise demonic vaginas and thwart them from operating like an altar call.
#IsThereAnyWhoWillCome

I just want to get to a place spiritually where I don't lose my shit if I glance over and peep that my kid's bottom lip is chapped or the spaces between the fingers are ashy as fuck.

Chapter 31: | THINKING | THINGS |
#StatusUpdates

19Mar2018

1:19 PM: There comes a point in life when you see a childhood friend holding a baby and you have to ask if they're a new parent or a grandparent because they were blessed with kids at a young age. Issa toss up.

1:34 PM: Boughetto is making ramen noodles in the microwave...but with bottled spring water. Live your life by design!

1:43 PM: Pussy Patrol: The story of a group of feminist prayer warriors on a mission to exorcise demonic vaginas and thwart them from operating like an altar call. #IsThereAnyWhoWillCome

20Mar2018

Princess Peach: The story of a young porn star struggling with gender identity issues while simultaneously working in the adult film industry and on a quest to gain the strength to confront the priest with whom he fell in love during years of sexual molestation.

Purp: The story of three teens who escape the horrors of poverty by smoking weed in their mother's basement and unleashing their rambunctious imaginations, thereby inadvertently creating a web series that myriad Hollywood bigwigs want to take to network television.

12:39 PM: Imagine whining about not being husky all ya life then BOOM, ya thyroid flips the fuck out on you, you puff up, and now you're mad at a red light because you can't pull ya sweater off and the temperature has spiked from what it was when you left the house this morning.

(I literally just sat at a red light and imagined this happening to me)

5:48 PM: What's the point of coming to the gym in a face full of RuPaul's Drag Race makeup just to sweat and look like your whole face is melting off in slow motion?

5:49 PM: People be lookin' like teddy bears without the stuffing when they get bariatric surgery and don't workout.

8:53 PM: Storefront Black churches will use a Chick-fil-A bag as a prayer cloth in a pinch.

21 Mar 2018

10:07 AM: If the girl I lost my virginity to had GPS on her pussy, there would've been a whole lot of "proceed to the route" going on. #YoungDumbAndFullOfCum

10:57 AM: I'm riding by a real life cotton field in Oklahoma and I'm so nervous and tense that my sphincter has a whole fuckin' Charlie horse!!! #ImScaryOfIt

11:05 AM: It's amazing how movies can contribute to the shaping of our perceptions of the world during our youth. It wasn't until recently that I stopped believing that all Russians died a stern death at home in bed under a homemade blanket while wearing a winter coat and a bonnet made out of potato sack cloth.

11:17 AM: I just got a brain freeze while simultaneously almost passing out because my durag was too tight. Surely there is a disability check with my name on it for that.

11:55 AM: Imagine occupying a home on a plot of land owned by your ancestors for thousands of years then BOOM, a group of muthafuckas who had to Huckleberry Finn from their place of origin shows up, bum rushes their way in, sits at your table whilst infecting your air with their foreign diseases, writes a set of rules, slaps them on the wall, acts like they're doing you a favor, then get irky when you say fuck them rules because they don't jive with your way of life. Colonialism can suck a rabid, pustule-covered dick with a slow drip!!!

12:03 AM: Any video showcasing a line of bikini-clad girls, who live solely on Starbucks coffee and Takis, doing back tucks into a pool can assuredly be made better by a full-figured girl in a short set standing at the end of the line, flipping the bird while saying "fuck this shit".

12:13 PM: My facial hair looks like a rat's pelt and it is making me want to snort antidepressants or butt chug promethazine.

1:05 PM: Dear Little Old Lady Driving with the Neck Pillow, if going the speed limit causes you to pee a little, perhaps you should hitch your wagon to public transportation, so you're not run off the road by the ever-growing road rage culture.

2:57 PM: I fuckin' hate when I go somewhere and the staff gets all confused & befuddled and asks ME questions about how THEY operate. "Sooooo you need a consent form so the mother can visit the chiiiiild?" Muthafucka why would the mother need a consent form to visit her own kid. I need one. "Sooooo you need a consent form to meet with the chiiiiiild?" BITCH I'M TRYNA FIND OUT FROM YOU!!!! If I'm not asking the right questions or presenting the correct information, then how about you tell me what the fuck your policies and procedures state cuz I don't fuckin' work here to know!!!!

3:52 PM: Stop puttin' on too little clothes if you can't handle road rash and yeast infections in your cracks and crevices.

26Mar2018 3:19 PM: She asked me why it is that when we go out it's always with a group of people and I politely informed her that it is so the one I truly want to be with can never tell that I'm actually on a date...then I kissed her sweetly on her forehead.

27Mar2018 4:01 PM: Warring with my body as it responds to the flirtation of sleepiness. Feeling the seductive numbness overcoming my eyelids slowly, but surely.

28Mar2018

7:58 AM: Somewhere in America someone woke up, threw something on that wasn't odiferous, swished a lil tap water around in their mouth, splashed a little on their face, then headed out to face the world with all the confidence of Khia on Miss Rap Supreme circa 2008.

8:05 AM: Every "woke" person seems to stake claim to Egypt, completely ignoring the fact that they could very well be descended from a tiny village near a hyena carcass.

8:20 AM: Muthafuckas complain about people showcasing the best moments of their lives on Instagram as though they'd prefer to spend their day looking at abject poverty (carpet that needs bonding glue for its edges, shurtains & candlelit microwaved dinners served on styrofoam plates) and shingles outbreaks. Not I. Find your best light and smile while you lie to me. 😬

8:25 AM: I lost a friend because I told him God scrambled his wife's DNA like a batch of three week old egg yolks.

8:45 AM: My coworker wants to set me up on a blind date with her friend. I told her it has to be a lunch date because the version of me she knows clocks out at 5 PM.

8:57 AM: The joy of being a single dad is mistakenly telling your boys that the tree in the front yard is a pussy willow then later finding them spanking it while chanting pop that pussy.

9:36 AM: Don't donate your birthday to a charitable cause if all you got last year was a handful of wall posts.

10:07 AM: The best thing about being a man is that even when the sex is the equivalent of Mariah Carey's dancing in the "Honey" video, you STILL bust a nut.

10:25 AM: It was very kind of Nene Leakes to loan Cardi B her ramen noodle lace frontal for her "Invasion of Privacy" album cover. #SisterhoodOfTheTravelingWig

11:22 AM: Black women don't have to be extra when sucking dick because they have full lips. And now we know why the Kardashians get lip fillers. #WorkSmarterNotHarder

29Mar2018

10:08 AM: She identified dick as the most wonderful counselor to whom she's ever opened her soul.

10:42 AM: My greatest pet peeve is when someone starts playing the well-rehearsed victim after I far exceed the level of disrespect they've hurled at me and not only chip away pieces of their soul, but also grind those pieces into dust and blow that very same dust back in their face while hoping it soils their tears. Y'all gotta stop thinking y'all can just say any and everything to people without retaliation. Hitting below the belt is my first line of defense. Fuck you thought?

11:32 AM: Black people have swimsuit parties, not pool parties. The pool is just there for decoration. Ain't nobody gettin' in it.

1:53 PM: Mass shootings and mental health issues have increasingly become problematic for the White community in maintaining the guise of moral and political superiority in this nation. #PrayForTheWhiteCommunity

3:40 PM: My hobbies include shouting "YOU'RE WELCOME MUTHAFUCKA" at the top of my lungs at people who don't say "thank you" and just walk through the door I have so graciously held open for them in an attempt to keep chivalry from dropping dead.

The Perfect Fit: The story of a con artist who loses his memory and tries out different personalities in search of a glove for his soul. Conning is the only memory he retains.

30Mar2018

9:39 AM: I'll be performing some of your favorite HipHop and RNB hits with my headphones on at the 40mph sign by China Wok Express this Saturday at noon for the culture. I don't mind the kind of tips that jingle, but I prefer the kind that fold.

Chapter 32: | WORD | VOMIT |

We are all now fully committed to the task of keeping one another entertained. We are all leads in our own production and supporting cast in others.{ William Shakespeare, 1564 - 1616. All the world's a stage, And all the men and women merely players; They have their exits and their entrances, And one man in his time plays many parts, His acts being seven ages. At first, the infant, Mewling and puking in the nurse's arms.}It's the game everyone can play if they so choose. Breaking free essentially means nonexistence. Nonexistence while existing sounds delightful. So I invited a weed in to spread its roots and kill my online presence. Let's see if it works. There's an enchanting sound that emits from the noise of my feet as I saunter away from toxic energy.

Parks and Recreation is my drug of choice right now.

Scraps and Stitches: The story of a 48-yr old farmhand who turns his Wyoming town into a fashion Mecca by transforming the residents' out of date duds into one of a kind masterpieces.

Some would argue that wealth has many faces. It can materialize as a billboard of health and vigor on a well-sculpted physique that possesses an equally impressive athletic ability. It can appear as an interweaving sprint and mosey emitting from the throat as unto an instrument. It can present itself in the many ships we forge in order to foster human connections. Yes, it can walk on many runways, but none gathers as large an audience as when it is fashioned in a manner that can be spent on goods and services.

The unbitten fruit of sexual activity remains a pivotal pedestal of propriety among humans. It is revered for its irrevocability. It is still perceived as powerful and redemptive. Though the reverence is somewhat hushed, we still champion safeguarding it as treasure, so long as it does not impede compilation. Adorn yourselves in white and proclaim your genital chastity. Just don't cause my erection to retreat.

The world would be entirely different if we were inherently good and had to work hard at being evil. Evil is easy...like microwaveable foods.

Living under the constant scrutiny of the questioning side-eye must be hard as fuck for the heterosexual minister of music with a lisp.

I don't think I'll ever not be phased by people deciding to be the owners of multiple pets over adopting children who have washed ashore in the system as the result of piss poor parents who lack the protective capacities that enable one to put the needs of a child before their own.

Shaking that ass in the middle of a circle of onlookers at dances throughout high school, college and the thotting twenties doesn't qualify you to run a dance studio featuring body rolls as the main course...but it doesn't disqualify you either. Random thought inspired by an Instagram video.

4Apr2018: I would much rather have a tie-tongued swamp person with a crippling stutter to assist me than a muthafucka with a foreign accent, so thick every gotdamn thing sounds like ingredients for some international delicacy. Don't get me wrong, I love an accent, but NOT when I'm ready to storm the corporate offices like the Tasmanian Devil and fuck up all the commas until my issue is resolved.

5Apr2018 8:18 AM: I am not a large mainly domesticated game bird native to North America, having a bald head and a red wattles, so I don't fucking understand why some white men choose to speak jive to me.

6Apr2018 10:23 AM: Vaseline Intensive Care Petroleum Jelly is the primary difference between Black Americans and our brothers and sisters from the international African diaspora. We combat ashiness like we're basting in preparation for being roasted...and I love it.

10:32 AM There should be a course committed to stoking the embers of creativity within children to garner the creation of new ideas that could potentially help improve the human condition, as well as advance modern society, but there isn't because the mysterious and looming elite cherry picks and grooms certain minds to make contributions to its agenda. There will always be great unrest if both our problems and solutions are manufactured by the same people.

10:38 AM: I absolutely hate it when pseudo-celebrities make charismatic promotional videos set to the backdrop of a brick wall and filmed on a camera phone.

11:01 AM : Taking the time to dress your baby like Ralphie from "A Christmas Story" only to leave the baby's head and feet completely exposed ranks highly on the unobscured idiocy chart.

12:19 PM: Far too many people are settling for brown paper towel love...love that functions as it should by definition, but is barren of all comfort.

1:23 PM: I wonder if the response time for obese people's farts is severely delayed due to the fact that said farts have to make a fantastic voyage through layers of fatty flesh before making contact with the air.

3:54 PM: I should not be as suspicious of the success of the Black Panther film as I am, but in a white supremacist world that thrives on suppressing Black people, I'm very skeptical of it like there is some unforeseen wicked scheme lurking in the shadows just beyond our ability to see it. Plus, Disney is making the bulk of the money from it anyway, not the Black people involved.

7:11 PM: There are literally white people in this world who think they can be Black...because they want to. Let that sink in.

6Apr2018 1050AM: You look like morning breath became a person.

7Apr2018 216PM: We, as a society of people, have become so morally bankrupt that we have mini photoshoots at people's funerals in order to commemorate our fashion choice for the "event". Our laurels are resting on a bed of quicksand above an abyss of crimes against humanity.

8Apr2018 209PM: I went out in public without underwear today. I did not feel liberated. I felt nasty. I liked it. Shaking after a piss has never been more essential.

412PM: There are times when the buzz from a group text will make you want to lacerate obscenities into someone's flesh.

447PM: Are you the type of person that buys all of their protein drinks from Dollar General? Do you consider yourself the surprise guest at every function attended by people you stalk on social media? Do you spend more time biting your fingernails than earning a living? Are you well-dressed, but are of poor hygiene? Do you memorize song lyrics backwards because you've always been a fan of dyslexia? Do you like to sing Country & Western songs with a wide vibrato like that of Jennifer Holiday? Do you listen to Crime Mobb's "Knuck If You Buck" before all religious holidays as a rule?

610PM: The Devil's greatest trick was convincing artists' fanbases to use streams as arsenal in social media Stan Wars. These people deserve sterilization by acid...or torture by way of Britney Spears' natural singing voice without a side of autotune.

1032PM: I fear that I've grown weary of traveling back to a time in which I starched creases into my jeans that turned them into bodiless mannequins to reflect on memories.

9Apr2018 1155AM: A nurse named Ashley: The story of an emergency room nurse who becomes jaded by trauma and commits to a life of pranks and practical jokes for shits, giggles, and small doses of adrenaline to curb her boiling desire to go on a euthanizing spree. #DarkComedy

949PM: She called her pussy "the projects". I laughed and pointed at it.

10Apr2018 1054PM: My hobbies include being sick and fuckin' tired of people coming into money and not fixing their mouth schematics.

107PM: Your breath smells like the womb of an aboriginal prostitute.

449PM: Something as simple as seeing someone driving down the street and enjoying the breeze it creates with their fingers makes me smile at odd times.

12Apr2018 0359PM: I'll say this of the day and you can go back and look at what was going on if you'd like; I hate when celebrities continually take the bait. Sometimes it's just easier to say "No comment because whatever I say regarding this situation will be taken out of context in some way." When people are caught up in drama they've created for the purpose of entertainment, it's always best to starve them of seasoning.

452PM: Cardi B makes music for girls/women who put their old weave inside a tube sock to wash it like laundry...and I'm here for the madness of it all.

12Apr2018: My hobbies include deleting songs from my Apple Music profile.

15Apr2018 0349AM: People keep peeking...speaking without thinking.

0536PM: I'm sick of housework judging me. It's just one of those nagging things that, if left unattended, make your character look like it's strung out on self-loathing. There are no kindred spirits for me. That sounds sticky and snobbish. I'm okay with that.

Chapter 33: The Lost Art of Mingling

To love a room full of skittish people nibbling on hors d'oeuvres rhythmically to the most knuck if you buck music. To allow your soul to swag surf to the low hum of small talk peppered with pettiness. A hive of flies on the walls, elbow serving as loofa to elbow, dancing the dance of extravagant hi's and byes with their inside voices. Documented day laborers of the pseudo-corporate machine, they settle for superficial associations because "deep and meaningful" is an investment and the market's ongoing love affair with cartwheels paralyzes the skittish. Woefully woke, they brandish smiles glistened by coconut oil.

They are soldiers of fuck yo bitch and the clique you claim. They are the former mime-dressed pop lockers from your local zoot suit Baptist Church who had the good sense to make the straight and narrow their bitch. They are sexual paths bloodied by abortions and lechery. They are fuck buddies with matching pill habits who don't see small doses of bussit here and there as a big deal. They are those who graduated from "Hi. May I take your order?" to "Good morning. Thank you for calling...". They are debutantes and sorors. They sell a little weed on the side. They have a food stamp plug because salary is a cock blocker.

She was just a girl a short while ago, but that ass and them titties skulldrug her to the front line of a personal brand of feminism that did not come to play with these niggas. She is familiar with the taste of pussy. She loves a cat eye and an attention-whoring acrylic. She refuses to work and bankrolls setting up camp on luxury's lap out of the wallets of white men who prefer their candy coated in chocolate. Her pussy is a venture capitalist.

She loves that the world is distracted. She thrives in social settings where people are so preoccupied with filters that they puncture their owns neck and let her drink freely. Her touch is a meditation in and of itself. It is a spell that inspects upon contact. What's a bad bitch to a succubus? Her pussy has an electromagnetic pulse. A crowded room is a puzzle. Imagine if orgasms were coy at times like sneezes. That special clusterfuck where perfume is a gateway drug and the 808 is the ace of spades.

HipHop is her native language. She is a master of punchlines and metaphors. Her mind is a turntable. She fakes a French accent to give context to her addiction to Newports. She uses fashion ads from Vogue as wallpaper. Her favorite shows are makeup tutorials and capoeira competitions. She considers yoga continuing education for her pussy power. She is allergic to cornrows. The droves that come are dark, muscular and street credible, but she hasn't made it to Trap Queen on her bucket list just yet. She is a hoarder of skills so as to make herself more interesting. She quilts when her pussy is on administrative leave.

She has lost count of how many times "Fuck a date. Just buy me some stocks and come be baptized by this pussy in the next 30 minutes" has rolled off her lips. She is bored because she wants to twerk, but despite the music, the Black Tie label is keeping her subdued.

A mouth is a terrible thing to waste. Passing around regret by surfing them on half-truths. People eat that shit up. A quick glance around the room is a field day. The skeptics have treated their noses and now la la land is a labyrinth hidden within a daydream. Birds in ball gowns singing like they were newly freed from cages. Body language of every dialect sends a pulse through the temperature-controlled atmosphere. He's having flashbacks of body rolls and her shoulders are tap dancing. The masters have charted maps of their conquests this evening.

He is country. His accent's cadence is unapologetically chopped and screwed. His hands have never been the Devil's playground. His best friend's wife is fucking him. That's how he rationalizes being the object of her Reverse Cowboy every time work supposedly Hershey squirts all over dinner plans. He's saved as Caprice Conservatory Prep in her phone. The conversations are always coded language. Every time is the last time. His intense infatuation commits suicide at the moment of ejaculation. He got someone else pregnant. His dick needed the drama to distract him from his ongoing Man Code Violation.

There's something disingenuous about a toothless smile.

16Apr2018 0812AM: The true mark of creative genius is sparked by the barrenness of fucks to give about what is coupled with an obsession about what could be. Living in a state of what's next is exhilarating and indifference, while suckling the teet of perfectionism, is a frenzied state in which to maneuver. Conditioned to thrive on function over form while trying to sully a laborious upbringing with fits of throwing caution to the wind, I take notice of the fact that these roads less traveled are ornate as fuck. I'm a wanderer given to sight-seeing and window-shopping all of nature's more opulent knickknacks. All the world's a corner store.

0254 PM: Faux panic, tentative rage against the machine, and bombardment by answers unrelated to the question are the order of the day. Stop hypnotizing yourself with the sound of your own voice and breathe a little.

0442PM: I can't stand people who are in a state of crisis, but have no sense of urgency. Rome wasn't built in a day, but they worked on the muthafucka daily.

17Apr2019

1030AM: People swear there's only one way to be a kid. Some kids thrive on building LEGO shit. Others thrive on dreams of being America's Next Top Model. Great parents honor their children's interests, not try to mold them into some cookie cutter version of what society deems is appropriate.

0825PM: Doubt. Your doubt. Your self-doubt, specifically, is blood to the sharks encircling the dissonant wavelengths radiating from consciousness.

0834PM: Nothing vexes my soul like going into a restroom after someone and being accosted by the malodorous demon of the aftershit.

0936PM: "It puts the lotion on its vocal chords" was my reaction to Britney Spears trying to sing Aretha Franklin.

Chapter 35: A Royal Flush and It Ain't No Card Game

Conversations of the Black Bourgeoisie: DOXI and O'BRIAN

Doxi: It vas hot time. Summer in city.

O'Brian: So that's how you want to play it?

Doxi: I vouldn't have it any other vay.

O'Brian: I don't know what kind of Russian poltergeist is reverse cowgirlin' on your tongue, but you sound as though your breath smells like vodka and sardine kraut.

Doxi: So you're just going to go full autopsy report on me like that?

O'Brian: These are the days of our lives and that bullshit gets met with equal amounts of fuckery.

Doxi: Touché, old sport. So what fantastics of life have you been tripping of late?

O'Brian: Just the same ole shit from the same ole me...upgraded here and there to remain in tune with the times, of course.

Doxi: Riveting...cough...sarcasm. You're suffering from a bad case of the groundhog's days if I've ever seen it. Your suit looks like it was tailored at a laundromat.

O'Brian: You're no one that I have to impress. You look like you're auditioning to be people furniture in a PBS sitcom written by local high school freshmen.

Doxi: You not impressing me is an excellence you manifest as though it were second-nature. So I heard that your little entrepreneurial venture tanked. Can't say that I didn't laugh. Can't say that I wasn't proud of myself for laughing. Have you bumped into young Chris Anthony anywhere? Did he point and laugh at you like I paid him to do? Money well-spent either way. I've been laughing about it without opening my mouth for days.

O'Brian: My greatest failures would be considered monumental successes when compared to your greatest efforts. Are you still passing yourself off as a stock broker?

Doxi: Do you mean am I still the most successful broker at the most successful firm you and your little friends drool at the thought of being represented by?

O'Brian: Oh, come now. Let's not pretend that this isn't just your gambling addiction jacking off while on steroids.

Doxi: Whatever it is, I could still buy and sell you five times over.

O'Brian: Interesting... and by interesting I'm referring to the Honda Civic I saw you park three lots over. I, myself, chartered an entire luxury bus just for shiggles.

Doxi: Sigh. I say the word rather than performing the action because you aren't deserving of an actual emotional response. You're worried about my mode of transportation when your soul has a micropenis...which might explain that bus.

O'Brian: But that Civic though?

Doxi: It's mine. It's efficient as fuck. I have an unspoken thing about efficiency. Why the fuck are you on a bus?

O'Brian: Because you can't be. What other reason would there be?

Doxi: An asshole through and through. Cheers to you, old sport.

O'Brian: Cheers, bitch ass nigga.

Chapter 36: You Drippin' Swagu...Not So Much

Conversations of the Black Bourgeoisie: ARILYN and ALWAYS

Arilyn: Excuse me.

Always: What's up?

Arilyn: From one Black girl to another, you have given the kitten heel new life in ways I couldn't have imagined. I couldn't let you pass me by without singing you a tiny A Selection of praise. I mean you paired those kitten heels with those gouchos and that blouse that screams "Sunday School in a southern zip code" in a way that would have Blanche Devereaux rethinking her entire approach to fashion. Give me PTA meeting or give me death. Am I right? AND YOUR OWN HAIR!!!! Pressed no doubt. I applaud you... in theory of course. We wouldn't want to make any more of a spectacle than the grandeur of your fashion excellence has already made now would we?

Always: Bitch, I was in a play today.

Arilyn: Like...earlier today ooorrrr...?

Always: Like moments before I was finessed with every bit of high-society loaded flattery a single, figurative breath could muster. You sure are dolled up. If I was a gambling woman, I'd put money on you donning the costume of a woman about to fake smile for hours and goop up the wealthiest and most dimwitted pinky's worth of penis you can seduce with that potpourri-scented compost heap you're packing in your Vicky's.

Arilyn: Ooooooh I like it. Can we be friends? I want to give you a second chance at...well...life.

Always: I don't know. I don't usually make friends with people whose knees require the attention of a loofah.

Arilyn: Some call them battle scars. I call them occupational hazards. For if hoe is not life, then what is life at all?

Always: Bitch, you have won my heart. Name's Always. Yes, I am eternally bitchy. Yes, I am appropriately named considering the couture line of coochie cosseting products that exist and just so happen to bear the same name as I. I have a pussy that is just as temperamental. Now you know.

Arilyn: What would my arsenal be without an upper echelon Bitch? My name is Arilyn. Former twerkaholic who washed her pussy in one last sink at the MGM Grand before writing a business plan for it. I am not a hooker. I am not a prostitute. I am not an escort. I am a professional fiancée and for $85,000 a month plus exclusive rights to my depiction in the breakup story, I'll turn your legend into the cum stain of every A-Lister's wet dream of prominence. That sounded more floral scented in my mind.

Always: Pleased to make your acquaintance.

Arilyn: Whatever, bitch...the term of endearment kind. Just so you know, I'm the type of friend that tells you the truth even when you don't need to hear it.

Always: I wouldn't have it any other way and I am the type of friend that lets you call her bitch once, even as a term of endearment, before I sweep your leg and snap a picture of you to post on social media.

Arilyn: Where have you been all my life?

Always: Probably popping my pussy for a real niggeur, and you have to blend nigga and nigger like that because they're white collar yet lowkey Black market, somewhere.

Arilyn: Same. Same. But we need to talk about your characterizations of Black and white.

Always: Check, please.

Chapter 37: The Dozens, the Breaks, & Bitch I Might Be

Conversations of the Black Bourgeoisie: COX and BRENNIGAN

Cox: Well if it isn't my favorite almost named after a working man's date night restaurant choice fuck boy.

Brennigan: And my second to least favorite person named after things he jacks off.

Cox: Much improved from our last joust. Been educating yourself on the blogs lately?

Brennigan: No, you haven't been in them much these days. I see the issue with your whole face hasn't improved much since last we met.

Cox: Nor has your ability to prevent your feet from contorting your shoes, thereby resulting in you walking on their sides.

Brennigan: Who's there?

Cox: I'll entertain you. Knock knock.

Brennigan: No, you're supposed to come with the punchline. Your knees already took care of the setup.

Cox: Weren't you intending to attend to that slurping sound you make when you pronounce "s" words?

Brennigan: I was waiting on a referral from you for the doctor who used a crank on the bags under your eyes.

Cox: It's the same doctor who took you from KRS-1 to Christine Baranski. Your nose looks like it needs a catheter.

Brennigan: This is always fun, but perhaps it's time for us to stop dillydallying over such trivial matters.

Cox: My pedigree views a truce with the same disdain as it does a defeat, so I cannot oblige you.

Brennigan: Why trifle with a truce when we can cause trouble with an unhealthy alliance? I'll never see you as more than an ash colored troglodyte.

Cox: The proposition drips with the ire of Supervillain latex accoutrements. Pause. I was referring to costumes.

Brennigan: And for my first trick, I will show you how to have a powdery Wonderland on a Midsummers eve. Shall we bump?

Cox: Does Kardashian pussy secrete voodoo venom?

Chapter 38: Admirations for the Spangled Populous

Conversations of the Black Bourgeoisie: HALO and SEAUXFEIGN

Halo: On such night's as this when weeping seems to be the calling card for God's holy wrath. Such a moist malevolence that drizzles over your consciousness. I am but the ashes of a burning heart. And I went searching for the flow of milk and honey, but every stretch of land I found was parched. And you may wonder why I claw at my flesh as though it offends me. Or dance naked in places that would bring shame to those who know my name. Passive-aggressive pettiness never did much to tickle my fancy. So I bathe it in the irony of my aloofness and solidarity.

Seauxfeign: I was the fifth echo you ignored when your brain finally processed that the caterwauling you were hearing was a rape in progress. I have developed a thing for lace gloves. They make me feel equal parts chaste and tawdry like crotchless panties worn beneath a burka or a habit. I am a beast unleashed...a djinn uncorked. Like humans, I can be good, evil, or neutrally benevolent. I surrender my body an erotic sacrifice for the profit of pearls. What's one soul I've never truly owned compared to an entire world?

Halo: Walk with me on particles of perfume. Kanye West. We'd rather remold mastery than to plummet into the depths of its tide and allow it to cascade us toward uncharted waters. We'd rather backspace the wavering paintbrush stroke than tilt our heads 13° and unearth breathtakingly cavernous captivation. We'd rather status update than craft soliloquies that caterwaul alarums of unrest within the soul. We'd rather spit-shine than refine. We'd rather chip than chisel. We'd rather critique than create; guzzle rather than sip slowly and savor. Imagination can't be a savior if our mindless behavior requires an IEP. I see me...reflected in erasure marks. Laughter can't be a savior if the lungs are handcuffed to coughing spells. I'm an adulterous conversationalist, trivializing the brokenness of lingering gazes. Crippling the artistry of drunken performance art. What molded, impoverishment of character befalls your smirking face? My soul rolls its eye...the third one with enhanced depth perception. My eagle soars with nibbled wings; a delicacy for the God of hubris. The abdication of banality absquatulating innocence. Bitch better have every cent of time invested in her melancholy animal magnetism. Rambling energetically about vacuous ideals that leave mankind's evolution at a standstill. I want to bleed my soul bare and showcase its nudity on billboards throughout Time Square. Such robust abandon weeping at the crest of the witching hour. Mindscapes carefully crafted from the cacophony of meritorious slaughter. The wicked don't slumber. They teeter at the precipice of unrest. The irony is that the deprivation only indoctrinates the primal urge and they molest artificial mood enhancers to function. We busily grieve out in the open. We allow our emotion to become the buffet of heathens. We kneel in prayer and subject our eternal to madness. We prefer our genius sequestered behind gilded, stained-glass. I've been searching for the thief who stole my heart while I was passed out drunk. Some stumble bum in a pencil skirt and Louboutins, no doubt. But that's neither here nor there and speaks nothing of my wanderlust. The tempest electric slides atop atmospheric pressure. The fowl scream in angst. Where does the cowering child nestle safely from the horrors of society's judgment? What treatment program will sedate his loathing? Freud married the death wish and the orgasm into a singular tingle within the medulla oblongata. When smiling is perverse and the compliments are venom. When impracticality begets innocence and the lullaby screeches to a halt. There arose a pompous poster-child for every douchebag, asshole, jerk off, and fucktard yanking his chain and serving his dick tears as the whipped topping on mimosas. A daring narcissist who temper-tantrumed his way into the hearts and minds of every would-be hipster toting a backpack and platinum grill this side of the Mason Dixon. He was as hollow as a shadow to some, but the second-coming to others. He was merely the conceptualization of our alter egos. He was a phantom, an idea at best. He was a night terror who loved strumpets. He didn't exist although he was visible...audible...reckless. They look you squarely in the eye, perspiring from the tongue ever so slightly, and tell you in their most evangelical voice that there's room enough at the top for every supplicant with a sweet-tooth for karma's...epiphanies, if you will. We prefer things tidy, refusing to open our eyes to the debris sweeping across our lives in favor of selfies in hip places. We've thrown away our internal compasses. We are drifting in blissful ignorance.

Seauxfeign: Rihanna. Like diamonds dipped in the pewter blood of cherubim, these are the days of get the fuck out of here with that bullshit; an era in which reckless abandon is both an appetizer and a fragrance. The promenade of Prada-clad gazelles on cobblestone catwalks. The twerk of born again virgins with a lust for mink eyelashes. She freestyles in patois over trap-infused dubstep and she ain't even Jamaican. Her harmony a sixth sense; the fifth element. One middle finger saluting the genuflection of HipHop & B paupers. A dutty wine for dirty Sprite. Her apparition the template for stealthy side bitches. She likes to pass the dutchie on the left-hand side whilst sauntering on uncharted waters. Make no mistake about her slithering sedition. Demigoddess of adolescent domestic violence, strong with this one the clapback gale rages. What good is a good girl if she's not ripe for corrupting? What good is a harlot with no promise of redemption? Such majesty in her melancholy; things fall apart when she can't handle her liquor. And the beat goes on in steady syncopation. What wondrous merriment sways within the pendulum of those clairvoyant, emerald ocular fixtures? Her algorithm is an amalgamation of haute couture, strip clubs, the bando, and Carnevale. Never one to cower from sticky situations. Never one to defy the soul's exhibitionism. Never one to deny the lust of the flesh. Never one to obsess about entitlements, but quick to let a bitch know she's spoiled by the undergods of this world. She dances on the landscapes where the wild things are. Budding from the chrysalis of pop culture infamy; desecrating expectations with a Kanye shrug. A debutante for dope boys. An archetype for the anti-prim & proper establishment. We applaud her irreverent naughtiness. We celebrate her refusal to wave the banner of role model while she's pussy poppin' on the downbeat for dollar bills. Oh, the witch's brew that melds reflections of bitchiness and feminism into a befuddled fusion, thereby thwarting one's ability to perceive upon which tract the lioness is prowling. Bare midriff. Sheer blouses serving as the parental advisory sticker to bare breasts. Lipstick jungle. Girls just wanna have fun. Maybe she's born with it. Stiff-arming those with the unmitigated gall to question her purpose. Never bewildered. Never broken. Never bound by perceptions. Never bothered. So take this as a letter to all of the young ladies out there struggling to gain footing on the road to self-love. Be a paragon of non-conformity. Let your hair down in every sense of the phrase. Let caution earn its wings in the breeze of your defiant dogma. Tilt your tiara to the side and put a knot in the hem of your ball gown, exposing you cotton jogging pants and Ugg boots. You decide which descriptors best delineate your being. You are the goddess of your cosmos. Reign supreme while flippantly turning your back on every inconceivable expectation thrust upon you because you bear the gift of a double X.

Chapter 39: The Commander in Tweets

Conversations of the Black Bourgeoisie: BRAX and PETERSON

Brax: So how are you feeling about the whole Donald Trump presidency situation?

Peterson: I'm feeling that human existence needs to be reset to the factory settings. I'm feeling that the things that we cling to, to add value to our lives are about as insignificant as an obese person's under-booty cellulite and pimples. I still feel Black in America...and that's deep. Like I can literally feel the impact that the color of my flesh has on the world around me. I feel that people will continue to make excuses for misguided hatred. I feel that fear will remain a great motivator for mentality herding of sheeple. I feel that we are going to witness an abundance of toxic language and propaganda being spewed via various media outlets. I feel as though America will continue to be for them by us. I feel as though my life will continue to be a fight to rank among the strong who survive. My hope is that Donald Trump is a better, more benevolent president than any of us could have ever imagined.

Brax: Because surely the anti-Christ wouldn't be dusted with orange pressed powder.

Peterson: HAHAHAHAHAHA now that's what I call some funny shit.

Chapter 40: Sex, Trap Music, and Video Tapes

Conversations of the Black Bourgeoisie: EUDOXIE and SOLACE

Eudoxie: I feel bulletproof when he slithers inside me. My wicked warrior come to battle against the dark forces who have taken my orgasm to be their damsel in distress. Eyes the color of a sandstorm. Locs like whips with gilded tips. My Milky Way made easy by his possession. My obsession.

Solace: But if this is what love is intended to look like, then why the shifting of shapes? Your pussy being the mood ring that gives expression to his madness. A toxic meandering of passion and dominion.

Eudoxie: A longing seed planted for harvest when I was still searching. Yet I remain steadfastly untethered to sentiment. This is purely a carnal distraction from redundancy. Allow me to frolic blissfully ignorant of encumbrances for once. For too long I've been cuffed to propriety...a side chick to prudishness.

Solace: And in abundance you shall find that which you seek. I simply caution you to avoid landing in the position of settling.

Chapter 41: A Face Beloved by the Gods of Man

Conversations of the Black Bourgeoisie: Balm and Brandywine

Brandywine: No, but seriously dude, whatever gave you the impression I would do that?

Balm: I don't know. It's just like...you...sizzle when you walk.

Brandywine: Well, people pretty much think I'm going to rest on pretty anyway.

Balm: Maybe just lean on it a little bit. I can easily make a few calls if you'd like.

Brandywine: Yeah, but that would be inorganic and that's not my brand. You know how I like for things to happen.

Balm: We met organically enough...and were killer organic two weeks later.

Brandywine: I swear you remind me of that in every conversation we have.

Balm: She says with mild exasperation.

Brandywine: Not even. Consider that more reminiscing than bitching. That's not my brand either. Correction, that's not my ministry.

Balm: So, you do like it?

Brandywine: It's a keeper. Much like you when you still have moments where you question whether or not I want to be with you. I like that you're still on your toes.

Balm: I'd sprinkle egg shells in front of me like that dude sprinkled the salt in that video just to keep you happy.

Brandywine: Quietly hums Beyoncé's "Single Ladies."

Balm: You're so funny I should put you on stage.

Brandywine: I'd just make my ass clap to "Who's the Loser Now" by Brandy...dramatic pause...and fuck shit up.

Balm: HAHAHAHAHAHA I love you.

Brandywine: I love you more.

Balm: We'll see.

Chapter 42: This is California, not Kentucky?

Conversations of the Black Bourgeoisie: VIYA and SEIGHJAI

Viya: It was kinda surreal that I was actually having to stand there and ask a grown ass man if he truly believes the wealthy sit around and talk about outfits for our pups and caviar brands all day. Being perceived as vapid and lacking depth first then acknowledged for my brain's constant boner second shall be written on my tombstone.

Seighjai: Mmmmmm I don't know. People trust you more when they think you're stupid. It's like the time I met that guy at Cool Kids Only and he thought because my hair was glossy and happy to be alive, because let's be honest some of these bitches' hair looks suicidal, and my titties are fake that I'm not savage enough or shrewd, as they say in the boardroom, enough to clear out one of his offshore accounts and then Whitemail him with lightly filtered photos of him doing the Orlando Brown on my pussy.

Viya: Look at us complaining about being stereotyped knowing good and damn well that we write entire sagas with our eye rolls about girls who manage to pull off, and by pull off I mean go out in public with it exposed, a size 1 and a muffin top simultaneously.

Seighjai: While we are on the subject of being that bitch, I'm thinking of getting Botox in my pussy. They've been a little too emotive lately.

Viya: They've?

Seighjai: Yes, it has Dissociative Identity Disorder. It's a racked up enough alters to qualify as a full-fledged horde.

Viya: The saga of your vagina is 100% more enthralling than the autobiographies of 80% of the people we know.

Seighjai: Its legend definitely goes unspoken. Darling, what time is it? I try not to drink before five minutes after whatever time it is right now.

Viya: Sweetie, it's 10:28 in the morning. You invited me over for mimosas, strawberries and girl talk, so you kind of already broke that rule.

Seighjai: A Mimosa will only become an alcoholic beverage to me when I'm on so much medication that a drink of any kind would effectively control alt delete me.

Viya: No judgment here. Real estate guys were snorting cocaine out of my ass all last night...so.

Seighjai: Can I visit your ladies room? I've got this new vibrator and the last time I used it, it made me cum until I peed on myself and I'm kind of in the mood.

Viya: Knock yourself out, but stand in the tub if you're going to slowly leak all over the place. Oh, and don't be alarmed, but one of the nine guys I picked to fuck last night is still passed out in my bed. If you're wondering why nine, I'm thinking of treating myself to a $15,000 a pop abortion scam for my birthday.

Chapter 43: One Time for the One Time

Conversations of the Black Bourgeoisie: AMILLE and CAMERON

Cameron: So how was my beautiful princess' first day at her new school today?

Amille: I don't know. It was okay. I guess.

Cameron: What's wrong, baby? You sound like you didn't have the type of first day we expected.

Amille: It's not that big of a deal. It's just that people always make it seem like me wearing my hair naturally and proudly is some grand act of defiance against white supremacy, I mean white delusions of grandeur, and it's getting older by the "Stay woke, sis". My decision to wear my hair the way it grows naturally out of my scalp has everything to do with me loving me and absolutely nothing to do with anyone else's perception of me, whether positive or negative.

Cameron: And what have I always told you, baby girl?

Amille: That my beauty is defined by the beauty I produce in the world for others to experience and enjoy and not the physical attributes that I was born with and I get that and I love you for teaching me that. I just get tired of my subtleties of being getting magnified into some grand acts of defiance for a revolution that hasn't even been clearly defined for me yet.

Cameron: Baby girl, you have a regal presence and the sooner you accept this about yourself, the better off you'll be. It wouldn't matter if you had a bald fade, a curl, a finger wave, braids or an 18 inch weave, you'd still command attention.

Amille: Thanks, daddy.

Cameron: You're welcome, baby. Well, let me ask you this. Do you think your mother and I made the right decision in moving you to this school? Now that I think about it, we didn't ask your opinion on the matter.

Amille: To be perfectly honest with you, I think it was a horrible decision. I know you guys were just trying to do what you thought was best for me scholastically, but I feel like I'll be missing out on more culturally. I don't want to be one of those Black women who can only relate to a certain type of Black person. I don't ever want to feel out of touch or like I can't relate because it's unfamiliar. You and mom have always instilled such pride in me. You taught me to embrace my chocolate skin and to let my love for it to be the only way that I flaunt it. You also taught me not to treat it like something I would wear or can take off; like a thing that is separate from my being. This move makes me feel like I've been tarred and feathered; tarred with my brown skin and feathered with microaggressions.

Cameron: Microaggressions? WHAT ARE THOOOOOOOSE?

Amille: Alexa, play "Google Me" by Teyana Taylor. A microaggression is a word or phrase used to describe or express the unceremonious ignominy of individuals belonging to or any group treated as peripheral within society by persons outside that group. The term was coined by psychiatrist and Harvard University professor Chester M. Pierce, a Black man, in 1970 to give an account in words all of the relevant characteristics, qualities, or events pertaining to the insults and dismissals which he regularly witnessed non-black Americans inflicting on African Americans. By the early 21st century, use of the term was applied to the off-the-cuff humiliation of any socially marginalized group, including LGBT, the poor and the disabled. Psychologist Derald Wing Sue defines microaggressions as "brief, everyday exchanges that send denigrating messages to certain individuals because of their group membership". The persons making the comments may be otherwise well-intentioned, but you and I both know that the road to hell is paved with both good intentions and that's not how I meant that.

Cameron: Let me find out you've been attending Hotep University on YouTube. Baby girl, it truly delights my heart and soul to see young, Black girls and women embracing their blackness, natural hair in all of its varied textures, distinctive features and beautiful brown bodies. But like your mom and I have told you throughout your life, whenever we start openly celebrating and loving ourselves, there are those who have an issue with it. While we recognize that physical attributes do not determine a person's worth or character, unfortunately not everyone in this world has evolved to that level of wisdom. You should be proud of your melanin. It is the very thing that sets you apart like being Jazmine Sullivan, Beyoncé, Brandy or Keke Wyatt in a room full of tone deaf people. But Baby Girl, I hear you. And I apologize for not giving you a voice in this issue. We just wanted you to look good on paper.

Amille: I get it, but I don't live on paper. I live in a complex world that views twelve year olds like Tamir Rice as threats before it sees them as children. I have two years left in school and I just don't want to live them like I'm an attraction at a museum like Sara Baartman.

Cameron: Say no more. I just want you to know that these talks make me so very proud of the young woman you're becoming. I love you, baby.

Amille: I love you more, daddy.

Chapter 44: A Bad Case of the Jungle Coodies

CONVERSATIONS of the Black Bourgeoisie: KING and GLORY

King: I hate when people diminish Harriet Tubman's significance by referring to her as a civil rights leader. She was a rebel!

Glory: Have you noticed that nine times out of 10 when you go to say something, it usually begins with "I hate when people..."?

King: BITCH, FUCK YOU!!!!

Glory: Well that escalated quickly...no...you want a dead son-in-law Miss Celie...no... it was at this moment that King realized that he was breathing his last breaths...that's the one I'm looking for. HAVE YOU LOST YOUR ALREADY FUNCTIONING BELOW NORMAL ASS MIND?

King: Cool your picket signs, Amber Rose. I was just testing it out to see if it was as emotionally liberating as friends have made it out to be and I must say that it was. So you're just going to steamroll past my heavily subdued and shortened rant about Harriet Tubman?

Glory: Please don't make me talk about Harriet Tubman again for the fourth time today. It's like your mind is set on a loop.

King: Why wouldn't you want to? There's a good chance you wouldn't be sitting there right now with your baby hair gelled down to the corners of your face were it not for Harriet Tubman!

Glory: King, listen. If you're worried about me snitching on you for that little one on one you had with Becky with the good hair under the bleachers two weeks ago...don't. I stopped telling on you when we reached the age that our business was no longer intertwined.

King: Well, didn't I see you posting the other day that any Black man that steps outside of the Black race to date, marry, and procreate is a disgrace and a deserter?

Glory: Scanned for lies. None detected. But that's how I feel. I'm not one of those people who tries to dictate how other people should feel.

King: So do you feel betrayed and deserted by me?

Glory: You aren't in my dating pool, little brother. This isn't Utah.

King: You know what I mean.

Glory: I can only know what you said and believe what you meant until you confirm what you meant.

King: Please don't do that technical thing you do.

Glory: Greater minds than yours have tried to decode my encrypted cognitions...and failed miserably.

King: HA! You know no greater mind than mine.

Glory: Agent Dario Asiatu.

King: Oh, we're pretending that you actually know him in 2017, are we? I must've missed the memo. Was it emailed or a hard copy?

Glory: Are you suggesting that I don't know the only man I've allowed to put a hickey on my inner labia even though we weren't dating?

King: Hands sister Skip card from incomplete Uno deck and looks away apathetically.

Glory: Like I said, a disgrace and a deserter. Rolls eyes in ratchet fashion.

King: LET ME BE GREAT!!!!!

Glory: I freed a thousand slaves. I could have freed a thousand more if only they knew they were slaves.

Chapter 45: Black Don't Crack

CONVERSATIONS of the Black Bourgeoisie: MECCA and MESSIAH

Mecca: These days it seems that dreams are filled with screams of horror and merriment in equal parts.

Messiah: What is to come of the overdone and underwhelmed when times do tell?

Mecca: It's not weariness. It's not some sadistic infatuation with coming up short. It's not a bloodlust for innocence or some shimmering phantom intended to bewilder.

Messiah: The ever-present dissonance; the cacophony of the hullabaloo; the upper echelon of the sleepless elite.

Mecca: And so we go into some distant dawn that's barely clinging to the abyss from whence it came. Blindly marching single file in syncopated rhythm.

Messiah: Lazy days of summer shriveling into glimpses of nostalgia that were once the template for complacency. Children shouldn't play with dead things.

Mecca: To quote the famed Kemetic Philosopher, Samantha Bridgewater-Phillips, "The truth is starting to seep & burst thru the seams. It's actually pretty self-evident... I mean, you can visibly see the traces of White supremacy. It's almost tangible it's so apparent. The general underlying current is that we've overstepped the boundaries they installed for us... Tamir Rice's case is absolute evidence. When a whole nation of folk will uphold a child's murder...you can visibly see the design. Police officers are the new overseers. Their role, is to keep us broken & in line with our notion of inferiority."

Messiah: It's like a hologram, you know? Or some fractured reflection of this dimension. Some overly filtered parallel universe.

Mecca: The truly superior don't have to use deceit in order to bring their superiority to fruition.

Messiah: A copy never reflects the true brilliance and resplendence of the original.

Mecca: This one time, at my place of employment, they wanted all the Black people to come together and plan a Black History Month Celebration. They were, of course, going to take the credit for honoring the contributions of African Americans...but they weren't giving niggers any funds to make the shit happen. Sweet land of liberty...of thee I sing.

Messiah: Yet, still I rise.

Chapter 46: The Broad Stroke

This is the story of the painter whose works of art killed people. No, the paintings themselves did not murder anyone. Don't be a dumb fuck. However, when she painted someone, they inevitably ended up dead within days.

She wasn't a prodigy. She didn't study diligently in school to become great. She didn't survive some freak accident and come out of it with an ability she didn't possess before. She was clever.

She knew how to sell herself with such understated intricacies so well that she stumbled into global phenomenon-dom. Stitched together with copious amounts of sneakiness, her personality was more serpent than unicorn. To be continued by someone I'll likely never meet...

Chapter 47: The Next One After That One

CONVERSATIONS of the Black Bourgeoisie: RHYME and REASON

Rhyme: I remember it...

Reason: Like it was yesterday.

Rhyme: Smiling faces dancing in the resplendence...

Reason: Of a sun happy to be serving its purpose.

Rhyme: And then it all turned to shit...

Reason: When the liquor kicked in.

Rhyme: These jiffies are made superfluous...

Reason: By the hankering of a salaciousness...

Rhyme: That feasts upon our complacency.

Reason: People often lack perspective.

Rhyme: My wilderness experience an experiment in existentialism.

Reason: I've been running in circles for what seems to be my entire existence.

Rhyme: Days aren't as significant as they used to be...

Reason: When cutting yourself is just another thing to do.

Rhyme: Everything macabre and predictably sadistic.

Reason: Repetitive surrender...the wanderlust of limbic resonance.

Rhyme: I've cried a thousand times and still I can't stop laughing at the pain.

Reason: A low and laboring cackle that erupts despite resistance.

Rhyme: I believe in things that no one should and search for answers in places that only lead to greater frustration.

Reason: But my calculated curiosity never lets me down, so I keep an ear in time with all the pretty little lies that we tell ourselves in order to cope.

Rhyme: I'm such a sucker for love that has been seasoned with danger and heartache.

Reason: I pour myself like pavement to be tread upon without regard.

Chapter 48: First of all, Papa Smurf didn't create Smurfette

I'm about to look like I'm auditioning for Urkel on Broadway.

I hate when people text "Call me" to me.

When using GPS, take a screen shot of the direction list and view it through your photos to save battery life on your iPhone. #CheatCodes

If you are buying anything of value, write down the serial number.

Replacing my heart with another liver so iCan drink more and care less.

I always have to have my Phone with me. If iForget it at home, iGo crazy!

Dear God, through whom all blessings flow, iCome before your throne of grace asking and praying that you hear my humble cry. Oh, Omnipotent Father, I've been tucking in my shirts and iLike it. Remove the blinders and change my heart Lord. Fix me Jesus.

Always remember that people are not simply the product of biology and environment --> but also of their own imagination, which is hidden within thoughts --> so you'll never truly know ANYONE because everyone keeps secrets about themselves to themselves no matter how real they tell you they are.

Evil seems to be inching ahead of good in this epic battle that we humans are caught in the middle of because evil "entertains" us and seduces our senses. We tend to associate good with rules & authority and let's face it, most of us have issues with authority.

Snaggle-toothed. Ashy. Underemployed. Disrespectful. Credit score 320. Convicted felon. Deadbeat dad. But his girl looks like Lauren London. How is that possible? #CheatCodes

Life was more exhilarating when classy girls saved their inner slut for special occasions.

No celebrity should be a part of your identity.

I'm about to overdose on people's excuses.

Study to show thyself approved before you try to tell me about me. #NARF

NEWSFLASH: iHavent changed!!!! So you can bet your sweet ass that whatever reason you deleted me before is still present in my personality and will be made manifest on Facebook. #NARF #StayDeleted #NotNow

FICTION: A Conversation iWish I'd Had!!!

Her: So what made you approach me at the bar tonight and decide that iWas the girl you wanted to take home?

Me: Well --> after iPhotoshopped you with six shots of vodka --> iNoticed you had respectable looking pinky toes. #NARF

iFeel like the only dudes who like 50 Cent's music now have synthetic hair braided into some cornrows and wear USPA religiously. #NARF

EGATS!!!! iThrew a fit about someone stealing my Bible at church and just noticed it's atop my file cabinet. How iOverlooked it amidst all that dry-hunchin I'll never know. #NARF

That prison of getting a notification from social media while your phone is locked knowing full well if you unlock your phone it's going to open whatever page you got the notification from but you're already almost over your data usage. (clearly this was during my iPhone 4 days)

Don't let people hold you in a place you're trying to move away from because they're comfortable there and you're comfortable with them. #NARF

I'll never understand the mentality of a man who perms his hair just to slick it back with gel and leave his struggle split-ends on full display.

iWasnt aware that iWas auditioning for your approval --> or iWouldve rehearsed. #NARF

People in church say stuff like --> Take me to a higher ground in YOU Lord. WTH does that really mean anyway? iBet Jesus be like "Daddy --> get your stupid kids." #NARF

This whole "Dumb It Down" movement has me pissed off. Whatever happened to encouraging people to "Smarten Up"? #NARF

You know what's embarrassing, frustrating, and disheartening? Inarticulate butchers of the English language trying to cheerlead you as you argue a point on social media!!!! #NoNewFriends #ArthritizeTheirFingersJesus #YoureHurtingNotHelping

Nobody really hates sluts and whores. People just envy their reckless abandon because it reminds them of the prison their inhibitions provide. People tend to pity pretty whores for some reason tho. It's like if you're an ugly slut, people encourage your vaginal exploits. #NARF

You have 33.2K followers on Twitter --> but you follow 33.1K people. Well isn't that special? Aren't you popular?

I'm predicting 'vocal cord injury' to be the new 'fatigue' --> which is code word for iWas still far too fucked up to perform in front of a live audience'. #RecordingArtistExcuses

Our youth really need to understand that the more fun you sacrifice now to get where you wanna be in life means the less you'll have to sacrifice when you're older and the more you can enjoy life then. Younger people should be working hard and older people should be enjoying life because they've already worked hard in life. #NARF

If only we could eradicate the fucktards --> the world would be most excellent.

iWant to be the first person to have his phone elevated to the status of national treasure because of its content. All the notes and voice memos and shit.

Weave --> single-handedly making African-American chicks look like they have bigger heads than other races of chicks.

I'll never understand how people tongue-kiss without first brushing their teeth. Morning breath is an extinction level event. #NARF

On the bright side, iAm not addicted to cocaine --> or mollies or xannies or acid or LSD and shit. Or meth can't forget meth OR heroin. Oh, and Krokodil. I'm definitely not addicted to Krokodil.

EMOJI LAMA: A SPIRITED QUEST

Chapter 49: PREFACE

My arguments with friends never end well...

Bro: Why you goin' so hard on Christmas? You mad because you're single and you're gonna wake up to no one on Christmas morning?

Me: Well, if I had to wake up to a chick built like a cobblestone patio deck, such as your chick, I'd take a lifetime of solo Christmas mornings. That bitch is built like a wad of snotty Kleenex. I bet when she undresses she just melts into like a pool of dimpled flesh.

He's currently waitin' on me in Burger King's parking lot. He said we can't move forward as friends until we catch a fair one. I told him I was on my way...33 minutes ago.

So there I was driving down the highway toward my favorite strip club with nothing on my mind except chafed netherbits and cum shot darts with dimly lit champagne room pretty strippers, but my life hasn't always been jacking off and butt chugging cough syrup. I've also been a very successful human furniture model.

The fact that I'm a heavy mouth-breather has never stuck out to me more than the time I lost consciousness eating Rayvyn Cummingham's pussy on the back row of the movie theater. She'd sprinkled a few honey barbecue bacon bits in her panties and before I knew it, I'd buried my entire face so deep in her chalupa, her left big toe had scratched the dude seated in front of us behind his left ear. The YouTube video he captured is still racking up views and likes. My tongue twerk went viral and suddenly this half-Botswanan/half-Guamanian man with a mullet and a physique like a run-over orthopedic shoe was poppin' all the pussy in a headstand.

But back to me driving across I-40 in my 3rd generation, highlighter yellow Kia Sorento, thumping through a playlist that features the Pussycat Dolls, Kendrick Lamar, Joni Mitchell and Kenny Chesney...I'm a sexy muthafucka who had to coat check his milkshake cuz I don't get down with the boys in the yard. Not since college and that bookie who threatened to feed my twig and giggleberries to his pit bulls. It was a dark and lonely time, but still I rise. But wait one second...

Officer: License and Insurance please? Do you know why I pulled you over this afternoon?

Me: There's a strong possibility it's either for throwing that bottle of road trip jizz out the window half a mile back or you've got a hankering to ruin a darkies day. Either way, I needed to fart just before you asked me that and I didn't hold back.

Officer: Step out of the car please.

Me: Oh, please don't make me do it. I'm not ready for another adult diaper change for another one twenty-eight miles, bro.

Officer: Step out of the car now, fag-slobber!

Me: How bout this? You punch me in the side of the face twenty times as hard as you can and I'll be on my way. No harm. No foul.

Officer: [Steps back from the car and looks over his shades.]

Me: [I smile then flick my tongue seventy-five times like Gene Simmons.]

Officer: So you mean to tell me...

When I woke up, "Best Friend" by Tokyo Vanity was wheezing through the speakers. The side of my face was having a sexy, little orgasm, so I threw back a BC Powder with the rest of my lukewarm Monster. There was a dead bird in my lap, but that's alright. Jesus died on the cross for that too. I took a few bumps of that premium grade, gourmet Ariana Grande (that's a special blend of cocaine and muscle relaxers) and my destiny became just a tad bit clearer all of a sudden.

The thing I love about the open road, besides the absence of society's judgmental eye as I pick and roll booger after booger between my fingers...and being able to jackoff into water bottles inconspicuously, is the laundry list of Tejano & Red Dirt stations to cruise to. Now I don't much speak the language of the tortillas, but that doesn't stop my taint from tingling. It was time for a gas stop and my chance at another piece of old chicken strip grease smelling gas station clerk pussy. My prey was knock-kneed and built very much like a peacock mascot. Her chubby face was painted with a face full of makeup like Mimi from the Drew Carey show, but I could tell I'd be able to see the contours of her cheekbones with a hefty blowjob.

Her name was something I only used once, so I forced it from my memory. I'm sure I'll get over it one day. But anyway, she wanted to lick my ass and I was like "I gotta change this depends first." And she was like "Okay, we've got wet wipes on the other side of the chips and shit." I was like "Okay, but let me shit first." She was like "Ew. Maybe a blumpkin?" I was like "Come through yuck mouth!" As I sat there, paying the penance for eating an entire box of Hostess Cupcakes while watching a pregnant woman twerk, rattle, roll, split, hydraulics, dutty wine and pussy pop on a kickstand followed by the ravenous deep-throating of my schfonz, I was reminded of the wise words of a homeless man who had more fingers on his right hand than teeth in his whole mouth, so I began to speak into her life: Don't chase people. Be you bitch, do your own thing and work hard. The right people who belong in your life will come to you, and stay. Always remember, God will never take anything away from you without the intention of replacing it with something much better. So if you find yourself pregnant, as you are now, the First Lady of the church your newly saved husband told you God spoke to him and told him to start, a working professional of corporate America for the first time, PTA President, a child care provider, a mentor, a 30-something grandparent, a role model not by your choosing or some other esteemed position, but your hoeness is still steadfastly intact, don't trip. Your hoe season just hasn't dried up yet and that means it's still a part of your ministry, so you should study to show yourself sanctioned. That way when the time comes for you to graduate from practitioner to testimonialist, you'll begin to rock steady! You're still a work in progress. Just remember to do your kegels for roadside maintenance while you're racking up all that mileage.

We wiped up the nut she didn't swallow (I geysered that hoe) and I was on my way. Bye, bye my precious toilet babies. Nourish your host body as best you can. This is what I was telling myself as I gawked at the dried up semen on the corner of her mouth as she said her goodbyes and farewells.

I stayed in town for a while because my crotch smelled like dirty feet, morning breath, and salmon croquettes, and I needed to shampoo, condition and flat iron my pubic hair. I was hungry as well and road food is like a perfectly timed queef when you're eating pussy and need to sneeze. I picked an old, piece of shit diner where they probably don't wash their hands as needed, but they ain't in the kitchen fuckin' up Food Network recipes and shit either.

An old neck pillow built bitch with a bouffant nesting on top of her head like day old cotton candy greeted me with that raggedy "nigger I'm just being pseudo-pleasant to your nigger ass because of the Obama and the Affirmative Action" ass greeting you get when you're a rooster built "Black" man with an S-Curl mullet and a fanny pack. But fuck that bitch. My dick game has a blue checkmark. Anyway, I was still reeling off of fresh bathroom sex and she had some juicy titty-fuck titties, so I laid low like Whitney Houston told me to.

Me: Say lil bih, what y'all got to eat in this blood-clot soiled Maxipad?

Her: Come again say what excuse me what did you say?

Me: My apologies. I was speaking the voice in my head. I was asking what fine cuisine one might fancy in this heavily messed swath of cushion placed in the seat of a woman's panties in order to serve as a receptacle for the seepage that runneth forth from her inner labia when she is menstruating.

Her (mouth hanging open like she was tryin' to smell between her teeth): I thought that's what the fuck you said and since your mouth needs a butt plug, you can just read the fuckin' menu.

Me: Thank you, ma'am. I admire your fupa...and the way you hock a loogie and swallow it after every few words. I'm lowkey erect.

Her: Well, what the fuck is a fupa?

Me: Fat. Upper. Pussy. Area. And I must say that yours has amazing girth to it. It gives you that nice Neti Pot shape I'm sure all the boys go crazy for.

Her: Now you wait one gotdamn minute there chicken shit...

Me *(waving my hands like I was trying to get her attention)*: Ma'am. Ma'am. Can you hear me? Ma'am. Hello? I was asking if you guys sold food here and you sort of just zoned out on me like you were having an out of body experience or something. Are you okay?

Her: What the fuck is wrong with your Black ass?

Me: *(excitedly)* THERE IT IS! (sociopathically) No, seriously can I just get three orders of 3-piece chicken strips, two orders of 2-piece chicken strips, two orders of single chicken strips, and one order of a six piece chicken strips to go please? YOU are a peach and I'd bet my life savings your clitoris is enlarged #FlicksTongueAtHerSeventeenTimesLikeGeneSimmons.

Her: I CAN'T DEAL WITH ALL THIS COCKAMAMIE BULLSHIT! Are you telling me you want 20 chicken strips to go or what?

Me: *(sociopathically)* No, seriously can I just get three orders of 3-piece chicken strips, two orders of 2-piece chicken strips, one order of a single chicken strip, and one order of a six piece chicken strips to go please? YOU are a peach and I'd bet my life savings your clitoris is enlarged #FlicksTongueAtHerSeventeenTimesLikeGeneSimmons.

Her: You just wait right there.

Me: OK. I'll just wait right here. Well, actually I'm gonna step over here these one, two, three, four, five, six, seven, eight, nine, ten, eleven, twelve, thirteen steps and read one of these magazines from this little bin that says "This ain't no library. Don't touch the magazines unless you're buying one." And you can....suck it. No seriously. I'll lay it on the counter.

So I'm standing there playing with the tip of my dick on the outside of my basketball shorts reading some dumb, fuck shit about rutabagas in <u>Better Homes & Gardens</u> and this bitch comes back with some Big Show built, the "Hills Have Eyes" lookin' somebitch. PAUSE: Who in the fuck came up with the word rutabaga? That is one of the ugliest words I've ever heard and I've heard some words that sound like a muthafucka is chokin' on squirrel bones. Unless rutabaga is from another language, amen. We want to be respectful. I love the foreigners over there where they're from and stuff. But yeah, so this slack jaw bitch comes draggin' this choke-chain needin' muthafucka from the back and he's all like...

Sloth from Goonies Lookin' Muthafucka: So as I'm hearing it here recently as I've been told, you're out here being a twat mouth to my momma.

Me: First of all, fuck you and that dirty dish rag built bitch. Where's my muthatfuckin' chicken strips hoe?

Foghorn Leghorn Built Muthafucka: I'm saying excuse me right now to you motherfucker. What did you just say to my momma?

Me: I said that bitch is built like dirty socks scrunched up at the bottom of a clothes hamper and you look like you're stuck somewhere between deformity and Lord forgive me for talking shit about this man who might be chromosomally challenged. Where the fuck are my muthafuckin chicken fuckin' strips nigga? And, why yes, I'm feelin' froggy.

The Blind Side Starring a White Man Instead of a Black Man: Well, that fuckin' does it. You and me officially have a problem, son, and I'm about to open a can of whoop ass on you.

Well, if a muthatfucka thinks they can talk to me any old South Dallas kinda way and thinks I won't Kung FU Panda that ass that muthafucka is sadly mistaken! So I pushed my nuts to the side and said "Let's tussle!" This big It's a Small World After All built bitch charged me and I kindly slid my happy ass out the way. Big boy dove head first into a display case and took a tumble, and I proceeded to stomp a mud-hole in his bitch ass about three good times before I was outta breath. That's when his momma pulled out a double barrel shotgun, y'all.

Her: You get your monkey ass outta my store right fuckin' now boy or I'm about to cast you in a murder scene.

Me: Haha. You right. Y'all funny. Y'all be playin' too much. Laugh. Out. Loud. And stuff. Ummm, yeah, so I quit. I throw in the towel and forfeit or whatever. Y'all win. But if I can get some chicken strips, I swear to God I'll pay for that gas I was about to steal.

Her [cocks the gun]: Get out.

Me: Vaya con Dios.

So now I'm hungrier than a bitch. My adrenaline is pumping. And I still have a nice stiffy because I never stopped playing with the tip of my dick on the outside of my basketball shorts. What to do? What to do? Fix it Stomach Acid Jesus. And just like the scripture promised, ask and you shall receive. A muthafuckin' mom and pop, soul food restaurant was sittin' off in the cut like somebody's been late on rent or property taxes for five years. When I walked in it was like the smell of pig parts and brown gel laid on top of me and died. I was in Heaven y'all.

Me: WHAT THE FUCK IS UP? WHO THE FUCK IS TAKIN' ORDERS AROUND THIS BITCH? HELLO? IT'S ME!

Pug-Faced Bitch with the Big Booty: Uh uhn sir, this is a Christian establishment. You cannot do all that cussin' up in here.

Me: Oh, my bad. I didn't know this was the Lord's house. Why the fuck y'all playin' Migos in this bitch then?

Pug-Faced Bitch with the Big Booty: Cuz we support Black-owned businesses around here and Dougie who owns the bootleg mechanic shop just figured out how to nigga rig a whole radio station from his iPhone and we're showin' love because that's what Jesus would do. Now may I help you?

Me: Yeah bitch, can I get a brisket sandwich and some sweet tea?

Pug-Faced Bitch with the Big Booty: You gon want some dessert or anything daddy or nah?

Me: Shit, I might. Let me see if y'all food is nasty first.

Pug-Faced Bitch with the Big Booty: You gon stop all that cussin' up in here. God don't like ugly.

Me: Bitch, I'll eat yo pussy and fuck you in the bootyhole on top of this table if you don't go make my plate. And if God don't like ugly, why the fuck are you wastin' yo time tryna be saved? You ain't gettin' up in Heaven witcho cockroach wit Down Syndrome lookin' ass.

Pug-Faced Bitch with the Big Booty: Ha. Boy whatever. I know I'm cute. I'll be right back with your order. Did you say you wanted sweet or unsweetened tea?

Me: Dunk your pussy lips in it and we'll call it halfway.

Pug-Faced Bitch with the Big Booty: Niggas.

Me: So what the fuck is there to do in this neighborhood?

Pug-Faced Bitch with the Big Booty: You mean this town? Cuz we right on the outskirts.

Me: Bitch, this whole shit is the size a neighborhood. The "Welcome to" and "You are now leaving" signs are in walking distance.

Pug-Faced Bitch with the Big Booty: Don't come for my town.

Me: Cumming is for bitches. I nut. Is there somewhere around here to do that?

Pug-Faced Bitch with the Big Booty: I mean...

Me: Tell you what, wear the head of the pig y'all slaughtered this morning as a mask and I'll beat that pussy up right now.

TWENTY MINUTES LATER...

Pug-Faced Bitch with the Big Booty: Oh my God, I can't believe I just did that. I don't do stuff like that on the regularly. Now I got pig insides in my hair and I let you fuck me raw, but yo sex is bomb tho. I gotta go reprent.

Me: And this is the house that Jesus built. Anyway, thank you for the pussy. Since it smells like Hobbit feet, can I get my meal for free?

Pug-Faced Bitch with the Big Booty: That was not my pussy. That was the pig parts.

Me: No, I caught the pig parts. What I assigned to you was that deep fried assholes and asparagus smell.

Pug-Faced Bitch with the Big Booty: Nigga please. Yo dick was stankin' too.

Me: So you acknowledge your pussy smells like death by dishonor? And you sucked my dick anyway, so....you're making a strong case for me to get a free meal.

Pug-Faced Bitch with the Big Booty: Whatever. Take this food and leave before my husband gets back from the feed store.

Me: You mean to tell me you fucked me knowing your husband was coming back?

Pug-Faced Bitch with the Big Booty: I knew it was gonna be quick. You were outta breath just asking me for the vagina.

Me: Oh, vagina. Vagina. Vagina. That's what the saved hoes say? Vagina. Anyway, you ain't lyin' on me. Bye. Be blessed and highly favored in the Lord.

Pug-Faced Bitch with the Big Booty: Bye, daddy.

Me: Why you keep callin' me daddy?

Pug-Faced Bitch with the Big Booty: Because that's what I call my husband and I don't wanna fuck up and call him by some other man's name.

Me: So you do this often? Well, at least you're a well thought out bitch.

I still needed to shampoo, condition and flat iron my pubic hair, so I decided to get a room at a pay by the hour motel to do just that, but first...DOLLAR GENERAL!

PAUSE: Allow me to take a moment to spit some shit about one of the many places I love to hate. As a person living off of a disability check, Dollar General is a utopia for my pockets, but I absolutely hate the staff there. These muthafuckas obviously took slow classes...or Master's classes in meth use. Brown teeth and bug eyes at every turn. Bad bodies of the Eddie Bauer Edition and awkward, grimace-worthy conversations in abundance. And often, some of the most fucked up attitudes you'll ever come across. So I make it my ministry to give these hoes pure hell each and every time I venture into one, regardless of the host city.

Doo Doo Mouth Clerk: Welcome to Dollar General. May I help you...sir *(rolls eyes)*?

Me: No, you can't help me. I've had enough pajama bottoms pussy for a lifetime. I didn't come in here for your faux pleasantries and eyeball gymnastics. I just stopped by for some genital hair care products and some cup o'noodles, and to tell you bitches that y'all got some fucking nerve trying to have a fucked up attitude all across America when y'all work in a place with the word dollar in its name. Y'all ought to be the most humble hoes known to man on the off chance that somebody who can actually hire you for a better job might come in this bitch and see that you have exemplary customer service. But no! You bitches walk around on these black footprint havin' ass floors like y'all are the fucking walking dead of orange county and the lie detector test determined that was a lie. Not saying there's anything wrong with earning an honest living here, but let's be honest. It offers no retirement plan. This is a Visa, not an EBT card. Chop, chop.

Doo Doo Mouth Clerk: First of all, don't come up in here poppin' yo gums about me and my coworkers when you don't know us like that wit ya fat ass.

Me: Bitch...FUCK Y'ALL! All you Garbage Pail Kids lookin' muthafuckas can suck my ashy, chubby dick. I'll spit on you hoe!

Doo Doo Mouth Clerk: Sir, you need to buy whatever the fuck you came in here to buy and get the fuck outta my store before I lose my temper and go Solange Knowles on yo Buddha built ass.

Me: Oh, this Notorious B.I.G. lazy eye bitch got jokes. Imma buy my shit, but this ain't over.

I'm not gonna lie to y'all. I stole a bunch of shit on GP, but that's just because it's my right as an American citizen and especially a man that ain't really Black who gets treated like a Black man to stick it to the man whenever I can. Now you might be asking yourself when the fuck did Dollar General become the man, but I'll ask you where else do you see these muthafuckas except in poor, Black neighborhoods? Dollar General and Family Dollar are two of the biggest contributors to the welfare mentality! There I said it! And I know this to be true because I PROUDLY suffer from the welfare mentality, so if you know anybody selling food stamps, fuck wit me! My Section 8 might get cut off. Anyway, I steal to level the playing field. I figure paying for less cheap shit increases my chances of stashing a few dollars here and there and gets me an inch closer to being freed from the bliss of the welfare mentality each month. But back to this body by cream filling built bitch!

Me: Say bitch! I need some muthafuckin' Tussy for my underarms. Where it's at?

Doo Doo Mouth Clerk: Behind the preposition!

Me: Bitch, spell preposition. I'll wait.

Doo Doo Mouth Clerk: I ain't spelling shit!

Me: Because you can't, bitch! I bet you're still on sight words, hoe! I bet you count on your fingers when you're reading, bitch; tryna figure out how many syllables the words have and shit! Bitch I bet you have to phone a friend to read the labels in this hoe. Ol lifeline needin' ass bitch!

Doo Doo Mouth Clerk: That did it! Jerome! JEROME!

Jerome: Yes ma'am, Mrs. Holloway. What's up?

Doo Doo Mouth Clerk: Get this bread bowl built bitch up out my store before I catch a case!

Me: A case of what? Bitch, you look like you've been treated for everything from jock itch to athlete's foot in the pussy, hoe!

Jerome: Sir, what seems to have you so mad?

Me: Don't talk to me fuck boy unless you want these paws!

Jerome: HAHAHAHAHAHAHAHAHA! I can't do nothin', but laugh at this senile old man.

Me: BITCH! I'm 23-yrs old nigga! A nigga just been up all night traveling and shit.

Jerome: Nigga if you 23, I'm 12.

Me: Well, mongoloids do age fast as shit in the face. Look at Lebron James. That nigga been lookin' 53 since he was in the 8th grade. I'd bet money y'all suffer from the same strain of mongoloidism!

Jerome: Sir, it's taking a whole lot of restraint for me not to slap the shit outta you.

Me: Well bitch, what's wrong with ya slapper?

Y'all, this apelike bitch slapped me so hard I started doin' the Tootsie Roll in that hoe. Nigga slapped me so hard I started speaking Swahili. Nigga slapped me so hard I had to check and make sure I hadn't shit on myself. Oh, but when I stopped seeing stars and clinching up to keep from pissing on myself, I kicked that niiga in his nuts so hard they wrapped around his tonsils. But then the nigga started laughing and taking his shirt off and I had to be quick on my feet...and by that I mean I ran when the shirt was covering his face. I had just gotten safely in my car and locked the doors when this big, brahma bull somebitch ran head first into my driver's side window. I screamed in a c above high c. It was a defense mechanism cuz I ain't no punk bitch. My blood curdling scream distracted that hoe ass nigga long enough for me to entangle him in my seatbelt and drag that ass a few yards. I skinned his bitch ass up like my uncle used to do squirrels in the front yard for stew that evening. Let a nigga try me. Try me. I'll fuck around and skin his whole family!

So that's my life. That's what the law of attraction does for me. I live each moment in corny, profanity-filled verbal fisticuffs with the bottom-feeders of the world. Won't you be my neighbor?

Chapter 50: MASHTINIS & XANAX

Englebert Maserati O'Shea Johnson-Ingram the Eighth, aka Emoji, is the textbook definition of an ain't shit nigga. This nigga is an entire glossary of ain't-shitness. In addition to collecting disability checks for successfully masquerading as one who suffers from Dropfoot, IBS, Bipolarism and Schizoaffective Disorder, Emoji, as his friends, enemies, lovers and haters call him, is every bit of the two bit hustler. At any given point, you are likely to find anything from tampons to DVDs to costume jewelry to prosthetic limbs in the trunk of his car...for sale. Not only that, but this muthafucka is a muthafuckin' lottery winner. Dig that? Ping. ping. PING! Ping. ping.

Emoji is the only child of a Back Pages prostitute and a shade tree mechanic who decided to launch his rap career in his late 30s. As far back as he can remember, Emoji has been haunted by the taunting he received from both his mother handing out $12 blowjobs to every Tom, Dick, and Dequan in the trailer park community he grew up in just outside of Schenectady, NY and his dad handing out his mixtape to kids at the bus stop and to parents & teachers during open house. He is also poltergeisted by memories of his father giving him and his friends copies of his mixtape for birthdays and Christmas. Growing up in such a, ahem, festive environment taught Emoji to use what he's got to get what he wants and he began to implement his wiles as early as kindergarten.

Life wasn't easy growing up for little boys who had to get their clothes out of the Huskies Section at K-Mart. Kids are brutal little shits that really don't give a fuck if your mom has ashy pussy and chitterling knees, so her prostitution game is a tad bit lacking...and they sure as hell don't give a fuck if your so-called mechanic of a father uses more duct tape and Gorilla Glue than tools in his repair shop, thereby fucking up his reputation and thusly forcing him to lowkey cyber-pimp your momma to keep the utilities on and your fat ass full. Emoji was exposed to all kinds of fuckery as a child and this began to both shape and warp his young mind in tandem. During the first week of school his kindergarten year, his teacher, Mrs. Scholowowitz, wanted the kids to participate in Show & Tell as a way to get to know one another. Emoji's requests for something cool to show off to his classmates, like his father's only expensive power tool, had gone ignored all week. So on the morning of Show & Tell day, he got a little creative and grabbed a 13 inch purple dildo out of the dishwasher thinking he'd present it as a light saber and gain favor with his snotty little classmates.

So there he stood before 21 crumb-snatchers in a Transformers t-shirt that coyly put his belly button on display and a pair of shorts that gave him a most glorious inner thigh wedgy. Reaching down into his Super Mario Bros. backpack, he began randomly reciting lines he believed to be from Stars Wars (having never actually seen a single installment of the franchise), brandishing an enormous, purple schfonz with specks of dried up semen an booty juice on it because it hadn't actually been run through the dishwasher yet.

Emoji: LUKE! I am your father...correction, I know your father. Retailing, retailing, where the real gwop from these fuck ass movies is made around this bitch, Hans Solo. I'm tombot Star Wars the T-shirt, Star Wars the Coloring Book, Star Wars the Leggings, Star War the Gold Fronts, Star Wars the Lunch Box, Star Wars the Breakfast Cereal, Star Wars the Blunt Wraps, Star Wars the Flame Thrower. It'll be like a mufuckin' dream that spread throughout our hoe ass galaxy Mister Spock. When you see Jabba the Wockee I need to holla at him bout this lil business thang. Aye, Aurora come suck my..."

Mrs. Scholowowitz: That'll be enough Englebert.

Emoji: BITCH, don't kill my vibe. And don't you ever in yo Falkor the Luck Dragon face ass life call me no muthafuckin' Englebert, hoe. My name Emoji!

Mrs. Scholowowitz: Okay then, Emoji, how about you and your adult toy take a trip down to the principal's office?

Emoji: How about you gum on my balls and we'll call it a day?

Emoji's entire class erupted with ear-piercing laughter and it was at this moment, Emoji realized that he had been blessed with the gift of shit-talking from his daddy's side of the family. And from then until the end he vowed to never bite his tongue because the shit hurts.

Emoji tried to express an interest in elementary school, but it just wouldn't stick because he'd never really had to live according to structure and rules. On the morning of his first day of kindergarten, he had the backwash from one of the beer's his daddy drank the night before and a bowl of Blue Bell vanilla ice cream mixed with Cap'n Crunch Berries as breakfast. Anyway, rather than going to the principal's office as he had been so sternly instructed to do, Emoji bypassed that bullshit and went to recess with a different kindergarten class.

Gail Freidmont, Gym Teacher: Good morning children, I trust that you are in good spirits and fully prepared for today's field, strength and training maneuvers.

Emoji: Say patna, what the fuck that bitch tombot?

Gail Freidmont, Gym Teacher: I am speaking. There will be no speaking. If I hear speaking that is not my own speaking, I will be speaking to the entirety of the class in the form of suicides. Is that understood?

CRICKETS

Gail Freidmont, Gym Teacher: Oh, perhaps I'm just a whisper because I swear before the God who guided me through three tours in Syria and blessed me, hobiyahshahtah chaturanga dandasana Dasani, to not only purge the Earth of mine enemy, but He also gave me the ability to rip a man's throat out with my bear hands. I said is that understood?

CLASS: Yes, misses Gail Freidmont, Gym Teacher.

Emoji: Oh, y'all on the microwaved bullshit. I'm out.

Gail Freidmont, Gym Teacher: Young man, where on God's green earth do you think you're going. I have warned you about what I can do to a fully grown man and still you defy me?

Emoji: Bitch, I'll kill you. Fuck up out my face. Fuck you, these ugly ass kids, this raggedy ass school, y'all nasty ass off-brand lunches and more than anything this funky ass recess. I'm goin' home...BITCH!

Gail Freidmont, Gym Teacher: Go right ahead. I'll see you in a group home near me coming soon.

Emoji: Watch out lil bih.

[AT EMOJI'S HOUSE AFTER IT TOOK HIS FAT ASS THIRTY MINUTES TO MAKE A SIX MINUTE WALK]

Momma: Hello my beautiful, Nubian Prince. How was your first day of school today?

Emoji: I quit school cuz they had recess, hoe and don't try to kiss me with that nut dried up on the corner of your mouth neither. Where the fuck is my old punk ass daddy?

Momma: You rude.

Emoji: And you a nothing ass bitch, you NAB.

Momma: Why would you say that to me, Emoji? Don't you know I'll fuck you up?

Emoji: I'm sorry momma. I just had a really bad day. Plus, on my way to the bus stop this morning I heard that fat white man with the mustard stains on his shirt calling you that when you was gettin' hit from the back. I figured the shit was cool because you didn't use the safe word. My bad.

Momma: Oh my God. You saw us?

Emoji: Duh, the door to the shed was wide open. We all stood there watchin' as you did a crossword puzzle while he tried his best to bang you out with that booger-sized dick. Anyway, how much money he pay you? I want some muthafuckin' honey buns from the convenience store.

Momma: Here you go baby. And can you bring momma back some Magnums? Dean Pointer is stopping by for a Bible study this evening and he packin'.

Emoji: I got you momma. Now go soak in some vinegar so your pussy can tighten back up. You all we got until that non-rappin' ass nigga you let get you pregnant with me realizes he sound like Sling Blade impersonating Silkk the Shocker when he raps.

Momma: HAHAHAHAHAHA you ain't never lied.

Emoji: And don't plan on startin' no time soon. Oh, momma...did you record my stories for me?

Momma: You know I did baby.

Emoji: Love you momma.

Momma: Love you too, lil nigga.

Emoji: Not too much bitch. We ain't figured out if you White or just hella albino, so miss me with that nigga shit til the ancestry.com results come back.

Momma: Bye boy! I'm biracial.

[ON THE WAY TO THE STORE]

Creawnshalique: Mornin' Emoji.

Emoji: Fuck you bitch.

Creawnshalique: MOMMA!!!!! EMOJI SAID FUCK YOU BITCH TO ME!!!!! MOMMA!!!!!!!!!!

Emoji: Fuck her too.

Omarquion: Emoji, you goin' up to the park later?

Emoji: Fuck you Omarquion. I don't fuck witchu like that. Fuck you White boy.

Omarquion: Fuck you too Emoji witcho fat ass. I'll bomb on you bitch.

Emoji: Whatever Omarquion. I drug you and yo bike for seven trailers last week and you ain't do shit. You better be glad I'm on a mission for some muthafuckin Honey Buns or I'd fuck you up bitch.

Omarquion: We'll see. Catch me at the park later after I get home from school and see these hands.

Emoji: And I might if I'm not still outta breath from walkin' to this muthafuckin' store bitch!

Omarquion: I hate yo fat ass.

Emoji: And that's cool too. Let me place you on hold for that ass whoopin' real quick.

[AT THE CONVENIENCE STORE]

Emoji: Ummmmmmmmmm...mmmm...mmmmmmmm.mmmmmmm... why the fuck does it smell like an Alpaca gave birth up in this bitch? Y'all muthafuckas need to start moppin' y'all's muthafuckin floors.

Ondondre: Say lil Black ass Indian boy, don't come up in these people's store disrespectin' my place of employment.

Emoji: Fuck you Orlando...and this store as a matter of fact.

Ondondre: My name is Ondondre lil boy. Get that shit understood before I ban you from comin' in here.

Emoji: Whatever Ontario, my money spend just like everybody else's. You can try to ban me, but then I'll just send one of YO ugly ass kids in here to get me my shit.

Ondondre: My kid's aren't allowed to play with you lil boy. Get what you need so you can hurry up and leave.

Emoji: Imma get what I need Obituary or whatever the fuck yo name is and ain't nobody said shit about playin' with yo lil musty ass snail lookin' ass kids. Imma throat punch one of them lil fuckers and punk they bitch ass out. Here, ring up my Honey Buns and give me some Magnums.

Ondondre: Keep my kid's names out of your mouth and I won't even ask about the condoms.

Emoji: Three things: 1. Don't nobody know them lil yuckmouth ass kids of yours names. 2. Your best bet would be to worry about getting' off in time to get your kids dewormed and NOT worryin' about what the fuck I got goin' on. 3. Jesus hates you.

Ondondre: Don't come back.

Emoji: I might and I might not, Octagon.

Ondondre: I swear I hate kids.

Emoji: That's cuz yours look partially aborted and subnormal.

[ON THE WAY HOME]

Keighsha, She Thinks She's Fancy Because of the Way Her Momma Spelled Her Name, But Emoji's Momma Skulldrug That Bitch Last Week: Hey, lil Emoji. What you doin'?

Emoji: Bitch don't speak to me. You know we don't fuck witchu and I don't like fake shit.

Keighsha: My bad. I was just tryin' to be friendly.

Emoji: Fuck yo friendliness, Keighsha. You just wanna know if my momma is still cool on you and she might be. That's right. Take yo awkward built ass in that dirty ass house you live in.

Omarquion: Wassup then Emoji? You tryna bang?

Emoji: Fuck you, Omarquion. I'm tryna get home to watch my stories and eat a box of Honey Buns. Ain't nobody got time for yo reindeer games, pussy.

Omarquion: That's right. Scurry you scary ass on home before you get this work.

Emoji: Scurry? That's an awfully big word for you Omarquion with that ol faggot ass name. Bitch, I bet you got twerk videos on Vine. Bitch, I bet you be tryna make them unseasoned, chicken cutlets clap. Just remember, White boys bruise easily. You invited me to the park so imam oblige yo Twizzler built ass.

Omarquion: It's on.

Emoji: And is.

[EMOJI'S HOUSE]

Emoji *(slamming the door)*: I CAN'T WAIT TO MOB ON OMARQUION'S OL DUCK FACE ASS! I don't like bein' tested in these streets.

Daddy: Boy don't come up in here slamming doors like you ain't got no fucks to give.

Emoji: Well muthafcka, not giving a fuck is my default setting, so you will deal and pay a bill before you tell me what I can do in MY momma's house. How was work witcho I like bread and butter I like toast and jam lookin' ass.

Daddy: HAHAHAHAHAHAHA you better be glad I love yo lil fat ass or I'd tackle you.

Emoji: I mean I almost shit on myself I got so scared. Where's my momma at?

Daddy: Out in the shed, having Bible study with Deacon Pointer. He prayed for me and told me this was my season.

Emoji: Yo season to be about as dumb as a box of rocks.

Daddy: What you mean, junior?

Emoji: Don't even worry about it. Did you get "The Road to Wealth" by Suze Orman from that baked potato built bitch whose pussy you be eatin' lowkey *TONGUE POP* or nah?

Daddy: Don't be doin' that gay ass shit. Real men don't pop they tongues.

Emoji: Real men run their households too, soooooo you were saying? My book? Suze Orman? How Not to Be a Broke Bitch Like Your Daddy: Volume One, please?

Daddy: Now you ain't just finna talk to me any old kinda way.

Emoji: I'm sorry father. I think I'm in the early stages of Conduct and Oppositional Defiance Disorder. Maybe y'all should get me some pills to pop.

Daddy: Boy, you funny as hell. Daniella is bringing the book by in the mornin'.

Emoji: Okay you know we got chives, shredded cheese and sour cream in the fridge, right?

Daddy: For what?

Emoji: Thought you might like some toppings on your baked potato.

[SCREAMING OUT THE BACK DOOR]

Emoji: MOMMA!!!!!! HOLLA AT ME WHEN YOU FINISH LETTIN' OLD ASS DEACON POINTER JAB YOU IN THE PUSSY WITH HIS OL MIDLIFE CRISIS ASS DICK! I NEED YOU TO ORDER ME SOME BOOKS AND MAGAZINES ONLINE SO I DON'T END UP AS DUMB AND DESPERATE AS YOU AND MY DADDY'S OLD SEMI-PART TIME EMPLOYED ASS!

Momma: OKAY!

Emoji: AND KEIGHSHA SAID SHE GON BEAT THE BRAKES OFF YO, AND I QUOTE, "OLD LOOSE LEAF PAPER, HALF-EATEN CHALUPA PUSSY HAVIN' ASS".

CRICKETS

Emoji: MOMMA, YOU HEAR ME?

Momma: YEAH BABY, HE WAS JUST NUTTIN' REAL QUICK.

Emoji: Y'ALL NEED ME TO BRING Y'ALL A WARM TOWEL?

Momma: YES, PLEASE. AND MY MAGNUMS! THANK YA, BABY.

Emoji: OKAY! [LOOKS AT HIS DADDY WHO'S WEARING BEATS BY DRE] You know what? I quit.

One day of kindergarten and Emoji never returned. He learned all there is to know from blogs, magazines, and gossip. And though he can hold an intellectual conversation on more topics than most certified geniuses, if you put a quadratic equation in front of him, he'll need a 51/50 psychiatric hold. Emoji's life was filled with nothing more than hours upon hours of reading and absorbing as much information about the world in which he lived as he could. That is until he accidentally discovered jacking off at age 11 one Summer's afternoon while taking his first shower in three days.

Emoji: MOMMA! MOMMA! HURRY UP! MOMMA!!! COME SEE ABOUT ME!!!!!

Momma: Boy what is it?

Emoji: Fuck you.

Momma: Wait a minute. Hold up. What the fuck did I do to you?

Emoji: You never told me my dick was a magic wand of Happy Birthdays and Merry Christmases.

Momma: Don't tell me you've been in my shower playing with your little dingaling.

Emoji: It's raw.

Momma: Bye boy. ENGLE COME TALK TO YOUR NASTY ASS LITTLE BOY ABOUT HIS DICK!

Engle: Mona Lisa don't come at me with that gay ass shit. I don't give a fuck about his dick.

Mona Lisa: Well he just sprayed down the shower with nut, so you might wanna think about talkin' to him about girls and sex.

Engle: COME HERE BOY!

Emoji: I'LL BE THRE IN A SECOND MUTHAFUCKA! I'M DRYING MY ASS CRACK OUT!

Engle: DON'T NOBODY WANNA HERE ABOUT YO ASS CRACK BOY!

Emoji: SO!

[THIRTY-THREE MINUTES LATER]

Emoji: What it do young swerve?

Engle: Boy what took you so muthafuckin' long? You fat, but yo ass crack can't be THAT long.

Emoji: Muthafucka, I was in there doin' magic tricks. What you want?

Engle: Your mom wanted me to talk to you about sex, so that's what we bout to do.

Emoji: Muthafucka I was suckin' momma's titty while she was suckin' strange dick. I know all I need to know about sex. Anything else?

Engle: Did? Did you? Did you just? Did you just say? Did you just say what? Did you just say what I? Did you just say what I think? Did you just say what I think you? Did you just say what I think you just? Did you just say what I think you just said?

Emoji: Bitch you tried it.

Engle: Is that right? Tell ya momma I'll be right back. I'm about to run and grab some cigarettes.

Emoji: I might.

[NINE YEARS LATER]

Engle: EMOJIIIIIII? WHERE'S MY BOY AT? EMOJI? MONA LISA? WHERE Y'ALL AT? DADDY'S HOME! WHERE THE FUCK Y'ALL AT?

Emoji: Man if you don't shut the fuck up with all that hip hip hooray bullshit. I'm in here tryna set up this website so I can sell mixtapes on it and shit. You got $42.29?

Engle: Emoji, it's your father. Aren't you glad to see me?

Emoji: I mean I guess or whatever. No, not really. I mean It's cool. Hi. Um, so you got it?

Engle: Here boy. Where's your mother? Can I get a hug and shit?

Emoji: I guess I'll humor your Cliff Huxtable fantasies for this money. I think momma is in the bathroom washin' her pussy with antibacterial soap out of one of them little bottles you get at Dollar General. You got some weed, pop? Some drank? I know you didn't roll up in here with them ashy ass ankles and ain't got no muthafuckin' olive branch.

Engle: I...I...I...

Emoji: Shut the fuck up with all that stuttering. Yes or No don't even start with the letter I, you dummy. It's cool. You can come smoke a blunt with me until momma finishes deep cleaning her pussy in the sink. I always got weed. I was just tryna conserve my shit. DO you know what conserve means or do you need me to look that up for you?

Engle: Damn Emoji! Let a nigga breathe.

Emoji: Oh, my bad pop. Do you need some muthafuckin' breathing room? Am I impeding upon your respiratory situation by being in your presence? Did you not find you a few wide open spaces for you to have some breathing room in during the course of the last nine years, pop? You roll up in my momma's muthafuckin' house dressed like Paddington Bear and you expect me to jump in your arms singin' "What About Us" by Brandy? ARE. WE. ABOUT. TO. HAVE. TO. CATCH. A. FADE. POP? Cuz I been waitin' to Karate Kid yo ass for a minute.

Engle: Son, just let me apologize...

Emoji: No need, pop. I'm just fuckin' witchu. I'm really not in my feelin's about it. I mean I'm still gonna fuck you up as soon as you say honey I'm home to momma, but won't no hard feelin's will be involved. I promise you that.

Engle: You seem angry.

Emoji: Child boo. Get the fuck up out my face with that PBS bullshit and hit this blunt. I'm tryna relax you for this ass whoopin'.

Engle: Let...me...go...say hi to your mother really quickly.

Emoji: Ok, pop. And pop?

Engle: What's up son?

Emoji: I like how you've been working on your Queen's English, but you over-pronouncing your vowels and consonants isn't going to negate this ass whopping. Okay?

Engle: As you wish, son.

[RUSHING UP IN HIS FATHER'S FACE WITH HIS FISTS CLINCHED AND AT A VAMPIRE'S SPEED]

Emoji *(through clinched teeth)*: See that's that Billy Goat's Gruff bullshit I'm talkin' about right there! I'm extending you all my bacon grease-stained grace and mercy right now. True story.

Mona Lisa: EMOJI WHO THE FUCK IS YOU CUSSIN' AT IN MY HOUSE?

Emoji: A BITCH!

Mona Lisa: WELL TELL THAT BITCH TO HAVE A SEAT AND I'LL COME SHAKE HER HAND AS SOON AS I FINISH SHAVING THIS PUSSY. HAAAAAAAANNNN!

Emoji: HAHAHAHAHAHA MOMMA HURRY UP. THIS IS A VERY SPECIAL BITCH.

Mona Lisa: CHILD, AIN'T NO BITCH SPECIAL, BUT ME! TELL THAT HOE TO WATCH TIME!

Emoji: You heard my momma nigga. Watch time.

Engle: Clocks on the wall would be helpful. Why do I feel like I'm in a made-for-TV movie?

Mona Lisa: Because you're an ol made-for-TV ass nigga. What the fuck are you doin' in my house you sunburned prune?

Emoji: Hold on let me get some popcorn.

Mona Lisa: You got yo muthafuckin' nerve sittin' up in my gotdamn living room in a gotdamn track suit lookin' like you just left a Men's Meeting at ya local Baptist church.

Emoji *(from the kitchen)*: I SAID WAIT ONE GOTDAMN MINUTE I'M MAKIN' SOME MUTHAFUCKIN' POPCORN, MOMMA!

Mona Lisa: Well hurry the fuck up. I got shit to do, shit.

[THAT AWKWARD MOMENT WHEN LIFE IS BUFFERING BECAUSE YOU'RE WAITING ON A MUTHAFUCKA WHO IS EQUAL PARTS CRAZY AND IMMATURE]

Emoji: Carry on.

Engle: Mona Lisa, I just...

Mona Lisa: Called to say you loved me? No. Can't stop lovin' me? Noooo. Want that old thang back? Hello? Who is it? BITCH please. How you doin'? CLICK!

Emoji: That means kick rocks nigga. You're so nine years ago.

Engle: But don't you guys want to hear why I...

Emoji: I don't even think you want to. I think you already knew you were comin' back to a bunch of bullshit and you just did it so you can further convince yourself that you didn't abandon your family. You made me a statistic, pop and now I'm on a mission to be the best fuckin' statistics this world has ever known. I'm fourteen and about to have my third child all by different bitches. One is White. Her name is Cambridge. One is Puerto Rican. Her name is Balenciaga, but I call her Ciggy. And we still fuck sometimes, but that's another episode. And my baby on the way is by n Black Queen named Ankha. It's pronounced on some ol Russian Ukrainian Soviet Union Norwegian shit, but it represents the ankh. The ankh, also known as breath of life, the key of the Nile or crux ansata (Latin meaning "cross with a handle"), was the ancient Egyptian hieroglyphic character that read "life", a triliteral sign for the consonants Ayin-Nun-Het. This sacred relic represents the concept of life, which is really the general meaning of the symbol when you think about it, but I'm sure you aren't aware of the existence of things such as this, pop. Anyway, the Egyptian gods are often portrayed carrying it by its loop, or bearing one in each hand, arms crossed over their chest like a muthafuckin' G. You understand where I'm comin' from? The ankh appears in hand or in proximity of almost every deity in the Egyptian pantheon (including Pharaohs). Thus, it is fairly and widely understood by muthafuckas who know shit, unlike you, as a symbol of early religious pluralism: all sects believed in a common story of eternal life and shit, and this is the literal meaning of the symbol on that ass. This rationale contributed to the adoption of the ankh by New Age mysticism in the 1960s. I ain't even about to get into cultural appropriation with you because I don't want you to get a nose-bleed. But yeah, lastly, muthafucka, the ankh symbol was so prevalent that it has been found in digs as far as Mesopotamia and Persia, and even on the seal of the biblical king, Hezekiah. And some more dope shit. But before you say anything, I'm sorry momma. I was waitin' for the right time and shit and it was like God itself wrapped this chewed up chewin' tobacco in the face lookin' ass nigga and dropped him in my life like a present like, you tight. Shrug Life.

Engle: Well hasn't this been a great deal of fun? It was so great seeing you fine folks again. Mona Lisa, please sign the divorce papers I dropped off earlier this week while Emoji was volunteering at the homeless shelter.

Emoji: In that pussy.

Mona Lisa: I just dried my pussy off with them dumb ass divorce papers, nigga. And just so you know, we know about the lil Rodeo Drive bitch you've been fuckin' in the booty. I'm glad that bitch saw fit to hire yo old ass a speech therapist.

Engle: Awesome. Look, Emoji, you're more than welcome to come visit me in Beverly Hills anytime you please, okay?

Emoji: Momma, did he say Beverly Hills?

Mona Lisa: Fuck you, Emoji.

Emoji: HA! Look pop...I might. Thanks for stopping by. Bye.

Mona Lisa: I second the motion.

Engle: Y'all be blessed.

Mona Lisa and Emoji: Nigga, fuck you.

Emoji didn't see his father again for another three years and during that time he developed a very unhealthy addiction to porn and prostitutes. Spending much of his time trying to buy, sell and trade varying types of thingamabobs and silently building up quite an impressive bank account for a teenager who got the bulk of his knowledge from Dave Ramsey and Suze Orman books. Emoji eventually became bored with trailer park life and, now a licensed driver, decided to take his growing list of talents elsewhere in search of a father who wrote him from time to time, continually extending an invitation by way of letters with no return address or phone number or specific contact information of any kind. But Emoji had become quite an impressive little hacker and managed to track down the mangy bastard anyway. Beverly Hills, here he comes!

Chapter 51: We're Off to See a Deadbeat...

Emoji: Momma, what you doin'?

Mona Lisa: Nothin' big baby. What's good?

Emoji: We need to talk about me going to visit pop.

Momma: Oh, here we go with that bullshit again. You're over it here and now you think you're about to chase down some phantom menace and have a reunion special.

Emoji: Momma, I just feel like there's more to life than this trailer park. I've been living in this bitch seventeen years and ain't much changed. I just can't see myself growing old and rottin' in this bitch like your pussy is doin'.

Mona Lisa: Fuck you Emoji! My pussy still pops...severely.

Emoji: It might, but that hoe gotta be losin' its elasticity by now.

Mona Lisa: Muthafucka don't be throwin' them salary ass words at me when you know I'm a paid by the hour type of bitch.

Emoji: I'm not tryna make you feel like stupid or like a cheap hoe. I know you've done everything within the power of your pussy to provide me with as good a life as you possibly could, but if that muthafucka out in Beverly Hills ballin' like it's a hobby, I need some muthafuckin' reparations...an abandonment tax or some shit. I just wanna take the world by its clitoris and nibble on it a little bit. Momma, tell me you understand that I'm just tryin' to be all that I can be.

Mona Lisa: Boy, you're too fat to join the fuckin' army. You tried it.

Emoji: Momma, be serious for just one second. I've got it all planned out. I'm leaving at the end of next week.

Mona Lisa: Big boy, I get it. This world in which we currently live just ain't enough for you and I refuse to be the one to hold you back. You just need to understand that the world is a cruel place and well, you really haven't developed the social graces to exist beyond this trailer park.

Emoji: Fuck that. I'm a fast learner.

Mona Lisa: That you are my precious cherub, but you lack a desire to be any different than the roughneck I've raised you to be. Do you honestly think they're just going to embrace you with open arms out there in Beverly Hills?

Emoji: Shit, they better or they're about to get this work the hard way.

Mona Lisa: Well, since it seems like you've got your mind is made up. I won't say another negative word about the idea other than it's stupid than a bitch. You go out there and take this bitch ass world by storm, big baby. Leave nothing to chance and never let em see you sweat.

Emoji: Momma, I'm about to fuck shit up.

Mona Lisa: I know baby. I know.

That night, Emoji drafted quite an impressive "GET THE FUCK OUT OF THIS SHANTY ASS TRAILER PARK" Bucket List. It read as follows:

1.   Fuck mad bitches. Welfare Bitches. Argentina Bitches. Scarce Headed Hitches. Expensive Weave Ass Bitches. Fake Booty Ass Bitches. Cheerleader Bitches. Knock-Kneed Bitches. Anorexic Bitches. Strong Jawline Havin' Ass Bitches. Midget Bitches. Just a Smorgasbord of Bitches.

2.   Let a crack head who used to be cute back in the day suck my dick for $3.

3.   Beat up Pastor Anderson for lowkey making fun of how I always get inner thigh wedgies.

4.   Slap the shit out of that Asian man who owns the convenience store because he said he felt sorry for my mother.

5.   Pay for breakfast at Golden Corral and stay there eatin' until they close.

6.   See what auto-erotic asphyxiation is really about.

7.   Lick peanut butter off of Anastasia Boston's booty-hole just because she won Homecoming Queen this year.

8.   Do hoodrat shit with my friends, starting with joyriding in the Mayor's Maybach.

9.   Nut inside a history book at the public library.

10.   Buy a penis pump and use it extensively...for research purposes.

11.   Become a member of the Nation of Islam and quit.

12.   Lead a song in the choir at somebody's church then dance in the spirit. Shout I think they call it.

13.   Do all the drugs.

14.   Dress up like a vampire and go swag surfin'

15.   Stick a habanero pepper in my booty hole while I'm jacking off...for research purposes.

16.   Get my nipples pierced.

17.   Let Angelo's cousin, Raul, arch my...I mean "clean up my eyebrows" like them and all their Puerto Rican homeboys do.

18.   Make a krumping video and post it on YouTube.

19.   Steal about 50 packs of Gummi Bears for my road trip.

20.   Get the Jordan logo shaved into my pubic hair...or tattooed on my fupa.

21.   Run through the grocery store butt ass naked.

22.   Get a lap dance from Ondondre's momma and fart in her mouth.

23.   Jackoff to as many episodes of America's Next Top Model as possible.

24.   Get a pussy tattooed in each armpit

25.   And some more shit.

Not to Emoji's surprise, he was able to complete his list and then some. I now take you to the time Emoji sought to fulfill his wish to ravage Ondondre's mother.

[KNOCKING FEVERISHLY ON ONDONDRE'S DOOR]

Emoji: OCTOPUSSY, OPEN THE GOTDAMN DOOR HOE! OCTOPUSSY!!!!! OCTOPUSSYYYYYYYY! COME OUT. COME OUT. WHEREVER YOU ARE. HERE PUSS PUSS PUSSY!

Ondondre: Why the fuck you knockin' on my door like the muthafuckin' police fuckboy.

Emoji: Fuck all that Octopussy, where yo momma at?

Ondondre: Fuck you mean where my momma at? Where yo momma at?

Emoji: Man look Octopussy, I got business. Where she at?

Ondondre: Don't worry about where the fuck my momma is. Worry about...

Emoji: See you done made me throat punch yo bitch ass. Ondondre's momma where you at?

Collene, Ondondre's momma: Oh, hey Emoji. Are you boys playing the knockout game again. Y'all know that shit is dangerous, right?

Emoji: Fuck that. Can I get a lapdance and fart in yo mouth? It's on my get the fuck outta this trailer park bucket list.

Collene: What the fuck did you just say?

Emoji: Lord, this bitch is lowkey slow just like her son.
May.......I.......get.......a.......lap.......dance.......and.......fart.......in.......yo.......mouth?

Collene: What you can get is the fuck up out my house with that bullshit.

Emoji: Okay, I mean I had $440, but that's cool.

Collene: Wayment. Wayment. Wayment. Hold up. Boy you is soooooo crazy. You know I was just playin'. Come on in here.

When Ondondre awakened from the throat punch that sent him night night nigga, the sight he beheld was almost too much. He found Emoji crawling on the ground letting out a steady stream of farts and his momma zigzagging to and fro, gobbling them up like Mrs. Pac-Man.

Ondondre: Momma, what the fuck is you doin'?

Collene: Makin' money for them Roshe's you want by eatin' farts and I'm about to give ya lil homeboy a lapdance. Anymore questions?

Ondondre: Make sure he cums in his jeans.

Emoji's momma cried and cried as he drove off into the sunset, giving her the middle finger until she faded from sight. This was to be a new chapter in his life; new adventures; a new beginning; his muthafuckin' manifest destiny.

[EMOJI'S JOURNAL]

Dear Diary,

What up bitch nigga? It's been a hot minute since I slid through and dropped some hot lava up in this bitch. Since the last time we spoke, a young nigga been makin' boss moves like a muthafucka. I don't know if you had heard or not, but a nigga chunked the deuce to the trailer park and shit and now I'm about to go reconnect with my daddy and creep on a come-up. I know that bitch nigga kinda like dipped out on ya boy a few years back and shit, but I forgive him and shit. And if I see him and find out I still got like two or three fucks left to give about the situation, Imma just steal all they silverware and jewelry and dog collars and shit and pawn that shit. Anyway, the story goes that the night the nigga left the house when I busted momma out for takin' dick from Deacon Pointer while pops was in the house, apparently the nigga got hit by some broad in a Murcielago and shit. Turns out the bitch is an entertainment attorney who was just in town visiting her peoples. Well, apparently when she hit pop, his dick print through his grey sweatpants caught her eye and she sucked his dick right there in the street until he regained consciousness. Super Muthafuckin' Head to the rescue out this bitch, ya dig? Anyway, for as much ass and pussy that she sell, momma ain't suckin' no dick and since her and pops been together since like fifth grade, I don't think that nigga ever had his dick in a mouth. Changed that nigga's life. You hear me? Made that nigga forget he had a family for three whole years. I mean I'm mad, but lowkey I'm like

STEPMOMMA...WHAT THAT MOUTH DO?

Truth be told, I'm scared shitless. I'd be lying if I said I haven't been overcome by both kakorrhaphiophobia and athazagoraphobia as of late. There I was, meandering my way through a subpar life and then all of a sudden, skeletons and demons started escaping from their closets. But I will not succumb to these feelings of anger and rage. I will face my fears head-on and mollywhop any muthafuckas who stand in the way of my happiness. This is my season.

Sincerely,

Emoji

It was during this quest to reunite with the father that had so flippantly vanquished himself from Emoji's life that Emoji discovered his love of the open road...and his penchant for the pussy of women who were the pariahs of a hard-knock life. Bitches with recovering meth face and shit.

It was within these days that Emoji became a shadow of his former shadow's shadow. The ever-hovering duality that was born of his lack of supervision began to erode into a singular thought...pleasure. It was as though Emoji's soul had been dipped in gilded debauchery and fortified in the eroticism of operating as his lower self. During his years of study, Emoji had once become deeply obsessed with the teachings of the Dalai Lama. He even shaved his head bald except for a ducktail that eventually grew down to the crack of his ass and wore burgundy bathrobes year round. Amidst his growing, maniacal fixation on the Dalai Lama, he learned of Calm Abiding or Single-Pointed Concentration. It was a fruit of the spirit he so maliciously endeavored to give birth to that he abandoned bathing for the entirety of a year. Mona Lisa should've bought stock in car air fresheners, but that's a different tale altogether. Emoji found himself possessed by the desire to master this form of existential, transcendental rumination whereby you choose a curious object and fix your mind upon it. Assuredly one who greatly overestimated his own genius and spiritual center, Emoji elected his pleasure center as the thing upon which he would focus. If I recall correctly, it was around this time that Emoji developed his love of playing with Barbie Dolls, but back to that pissy ass year of meditation. Calm Abiding isn't by far a punk. The degree of focus required to arrive at this spiritual state cannot be achieved in one, introverted sitting. It's not that microwavable New Age shit Miss Cleo was on or no shit like that. In speaking of degrees, it should become apparent that in order to achieve Calm Abiding, the student must train his/her mind by degrees. There're levels to this shit and stuff. The goal is to make your mind capable of greater and greater concentration and focus. The calm that is free of distraction became so deeply rooted within Emoji that over time, it was almost like pleasure-seeking was the chauffeur and Emoji was merely the limousine. Oh, Emoji told me to say shout out to page 129 of An Open Heart by THE DALAI LAMA; published by Little Brown and shit. Ain't no plagiarism bih! He's standing right here.

I'm sure you've often heard it said that people are like onions and the more layers you peel back, the more tears will abound. Emoji is no different. Once you get beyond all of the body odor and dried up semen, therein lies a complex man; quite possibly the most interesting chap in the whole, entire universe. This was a man who loved Pooktre Tree Shaping. And if you don't know what Pooktre Tree Shaping is, as I suspect you don't with your grossly uncultured ass, Pooktre tree shaping is a unique eco-art form created, developed and perfected by Peter Cook and Becky Northey in South East Queensland, Australia. I bet you haven't even ever heard of South East Queensland, Australia with your IEP having ass. Pooktre Tree Shaping is a fantastical, trance-inducing mindfuck for Emoji. It affords him the opportunity to reach down into the very depths of his imagination and transform his little brain spasms into a reality through muse, a stimulus package of wonder about the world, love of fauna and flora and rosa nem, tree finesse from the very hands that beat his meat, doggedness and communing with nature. This is a man who absolutely loves duct tape art...like literally making shoes, clothes, jewelry, cards sculptures, a model of Shakespeare's Globe theater and shit. This is a nigga who has a passion for and enjoyment of cemeteries. Yeah, you read it right. My nigga is a taphophile who undergoes protracted bouts of Taphophilia. Who don't love no epitaphs? Not Emoji. Who don't get an erection from gravestone rubbing? Not Emoji. Who don't have a cemetery photography, art, and history of famous deaths brainer boner at least three months out of each year? Who don't watch the 1971 movie Harold and Maude every third Sunday in all the months that end in –ember? Not Emoji. This is a man who collects handcuffs (even the mitten ones), elongated coins, cigar bands, and tea bags. This is a man who once said the beetle is his spirit animal. I don't know when bugs became animals, but I went along with. This is a man who once said the beetle is his spirit animal because they are natural brawlers and never shy away from a fight. This is a man who is a master at javelin...catching. That's right you read it correctly ladies and gentlemen, this man catches javelins with his bare hands and lives to tell about it. I ain't lying. This is a man who carves egg shells. I want you to let that marinate, so count to twenty-eight then start reading again. Okay, so Egg Art is one of the earliest forms of art. Now that could be a lie, but I'm going off of what Emoji told me. He said early civilizations regarded the egg as a fertility symbol and decorated it as part of their fertility rites, so whenever he was, and I quote, "About to raw dog the chitlin juice out this ol thick somethin' [he] ran into down at the [INSERT WHATEVER YOU THINK OF AS EQUAL PARTS GHETTO AND WHITE TRASHY]", he would carve an egg in the hope that he could father a child, but it hadn't happened since he started fucking at age 12. But his favorite of all was noodling. He felt that catching catfish he described as the size of his dick by hand unleashed his buffet of magical powers. That's right. This nigga is enchanted. And now a list of Emoji's magical powers...according to Emoji and in alphabetical order no less.

Okay, so let me hop in the driver's seat up in this bitch for a minute. So, first we have the A's. Acid Secretion - The ability to generate corrosive acid. I can control my nut though, so ladies don't even trip. You can swallow. Adjusting - The ability to resist and fight through molecular powers. I use this right here for the specific purpose of doing thangs to the pussy you probably didn't even bother to imagine because you thought you knew yo pussy...but I know pussy. Advanced Electrokinesis - The ability to shoot extremely powerful beam-like blasts of pure electricity. I ain't about to lie sometimes I do zap the clit a lil bit. Advanced Fire Throwing - The ability to shoot a beam of highly concentrated, torch-like fire. I mean y'all shoulda guessed I use this shit to light my blunts and shit. Advanced Telekinesis - An advanced form of Telekinesis. It allows me to move very large objects and create a powerful burst of sheer telekinetic energy. This shit comes in handy when you got like a real big chick like super heavy, but her pussy real good, so you still wanna smack her up, flip it and rub it down and shit. Aerokinesis - The elemental ability to create, control and manipulate the air and wind. Because I be blowin' the pussy kisses and shit. My breath be right though, so don't trip. Age Shifting - The ability to accelerate or reverse the aging process; to become younger or older. I don't know another nigga that can role play better than me. You want you a silver fox firefighter? I got you. You want a young nigga that's legal, but ain't got that much hair on his body? Fuck wit me. Agility - The ability to lighten one's body and make oneself more agile. You want that pussy beat up like a jack rabbit? I'll be like if Ginuwine, Chris Brown and Channing Tatum all was the same The Flash up in that pussy. Body rolls for days and shit. Apportation - The ability to teleport objects or people through space. One minute we fuckin' on a park bench in Compton. The next minute we fuckin' on liger rugs in the Taj Mahal. Ash Teleportation - The ability to teleport across short or long distances through ashes. Let me find out a bitch thinkin' bout the dick and imma transport myself into the ash droppin' off her blunt in a heartbeat. And you might be worderin' how I be knowin'. All I need is my Astral Premonition - The ability to astral project into your premonition. Astral Projection - The ability to project the consciousness into an astral form outside of the body. I can fuck my thoughts about you bitches. Atmokinesis - The ability to control and manipulate all various aspects of the weather at will. We can fuck in the heat. We can fuck in some snow flurry action. We can fuck by the window on a rainy day and shit. We can fuck wit high winds doin' what they do. Audible Inundation - The power to overwhelm someone's mind with voices. This is how I talk nasty to bitches because I be too busy bitin' my bottom lip to say the shit out loud. Augmentation - The ability to enhance one's and other's abilities. On me, you ain't never had an orgasm like the ones I be givin'. I put that shit on the set. Aura Choking - The ability to strangle someone through their own aura. I use this for something I like to call Aura Autoerotic Asphyxiation. And it's just what you think it is and bitches LOVE IT! Aura Manipulation - The ability to manipulate auras. I can fuck you through every phase of your period in one fuck from the cramps to the feelin' of relief when that hoe is over.

Okay, you know, so, by now I'm sure y'all know I can assassinate the pussy in a good way with just my A Abilities, but there are more to come. Now we at the B's. We got Banishing - The ability to cast someone out and forbid them from returning. This shit comes in real handy for stalker-type bitches. And I know it's my fault because my sex game is so bomb, but oh well. Beaming - A form of teleportation used by Cupids and Cupid-Witches. I don't fuck wit this one too much and shit cuz I'm just tryna get some pussy and love ain't on the menu and anything that has to do with Cupids...I'm not interested. I'll pass. I'm high already. Black Orbing - A form of teleportation used by Darklighters and Darklighter-Witches. I use this shit after a bitch slash my tires and I need to find that bitch for the money she owe me to replace them hoes. Black Telekinetic Orbing - The ability to teleport objects through the use of black orbs. This power is used by Darklighter-Witches. Either when she take off the waist trainer and the belly parts and the fupa spill all over the floor or when I pull down her jeans and her pussy smell like mornin' breath. I'm cool on it. I'll pass. I'm already high. Blinking - A form of instant teleportation, activated by thinking of a location and blinking the eyes used by Warlocks. I use it when I gotta go, but a bitch is holdin' me hostage with her conversation and shit. Bitch I don't wanna conversate. Blood Boiling - The ability to increase blood temperature to a boiling point. I mean shit. Some like it hot. Y'all would actually be surprised by how many bitches get wet off this shit. Body Insertion - The ability to physically transfer a person into someone else's heart and mind. Something else I use for role play when bitches wanna fuck celebrities and shit. No, you didn't really fuck Tyson Beckford lil momma. Bursting Balls - The ability to conjure a metallic sphere that combusts upon impact. Anal beads on FLEEK. That is all.

Okay, so up next, we got my C's. Calling - The ability to call or summon inanimate objects into one's hand at will. No more awkward pauses to go grab a rubber or some lube for anal. No more having to take breaks to run in the kitchen and eat a sandwich real quick. Camouflage - The ability to magically change one's physical appearance to match their surroundings. I've been known to transform into an action figure and crawl up in the pussy and do a dance routine a time or two. Catoptromancy - The ability to see distant people or places through mirrors. This comes in handy when I just wanna jackoff to Jasmine Sanders when she's takin' a shower or Viola Davis when she's getting' a Brazilian wax. Channeling - The ability to take control of and use the powers of others. I reserve this one for the super freaks who like to be misused and abused in bed. Them 50 Shades of Grey type bitches. If I got a mufuckin' Charlie Horse and she still on 20, I might need her to fall back a lil bit for about five minutes. Chronokinesis - The ability to control and manipulate time in all directions. I'll give you a two hour orgasm just for shits and giggles and shit. This helps to keep my dick hard longer than Viagara too. Clairaudience - The ability to hear what people outside natural hearing range are saying inside one's mind. That's how I was able to fuck them niggas up who thought they was gon rob me that time. Doin' all that high cappin' about pistol whippin' a nigga and shit, but I throat punched every last one of them niggas. Clinging - The ability to cling to solid surfaces. When a bitch wanna cuddle, but I just wanna blackout sleep. Cloaking - The ability to make someone invisible and unable to be detected. When I double book fuck sessions at the same time and shit and I don't want the crazy bitch wit the big ol booty and a pinch worth of titties to hurt the real pretty bitch, so I "I Dream of Jeannie" that bitch up out my muthafuckin' face real quick. Cloning - The ability to duplicate oneself. I be runnin' trains on bitches wit myself and shit. We be goin' hard than a mufucka too cuz our synchronicity be all on point and shit. Combustive Orbing - The ability to channel orbs into another object or being, causing combustion. I used this one time when a bitch told me she got crabs from me and she did cuz I had got em from her cousin, so I used this cuz she couldn't afford to go the doctor. She only ended up wit like first degree burns on her pussy for a lil bit and shit. Conjuration - The ability to instantly create matter from nothing. Sometimes I'm just super lazy and don't even feel like runnin' game on bitches or no shit like that, so I just Weird Science me a bitch outta thin air and shit. Them hoes be right too. Conjuring the Elements - The ability to conjure and control the elements of earth, fire, wind, water, and even lightning. I use this when I need to stand a bitch up cuz a badder bitch caught my attention in like the food court at the mall or some shit. Corporealization - The ability to change from spirit form to a solid physical form. When I like go Casper the Friendly Ghost inside a bitch pussy and shit. Sometimes I mix my spirit wit blunt smoke and fuck her wit that so her pussy get a good buzz and shit. Crushing - The power to surround an object or power with a force that ultimately squashes it. I mean I'm not proud of it, but I done aborted some freshly fertilized eggs in my day. Nigga either didn't want no kids right then or the bitch was just too ugly, but her body was tough, to have kids wit and shit. Cryokinesis - The ability to create and/or manipulate ice and cold. I use to have this bitch that was addicted to popcicles and shit, so I use to make my dick real cold and let her suck on it while we watched TV and shit. It was real cool for both of us and shit. We use to fuck to the ice cream truck music all the time too. Cursing - The ability to enchant an object or person, and produce highly negative effects. I remember one time I used this shit on a nigga that was hatin' on me and shit cuz all the bitches was lettin' me fuck one summer and he couldn't even buy no pussy. I think I gave him like bad feet and a high booty wit child bearing hips. Nigga was built like Big Bird in a wife-beater and some skinny jeans and shit. Shit was hella funny.

Up next is the D's. Dark Binding - Evil ritual performed by dark priestesses to bind two people as husband and wife. Bicthes be havin' too many side niggas these days and sometimes I just wanna be selfish wit the pussy and know no other nigga playin' in my shit. Dark Wisping - A form of teleportation used by the Angel of Death. Now, I ain't the Angel of Death, but he let me put some of his powers on layaway awhile back and this one is how I be killin' the pussy. Leave a bitch pussy wit rigor mortis for a few days. Pussy don't even piss for a minute. It just be queefin' my dead sperms and shit. Deflection - The ability to deflect the active powers of others. That's how a nigga keep from getting' sprung and shit. Yo pussy ain't got no power over me face ass. I'm a mufuckin' legend, baby. Ain't no seconds bih! Deviation - The ability to return attacks back to where they came. Like when a bitch be tryna throw it back at me and I backhand that shit right back to her like nah bih. Return to sender, hoe. Discord - The ability to create conflict between people. I be breakin' people up so I can fuck cuz sometimes chicks really be likin' they dude's dick and he be treatin' em right and shit, so they don't be givin' the kid no action and I be like...not so. Divination - The practice of predicting the future. This let me know when a bitch tryna trick me by offerin' pussy, but she really on her period and she just tryna get me to come over there and do boyfriend type shit like rub her booty and watch chick flicks and shit. I'm not interested. Not today. Dream Leaping - The ability to project into people's dreams and manipulate them. When I tell a bitch I'm her fantasy and her dream nigga and she be tryna act like I'm not. I fuck her in her dreams for about a good week until her pussy just start cryin' puddles as soon as she see me. Dusting - The ability to teleport through grey, dust-like particles. Good for when a chick's dude barges in and catches you hittin' it from the back and you can't really fight because yo pants are around ya ankles and ya dick is on sword.

Up next we have the E's. First up, Ectoplasmic Webbing - The ability to fire strings of ectoplasm. I often use this when a bitch pass out drunk, but I ain't no rapist type of nigga, so I just play target practice wit her clit if I get bored while she's passed out. Elasticity - The ability to stretch a part of your body like a rubber band. Some bitches just love big Lochness Monster dicks...so I oblige. Electrokinesis - The elemental ability to control and generate electricity and throw lightning. For the hoes that like to have they booty hole tasered. Trust me. They exist. Empathy - The ability to feel others' feelings and channel them, as well as to copy other's powers. This is good for havin' to play like you really got feelin's for a bitch before she'll let you fuck and she so fine that you really want her to fuck you without fuckin' with her thoughts directly. Enchantment - The ability to bestow magical powers on an object or an individual. I done been high on ecstasy a few times and enchanted a couple bitches pussies and they left before I woke up and could turn it off. I don't even be rememberin' they names and faces and shit, so they just walkin' around wit a deluxe edition pussy and shit. Probably gettin' all kinds of money and gifts from niggas wit it and shit. Y'all are welcome though. Energetic Fading - An energy based type of teleportation power. I like to use this when I get tattoos so it don't hurt at all. I thought I could handle all tattoo pain until I got a smiley face of the head of my dick, then this shit kicked in and I was all like...swaggy. Energy Balls - The ability to throw balls of electrically charged energy. Some more anal beads type shit except it's like playin' Skeeball up these hoes booty hole and shit. Energy Beam - The ability to shoot deadly beams of energy. I haven't used this since I was a little kid and thought I wanted to be a sociopathic killer like Christian Bale in American Psycho. I used to kill all kinds of trailer park opossums and armadillos and horny toads and shit. Energy Blast - The ability to shoot a powerful wave of pure kinetic energy. This shit right here'll light a mufuckin' pussy up like Christmas on a bitch and have her moonwalkin' like a slew-footed baby deer up out the bedroom and shit. Energy Bolts - The ability to throw bolts of energy similar to Light Darts and Laser Bolts. More anal beads type shit. Bitches are really into they booty holes these days...especially if they bleach it. Energy Magic - The ability to project energy and shape & manipulate it into various forms as desired. Man look, so I used to throw these orgy parties for like $50 a person right and this shit right here had me moppin' up nut and pussy juice and booty slobber all over the warehouse we used to have em in. Nigga was packin' knots in his pockets back then. I used to have all the high-powered freaks comin' through for that shit...judges and cops and state representatives and CEOs and shit. And ya boy got all the footage too and I blackmail me a muthafucka about once a month from em too. Energy Projection - The ability to control and be able to project all forms of energy. I use this mainly to put bitches to sleep so I can sneak out and fuck other bitches without drama and arguments and shit. Nighty night bitch. Nighty night. Energy Sparks - The ability to shoot short beams of red energy sparks. I mean it's some more anal beads type shit, but I primarily use this shit on the 4th of July, so a bitch can be all in the holiday spirit and what not. Energy Waves - The ability to send enormous destructive waves of energy. The only time I had to use this was when a group of ol hatin' ass nigga tried to jump me at a football game because I was fuckin' one of they mommas under the bleachers and shit. She was old as shit in the face, but she had some nice ass titties. Enhanced Intuition - The ability to anticipate or sense danger before it occurs. Most often this ability is developed from psychic powers such as Premonition. This shit right here came in handy when that cop was about to try to shoot me when I was unarmed because he thought I was Black and shit. I mean I am Black if you look at me, so I be screamin' Black Lives Matter just like everybody else. Yeah, but this hoe ass nigga was for real about to try to take ya boy up out the game on some ol fuck boy shit, but I peeped em and throat punched his bitch ass as soon as I rolled my window down. I used my energy wave ability to destroy the dash cam footage and shit. Enhanced Senses - The ability to have extremely advanced senses. I mainly used to use this when my momma use to make me go to funerals of people I either didn't know, didn't like or didn't give a fuck about either way. I just used the shit to blend in with the mourners and shit.

Nigga, we gotta get back to the story or I'll be goin' through these powers all day. Y'all just check out the glossary at the end of the book for the rest of my powers and shit. One!

So as you can see, Emoji is a multifaceted human being. A marvelous specimen of demigodness.

One of his very first stops on his long and tedious journey was at a Burger King. Stricken with a gourmet case of bubble guts, Emoji swerved into the parking lot rather quickly at the onset of his booty hole starting to twitch.

[BURGER KING]

Cashier: Welcome to Burger King where you can have it your way. May I take your order please?

Emoji: Well, what if I said my way was shampooing your hair in my dick snot. Would that make your pussy lips clap?

Cashier: Um, say what now?

Emoji: Look, I've been driving for seven hours straight and my dick is as hard as a sedimentary rock layer right now. I could run up in y'all's bathroom and jackoff with hand soap real quick, but I'd much rather plunge dick first into the depths of your lap infinity pool, ya dig? And from the way your booty is trying to exorcise itself from them Dickie's, my estimation is that you packin' that wet-wet and I'm eager to oblige myself with some pushin' in your cushion. So you want this dick or what baby?

Cashier: Boy you wild. I ain't never had a man speak to me like that in here before.

Emoji: And I bet you ain't never had a man give your pelvis a hairline fracture from good dick neither.

Cashier: You right, but having my pelvis fractured don't sound like a good time to me.

Emoji: So how about I don't fracture your pelvis and just bruise your cervix real good.

Cashier: That shit don't sound like pleasure either.

Emoji: Well, bitch I'm packing a tube of ground beef in these basketball shorts. I'm just providing you with a backstory to help guide your decision.

Cashier: I think imma pass.

Emoji: What if I throw in $50?

Cashier: MEAGHAN, I'M GOIN' ON BREAK! Can you get this done in fifteen minutes?

Emoji: If I can't, yo pussy will be like a jumpstart. I'll beat the nut out if you gotta go back before I bust.

Cashier: Deal! Meet me by that door right there. Let me grab the key to the office real quick. This dick better be good.

Emoji: Well, if it's wack, use the $50 and go buy a dildo that can treat you better. And bring me a muthafuckin' double whopper so I can snack on it while you lick my booty.

Cashier: Lick yo booty? We ain't negotiate for that!

Emoji: I'll give you an extra $25.

Cashier: Well, okay, but go wash it with some hand soap real quick.

[EMOJI'S DIARY]

Dear Diary,

I am officially in love with Burger King. Besides giving me some extra ketchup packets to jack off with later on tonight, I met a thick, young thot whose booty was hella swollen, but her pussy smelled like overcooked French fries floating in the Bog of Eternal Stench and she taught me a very valuable lesson. Not only is life too short to live beneath subjugation, but also money makes people do the most vulgar things with their mouths. Now I'm going to be staring into people's mouths when they talk to me, wondering what the hell they've sucked, licked on and swallowed during their lives. Life is, but a salty tear streaming down the cheek of a harlot whose wad of cash fell out of her pussy while she was running to hop in a cab really fast. Life is a pestering nuisance that presents itself as a jester and browbeats you at every gesture. I often sit back and reflect upon the type of man I've become. I'm rather in love with the emptiness that frolics in my heart. It has married me to a life of reckless abandon and I do so love the many spoils a glib and superficial outlook on life affords me. I look at the silly muthafuckas out here trying to reenact a version of the American Dream that is more scripted than the reality of the human experience can ever truly be. You lose something by trying to fit within a mold that was not designed by your hands. You must chip and chisel away tiny fragments of yourself in order to fit. I could very well be walking in a park somewhere with a beautiful girl who's become so intertwined with her reruns of ulterior motives that she has begun to believe that they are her character. I am a marvelous muthatfucka who literally had a funeral for the last fuck he found within himself to give. It was a handsome ceremony chocked full with black roses and black licorice and black, lace lingerie.

I feel somewhat like a prophet who has been sent to open the minds of those people who are crippled in their ears; deaf in their eyes; and tasteless to the perfunctory assaults the secrets people adorn themselves in so freely offer. I have no interest in wispy loyalty. I am a beast fueled by whisky and selfishness. Fuck them other niggas cuz I ride for my niggas. I'll die for my niggas and my niggas are me, myself, and I. People speak of caged birds singing melodies of the heart when they are merely lost souls in search of validation. I'm good enough. I'm smart enough. I'm pretty enough. My dick is big enough. I take dick good enough. My titties are suckable enough. And so on and so forth and stuff. Whispering lies makes them no truer words.

My journey to my father will be much like Calm Abiding. I am pacing myself for the perfect illumination and evolution of my soul. But in the meantime and in between time...I must body roll.

Chapter 52: I'm About to Get This Body Right, Tho

That following morning, Emoji caught a really good glimpse of himself for the first time in a long time and discovered that he was built like a capital G on legs. Overcome by the insatiable want of becoming an exotic male dancer, Emoji knew that he needed to tighten up in order to maximize his sex appeal. He used to tell people, mainly women, that science has proven that sexiness is measured in pounds, but none of the club owners he attempted to audition for were buying that research data. Initially he was incalcitrant, a bastion of apathy and defiance, but something stirred the leviathan of lewdness within his soul and he could no longer resist the urge to shake his groove thang in front of awed audience.

Emoji had begun his illustrious body rolling career at the age of 12, when he lost his virginity. From that day on, he dedicated himself to the mastery of gyration. His hips were a fountain of equals parts truth and perdition. Over time, Emoji taught himself to weave a most salacious web with his sexy bits, but he'd never invested much interest in perfecting his temple until one club owner told him that he was built like Cleveland Brown from The Cleveland Show and "no bitch in the United States of America wants to squander her hard-earned money on a nigga that's built like a mouse for a computer." Normally, Emoji would've throat punched that bitch nigga, but his passions overthrew his instincts and he took the club owner's caveat to heart. Emoji purchased a membership at Planet Fitness and threw himself headfirst into life-altering workouts and healthy eating choices regimen that gradually began to Altered Beast his body into a godlike version of its former lack of glory. The smell of mayonnaise, peanut butter, leg of lamb, tuna fish, ravioli and protein powder poots often filled the air as Emoji could be found sweating it out and striving for muscle failure. He slowly began to take notice of his stomach flattening and the pancake-like form of his glutes starting to both dissipate and lift into a nice little bubble for the ladies to run credit cards down like in Nelly's "Tip Drill" video. His chest stopped looking like oversized black eyed peas and he began to develop some perky man cleavage.

In a matter of six months, with tremendous amounts of hard work and a few steroid shots in the butt cheek for a full cycle, Emoji completely Decepticonned his body and committed to dressing in nothing, but Underarmor leggings and tank tops. Brimming with confidence, he arranged an audition with the largest male review in town, Le Schfonz, and worked up a nice little routine to "Falsetto" by The Dream. As he sat backstage, greasing his full body down with an entire jar of Vaseline and lovingly eying his Tarzan costume, he drifted into a trance, envisioning the greatness that was about to unfold.

Club Owner: Emoji, you're up next for amateur night. Many of our staff dancers got put on from their amateur night performance, so come wit it.

Emoji: Shit nigga, I'm about to slang so much cock, y'all are gonna need security to help a nigga pick up all them bills off the stage.

Club Owner: Shit, I hope so, so I can get my mufuckin' percentage off top. Is there a particular way you wanna be introduced?

Emoji: Hell the fuck yeah. Tell that nigga to read this...

Announcer: Coming to the stage ladies is that python penis dick slanger y'all know, love and affectionately call Deez Nutz!

Emoji: WAYMENT! Hold the music. Before I begin let me just say, giving honor to God, the pastor, first lady and the usher board. I stand before each of you on tonight both blessed and highly favored, amen. God has smiled on me. He has set me free, amen. There's a lily and it's in the valley of my well-defined gluteus maximus and it's as bright as the Morning Star. Like Warren Marvin Sapp said, I believe it was, Lord, I never would've made it; never could've made it without you. I could've lost it all, but now I see that you are here with me. And now I'm a child of destiny with independent beauty. Yes God in Heaven, I'm a survivor on you hoes (what?). I'm not gon' give up until I've body rolled that bank roll right up out y'all's hands (what?). I'm not gon' stop. Shit turn down for what? (what?). I'm gon' work harder (what?). I'm a survivor (what?). I'm gonna make it (what?). I will survive (what?). Keep on survivin' (what?). Because there's a voice that cries out in the silence, searching for a heart that will love Him.

THAT'S ME! Shatah! Longing for a broad that will give Him her all. Give it all, He wants it all. And when I say He, I'm talkin' about me and my acceptance of the kind that jingles with a preference for the kid that folds into origami if I want it to. So as I slither my well-oiled body all over this stage and leave Soul Glo-like stains on y'all's outfits, just know that I'm only doin' so, so that y'all hoes will Daft Punk a nigga and buy it, purchase it, acquisition it, bargain it, use it, break it, disrupt it, discontinue it, interrupt it, pause it, halt it, fix it, dose it, shoot it, inject it, hit it, answer it, hit it, trash it, waste it, junk it, scrap it, change it, mail, upgrade it, charge it, care it, junk it, point it, zoom it, rise it, press it, snap it, quick it, break it, work it, quick, erase it, write it, cut it, paste it, save it, load it, check it, quick, rewrite it, plug it, play it, burn it, rip it, tear it, split it, scratch it, cleft it, slash it, slit it, gash it, drag and drop it, zip, unzip it, punch it, pep it, spunk it, lock it, fill it, curl it, find it, view it, code it, jam, unlock it, surf it, spray it, sea it, top it, side it, scroll it, pose it, sham it, fake it, click it, cross it, crack it, twitch, update it, tic it, spasm it, jerk it, jolt it, name it, read it, tune it, print it, scan it, test it, probe it, send it, fax, rename it, touch it, bring it, pay it, watch it, turn it, leave it, stop, format it. Cue the music. POWZERS!!!!!

Emoji slipped, slid, blundered, glided, slithered, slinked, skidded, rolled, trundled, popped, locked, dropped it, rotated, whirled, twisted and gyrated himself into $4200 that night (he ate a lil pussy and licked a few booty holes in addition to full on fuckin' in the champagne room) and was hired for a probationary trial period to become one of the stable dancers of Le Schfonz. To treat himself, he decided to attend a campaign rally for Donald Trump. Now, I'm sure a lot of you feel a lot like Felix Dennis when he said "Nobody could like Donald Trump, surely, except his mother," but you've gotta love a guy who literally said out of his mouth where other people can hear him, "The beauty about me is that I'm very rich."

[DESPERATELY SEEKING THE DONALD]

Emoji found himself to be drawn to The Donald in ways that made his bowels do the Dougie, thereby causing him nausea. What he saw in The Donald was the uncanny ability to force Emoji to download Trump, watch and invest time in following him on varying medium, not because he wanted to see The Donald become president, but because he wanted to study the man, so that he could train that very same douchey muscle that lived within him. As such, Emoji devised a simple plan: STORM THE RALLY AND FUCK SHIT UP! The forecast predicted a warm day with no rain, so Emoji put plats in his hair like a young Miss Celie, A$AP Rocky, and Travis Scott, threw on a wrestling singlet (to show off his hot bod and bulge) and his cowboy boots, and headed out the door with a Boom Box so big 1990 called for it and asked for it back just before he left.

The stage was set and everything looked extremely Caucasian and tediously put together by some OCD-stricken up-and-comer who was trying to spare her knees from ruin from blowjobs in favor of being a Stepford employee. Everyone was dressed in their finest business formal attire, and then in comes Emoji in all of his life-sized action figure glory. He, of course, received a barrage of stares ranging from awkward to aghast to rapey, but he continued toward the front of the room unscathed and unbothered. Cognitive dissonance being the hell of the drug that it is, most people just wrote him off as a part of the festivities. Except for the security detail. With brains preprogrammed to attack and silence any person who looked out of place, three Agent Smith looking motherfuckers converged upon Emoji for a sorting out of things. It did not end as they had anticipated.

Guard One: Excuse me, sir, and I use that term as loosely as possible, but may I see your invitation please?

Emoji: Maybe.

Guard One: And what, might I ask, is the source of your hesitation in providing me with for what I ask?

Emoji: First of all...nigga...back back and give me fifty muthafuckin' feet, bitch. I felt the steam off yo breath iron my muthafuckin' sideburns cuz you too muthafuckin' close to my face, hoe. Second of all, nigga I don't know you. Who the fuck is you to be comin' up askin' me about my muthafuckin' invitation, bitch?

Guard Two: Sir, I'm going to have to ask you to remain calm and comply. We're simply doing our job.

Emoji: Oh, so it takes three muthafuckas to come ask me to see my muthafuckin' invitation? Ain't it the job of the person AT THE DOOR to ask to see my muthafuckin' invitation? Yeah, THE DOOR that I just walked through and showed my invitation. What you can see is the fuck up out my face wit that hoe shit nigga.

Guard One: Sir, let's not cause a scene. I apologize for not properly introducing myself and my colleagues. I am Agent Slaussen. This is Agent Eidexis. And that is Agent Rojas. We are here to attend to Mr. Trump and his guests.

Emoji: Agent? Man gon. I don't need no muthafuckin' loan. Y'all ain't about to fuck up my credit. So Agent Sausage, you, Agent Mexicans, and Agent Blowjob can run 'round. I'm cool on it. I'm good. I'm already high.

Guard One: And that I don't doubt' sir, but we provide security for the event, not payday loans.

Emoji: Oh, so because you look at me and I look all caramel with this wavy hair and hazel-green eyes, you think my daddy is Black and my momma is White. That's okay tho. Black lives do matter 'round this bitch! BLACK…LIVES…MATTER! Afro picks and glycerin on that ass as I hold my fist up and shout POWER TO THE PEOPLE. And scene. Would you like to make another one?

Guard Two: Sir, if you don't comply, we'll be forced to remove you and search you for your invitation.

Emoji: Well, may the force be with you then.

Guard One: As you wish.

Emoji: I SAID GET YO GOTDAMN HANDS OFF ME YOU OL DICK IN THE BOOTY ASS BOY! IMMA GIVE YOU MY MUTHAFUCKIN' INVITATION, BUT WHERE'S THE STENOGRAPHER BECAUSE I WANT IT ON RECORD THAT I'VE BEEN RACIALLY PROFILED AT A DONALD TRUMP EVENT TO WHICH I HAVE A PROPER

INVITATION THAT I BOUGHT FROM A BIG BOOTY BITCH WHO WORKS ON HIS STAFF BY THE NAME OF...

Andromeda Williams, Japanese & Black Event Coordinator to the Stars: What seems to be the problem here?

Emoji: AIN'T NO MUTHAFUCKIN' PROBLEM ANDROMEDA! YOU BETTA TELL THESE THREE MARK ASS NIGGAS WHO THE FUCK I AM AND TO BACK UP OFFA ME!!!!!

Andromeda Williams, Japanese & Black Event Coordinator to the Stars: Emoji, calm down before you cause my employment to be in jeopardy?

Emoji: What is I don't give a big fat rat's ass of a flyin' fuck for $1000 Alex? Imma quit yellin' cuz my throat hurt from eatin' all that pussy and booty last night, but what I won't do is calm down. Tell Huey, Duey, and Luey to back the fuck back and that's that. Especially that third one just standin' over there smilin' like he shit on hisself and don't wanna tell his momma cuz she won't give a fuck that they in church. She still gon beat his bitch ass.

Andromeda Williams, Japanese & Black Event Coordinator to the Stars: Gentlemen, this gentleman is here by invitation.

Guard Two: We have been ordered to see it with our own eyes.

Emoji: Well, who the fuck elses eyes is you gon see the muthafucka wit nigga? I tell you what. Here you go...

Emoji reached into the leg of his wrestling singlet and fished the dainty invitation from under his ball sack. A trick he'd learned that time he went to the juvenile detention center for throat punching a crossing guard who tried to escort him to the bus.

Guard Three: I'll take that.

Emoji: SEE...SEE...Y'ALL LOOK...TOLD Y'ALL...OL DICK IN THE BOOTY ASS NIGGA. AIN'T SAID SHIT TIL I PULLED THIS

INVITATION FROM ITS' NAP ON MY GOOCH. Now you sniff my invitation and you hold yo breath til forest fairies come sprinkle you with glitter and pixie dust and reactivate your dick in the booty holeness.

Guard Three: He's clear.

Emoji: But my nut ain't. It's kinda milky. Thanks for playing gentlemen.

Guard One: Enjoy you evening...sir.

Emoji: And I might.

Andromeda Williams, Japanese & Black Event Coordinator to the Stars: Emoji, look I know I let you beat this pussy up last night after you fucked three of my sorority sisters, but this is my job and I just can't have you being a disruption on a night for which I so painstakingly planned.

Emoji: Andromeda is my thumb still stuck up yo ass from last night?

Andromeda Williams, Japanese & Black Event Coordinator to the Stars: Just sit here. Enjoy the free food. Don't make eye contact with anyone and don't spark up ANY conversations. And most importantly, try to turn down the volume on your outfit by being as inconspicuous as you can be at the front of the room. I actually thought you were joking when you said you wanted to attend tonight.

Emoji: Can I get some head later?

Andromeda Williams, Japanese & Black Event Coordinator to the Stars: Yes, but only because I can see that you are fully erect and your penis is throbbing.

Emoji: He's sick to his stomach and needs to throw up. That's why I asked you to give him mouth-to-mouth.

Andromeda Williams, Japanese & Black Event Coordinator to the Stars: Good evening, Emoji.

Emoji: No, good pussy. Yeah you. Her bruh. Yeah that one walkin' off with the big ol booty. I can tell by yo face that you, like me, ain't never seen a Asian chick wit a ass sittin' fat like that. It's that Black from her mama's side of the family. Shit make you wanna blow spit bubbles in that hoe. BIG BOOTY JUDY!!!!

As The Donald took to the stage, Emoji could feel the excitement churning within him. The crowd detonated with applause and as the claps began to dissipate and The Donald parted his lips to greet his audience, Emoji stood, placed the boombox on his shoulder and pressed play. The 5th Ward Boyz filled the air...

"Pussy, Pussy-Pussy, Pussy weed and alcohol it seems to satisfy us all, indeed. Don't even trip, half of you bitches like pussy too. Love to smoke weed and get high, sip syrup and let the freaky shit up out. And suck the skin off a nigga dick. I's a playa. I's a never had to trick. Stupid fuck put the game down so well. Can have yo bitch playin' a good game of suck dick and tell. Nigga don't trip if you see me creepin' through yo hood. I'm pickin' up a shot of cock, some head, and it's all good. It just might be yo baby momma or sister, but then again, if it is, you better be tryin' to be a nigga friend. Cause see I do this shit only one way, nigga the "G" way. Blowin' my hair back, gettin' my dick sucked on the freeway. I never lie on my dick cause that's a playa rule. Smokin' weed, gettin' drunk, rockin' shows and then be ready to fuck somethin'. Pussy, Pussy-Pussy, Pussy (Pussy weed and alcohol) Pussy, Pussy-Pussy, Pussy, Pussy, Pussy-Pussy, Pussy (It seems to satisfy us all). Pussy, Pussy-Pussy, Pussy, Pussy, Pussy-Pussy, Pussy (We livin' like pussy, weed and alcohol). Pussy, Pussy-Pussy, Pussy, Pussy, Pussy-Pussy, Pussy (It seems to satisfy us all). Pussy, Pussy-Pussy, Pussy (That's how we playa's ball).

Emoji: I guess these hoes didn't hear me, when I said bitch please. Now it's five years later big faces, big sprees. Talkin' bout bad bitches up in condos. Smokin' mad swishers, bout to get some head pronto. Pussy, weed, and alcohol nigga, plus that cash go with it. Double "o" we clockin' hoochies; stick a bird up in her pussy. Smokin' cryptonite, rollin' in a benz. Souppin' up some tenz. Bout to break 'em for they endz. Tell 'em low man.

The Donald: "Oh, look at my African-American over here. Look at him. Are you the greatest? You know what I'm talking about? OK! I'm in a ninty eight, put it out. Gassed up to the fullest, b-e-n-z. Two bitches and me. A quarter pounder, weed, and Hennessy. They lookin' sexy. From the start, they under me. Too tough, I got they hearts pleased. Understand indeed. Ways to get yo ass, through the days with razor blades. Tight game you'll fade 'em all away. Peeped the laid out. Pussy, weed, and "D" fellas. Alcohol and "G" fellas. Bitches come in fleets fellas. Courtesy on me fellas.

Emoji and The Donald: Pussy, Pussy-Pussy, Pussy (Pussy weed and alcohol) Pussy, Pussy-Pussy, Pussy, Pussy, Pussy-Pussy, Pussy (It seems to satisfy us all). Pussy, Pussy-Pussy, Pussy, Pussy, Pussy-Pussy, Pussy (We livin' like pussy, weed and alcohol). Pussy, Pussy-Pussy, Pussy, Pussy, Pussy-Pussy, Pussy (It seems to satisfy us all). Pussy, Pussy-Pussy, Pussy, Pussy (That's how we playa's ball).

The Donald: Well what a spirited way to be introduced. You know, believe it or not, I actually have quite a bit of respect for Andre "007" Barnes, Eric "E-Rock" Taylor and Richard "Lo Life" Nash, so thank you for that. As matter of fact, Andromeda give this young man a backstage pass. I'd like to speak with him for a bit. You know back in 1984, I believe it was, the Simpsons accurately predicted that I would run for president and even eerily had me wearing the very same outfit I've been pictured in as well as accurately envisaged that I would be running under the banner of the GOP. Where they got it wrong is when they had the Simsoned version of me saying I would be doing so because the Republican party is full of idiots or something like that. While I cannot say they were wrong in the cases of Sara Palin and Anne Coulter, though I'd take them both for a long swim in my infinity pool, if you know what I mean, I cannot agree that the rest of my comrades in the Sect of the Elephant are anything other than pure genius. Some my decision to run for president has more to do with my loyalty to this country than anything else. You know it literally sickens me and gives me bubble guts to think about all of the whoremongers, thieves, rapist, bootleg CD & DVD salesmen, hot check writers, boosters, peeping Toms, male prostitutes, the gays, and civil rights activists invading our country from Mexico and Syria. I think if this country gets any kinder or gentler, it's literally going to cease to exist. My decision to run is more about protecting you from them, their thug friends, and all radicalized thinkers like Azalea Banks and Charlamagne the God from preventing us from making America great again. We're rounding 'em up in a very humane way, in a very nice way. And they're going to be happy because they want to be legalized. And, by the way, I know it doesn't sound nice. But not everything is nice. What I won't do is take in two hundred thousand Syrians who could be ISIS... I have been watching this migration. And I see the people. I mean, they're men. They're mostly men, and they're strong men. These are physically young, strong men. They look like prime-time soldiers. Now it's probably not true, but where are the women?... So, you ask two things. Number one, why aren't they fighting for their country? And number two, I don't want these people coming over here. You know, I had a long boring speech written that was probably going to make someone sprain their neck from dozing off, but since I'm always in a perpetual state of ad libbing anyway, me switching gears and taking a page from the 5th Ward Boyz and their amazing contribution to Hip Hop music, "Concrete Hell", should be accepted with open arms. You see, I'm running for all my muthafucking niggas, I put the "a-s" on the end, so don't blow your wad, that are in the penitentiary for any number of White Collar Crimes including bank fraud, blackmail, bribery, cellular phone fraud, counterfeiting, credit card fraud, currency schemes, embezzlement, environmental schemes, extortion, forgery, health care fraud, insider trading, insurance fraud, investment schemes, kickbacks, larceny, money laundering, racketeering, tax evasion, welfare fraud, weights & measures, telemarketing fraud, advanced free schemes, airport scams, auto repair schemes, check kiting, coupon redemption, directory advertising, fortune telling, gypsying, inferior equipment schemes, Jamaican switch, land fraud, pigeon dropping, odometer fraud, police impersonation, Ponzi schemes, pyramid schemes, quick changing, shell gaming, utilities impersonation, Western African Investment schemes, and all of the other gentlemanly ways to bend the law and not act niggardly. It's a real word in the dictionary. Pump your brakes folks. So yes, I am running for all of my motherfucking niggas that are currently on death row because some mystery Mexican got away with murdering everyone in their family in their sleep, except for my friends who landscape my gardens, and the Mexicans walking around on this great soil freely and illegally. I'm running for all of my motherfucking niggas that are trying to garner themselves some motherfucking bail for Pete's sake. I'm running for all of my motherfucking niggas that aren't down with the motherfucking police. I, personally, was not born in the motherfucking penitentiary because a nigga escaped by way of a small loan of a million dollars from my father, which really wasn't a lot of money even back then. Today, I stand before you in an Armani suit, but were you to look closer, you'd notice that I'm wearing checkers on my feet as I wanted to be prepared to creep through a long line of drug dealers and killers, thugs and hoodlums, and OG's all looking at me meanly, with an intense desire to point a finger because I know they're all from Tijuana. I will build a great, great wall on our southern border, and I will have Mexico pay for that wall. Mark my words. One thing you should know about The Donald is that I am always prepared and ten steps ahead in the game. I'm playing chess, while these lesser are playing checkers. I hold my nuts because these fingers have me tripping on a daily basis. I duct tape a shank to my inner thigh when I meet with a lot of you people just in case you fools develop the audacity to try fade me in my attempt to return America to her former glory. A time before baby momma and baby daddy were used on the news like they represent the core values for which so many of our forefathers bled and died. I don't foresee my lifestyle in the White House being any different than any of the many mansions I own other than my having to get accustomed to somewhat cramped living quarters, but I'm prepared to make that sacrifice for the land that I love. You know Killary Clinton and those other nobodies, hey I call them like I see them, Kanye shrug...but yes, the anti-Monica Lewinsky and those other dudes no one really cares about can eat, but they should prepare themselves to pick the scars from my throat later on down the line. They loved parading across the stage, spouting fortune cookie messages of the status quo like they're heroes for this great nation, but their words are like mist, they dry up quickly, which makes them a bunch of hoes in my book. I read a blog entitled 25 reasons The Donald Should Kill Himself and I laughed. They proposed to shed light on some alleged misdeeds I am reported to have committed in my mission to become wealthy. I hear they called me for a quote, but much like the United States of America, I don't negotiate with terrorists. It's not my ministry. I say all of that to say this, now that the good Lord above has seen fit to drive this Muslim-sympathizing non-American with not a credible birth certificate to be found out of office, it is time for not a new America, but the America of old. The America where people could own people and provide them with shelter and food and sustainable communities to worship their jiggaboo gods. The America where it was fucking awesome to be proud of being White and you could literally say that in public without a billion memes. I represent that America. The America that was built by Andrew Carnegie, John D. Rockefeller, J.P. Morgan, Henry Ford, and Cornelius Vanderbilt. So stand with me as I proudly proclaim that no wetbacks or towel heads formed against us shall prosper!

Emoji rose to his feet and shed tears like that time Jaden Smith cried after a Drake performance. He wasn't really listening to the content of the speech, but they were tears of pure, unadulterated admiration nonetheless. He immediately began rehearsing all of the fanciful words he would share with The Donald, hoping to arouse his veneration as well and maybe, just maybe land a spot on The Apprentice. Unfortunately, Emoji is Emoji and The Donald is The Donald and the clash of these titans was not the experiment in fraternity that either had hoped, but still a bond was forged.

Emoji: Donald Trump. Donald Muthafuckin' Trump. The Donald if you nasty, right?

The Donald: Aw yes, my disruptive little chocolate-covered Mighty Mouse with the captivating bulge, boombox and 90s HipHop jams. Tell me your name young man.

Emoji: Emoji.

The Donald: Well that's surely an interesting name. Let me guess, your mother's name is like Shasta or Shamwow, right?

Emoji: Now you wait one gotdamn minute you dandelion headed son of a bitch, Donald Trump. Don't you ever fix your wafer thin ass lips to say shit about my momma or I'll skulldrag yo bitch ass by them 27 hairs you've got Miracle Whipped on the top of your head, bitch.

The Donald: Calm down young man. I was just poking fun at you.

Emoji: This ain't no muthafuckin' Facebook bitch. Fuck you and them pokes. I'm real close to throat punchin' you right now.

The Donald: Now you and I both know that wouldn't be wise. I have the finest security detail on the planet.

Emoji: Fuck them ol dick in the booty ass glorified rent-a-cops.

The Donald: As dick in the booty as they might be, I'll have you know that my agents are highly skilled assassins with black ops training.

Emoji: Oh, that's real cute for them and shit. I grew up in a trailer park, so unless they replaced them shriveled up ball bearing ass nuts they packin' wit titanium testicle implants, my intestinal fortitude will find a way.

The Donald: I like your spirit. Care for a drink?

Emoji: Hell yeah, but I only fuck wit that brown. That white is for frat boys and bitches in pencils skirts.

The Donald: Gotta love a skin tight pencil skirt. We can thank the Kardashian whores for their popularity.

Emoji: Donald Trump, miss me with the bait of Satan, bro. You probably sucked on Kris Jenner's booty hole a time or two in the past.

The Donald: Without question, but you see I've developed a reputation for being rather cavalier when it comes to political correctness. It's my greatest triumph as a celebrity mogul. Everyone else dances on eggshells in their lace tutus trying not to offend people who could possibly add a few dollars to their portfolio, but I've graduated from the song and dance. I'm bigger than political correctness, the Beatles AND Jesus.

Emoji: See that's why I fucks wit yo pseudo racist ass. People always question me about why come I'm such a follower of you when I don't agree with most of the shit that comes outta yo mouth, but for a nigga like me, it's never been about the content. It's always been about the balls. And you, Donald Trump, must have elongated, veiny, liver-spotted, freckled, pimpled, patchy-haired balls and for that I give you a slow clap, sir.

The Donald: I appreciate that from a trailer park urchin. Most people don't believe that I connect with American citizens, but...

Emoji: Throat punch activated *pop pop pop pop pop*

The Donald: What in the name of Jesus, Mary, K-C, and JoJo was that for?

Emoji: Nigga you tried it with that trailer park urchin shit. And you see ya fuckboys ain't move a muscle.

The Donald: Touche'. I'll try to bide my tongue for the rest of our visit. Wet wipes please. I need to take a hoe bath before I venture out to shake hands and kiss facially challenged babies. So Emoji, what prompted you to come out to today's event...in a wrestling singlet and cowboy boots no less.

Emoji: Well, The Donald, it's like this. On my way to St. Ives I saw a nigga wit seven bitches. Each bitch had seven sacks. Each sack had seven cats. Each cat had seven kittens. Kitten, cats, sacks, bitches. How many were goin' to St. Ives? You feel me?

The Donald: Totally fetch. Go on. You know, it really doesn't matter what the media writes as long as you've got a young and beautiful piece of ass. All of the women on 'The Apprentice' flirted with me -- consciously or unconsciously. That's to be expected. I'm sexy and my hands are HUGE.

Emoji: Okay, so a nigga is sittin' in a pub feelin' rather broke, busted and disgusted cuz his big sister said she wasn't gon let him claim none of her kids on her taxes this year because he stole all of her Xanax and didn't give her no money for em and shit. He sees the nigga next to him pull a wad of one hundred dollar bills outta his Levi's and shit, right? The poor nigga turns to the rich nigga and says to the nigga, "Say nigga, I'm like America. I have an amazing talent; I know almost every song that has ever existed." The rich nigga laughs in the poor nigga's face. The poor nigga says, "And am willin' to bet you all the money you got in yo pocket that I bust out a genuine song with a lady's name of yo choice in that bitch." The rich nigga laughed again and said, "Okay lil nigga, how about my daughter's name, Joanna

Armstrong-Miller?" The rich nigga goes home poor as shit. The poor nigga goes home rich than a bitch. What song did he sing?

The Donald: Even in a race against Obama, Hillary Clinton was gonna beat Obama. I don't know who would be worse, I don't know, how could it be worse? But she was going to beat him – she was favored to win – and she got schlonged, she lost, I mean she lost. If Hillary Clinton can't satisfy her husband what makes her think she can satisfy America.

Emoji: Real nigga shit, The Donald. Real nigga shit. So you feel me when I say, Queen Elizabeth organized a royal party and to avoid uninvited, ratchet ass guests the royal family set a password. Kristoff, an uninvited gutter ass, hood nigga, plans to enter the party. He stands nearby the door and shit. The first guest comes, the security person said "twelve" and the guest replied with "six". The second guest comes and the security person said "six" and the guest replied with "three". Kristoff thought to hisself "Man, fuck this bullshit. I'm over it" and he walked to the entry point. The security person said "eight", Kristoff smilingly replied "four". He was immediately thrown out of the party. Why?

The Donald: She really has become a monster ... I mean monster in the most positive way. You know the funny thing, I don't get along with rich people. I get along with the middle class and the poor people better than I get along with the rich people. My fingers are long and beautiful, as, it has been well been documented, are various other parts of my body. Wow, Vanity Fair was totally shut out at the National Magazine Awards - it got NOTHING. Graydon Carter is a loser with bad food restaurants! Dopey Graydon Carter, who is presiding over dying Vanity Fair magazine, is also presiding over dying Waverly Inn—worst food in the city. Graydon Carter, whose reign over failing Vanity Fair has been a disaster, has acted in two movies—both bombed & got bad reviews.

Emoji: No short-fingered vulgarian here, bih!

The Donald: Mini Me. You complete me.

Emoji: I like the fat rolls on the back of your neck.

The Donald: Well, as fun as this has been, I've got other business to attend to. I sincerely want to thank you for taking the time to speak with me today, not really, but it sounds good.

Emoji: Fuck that Donald Trump. I ain't through witchu yet. I need to know if Omarossa's pussy smells like beef jerky. I need to know if you use Aquanet. I need you to let me hold like 40 racks til payday.

The Donald: Son, just stop right there. Time is money and money is time and because you don't have the money to make an investment of my time worthwhile, you need to be focused on using your time to build your wealth. So can I count on your vote?

Emoji: Niggaaaaaaaaaaaaaaaaaa...you better pay me like you paid them two shuckin' and jivin' Black ladies that look like they work at the water company and the elementary school cafeteria or that barely lingual Spanish lady. I'll take food stamps, pesos, Chuck E. Cheese tickets, coupons and all.

The Donald: Then I guess we're done here, but before I go. Take this cellphone. My number is already programmed in it. If I ever get a call from someone that isn't you, I'll know you gave out my number because the phone your phone rings to only has one number saved in it and that's your number. See how that works?

Emoji: Say my nigga, you ain't never gotta worry bout no shit like that. I'm a trill ass nigga. I put that on the set.

The Donald: Awesome. Now go put some pants on. That bulge in your singlet is making everyone uncomfortable.

Emoji: Ah nigga that's just because they want this dick and if I catch you lookin' again, imma fuck you up.

The Donald: Trust that I wasn't admiring. It was just staring at me and I never back down.

Emoji: Whatever nigga.

The Donald: And Emoji...

Emoji: What's good?

The Donald: Always remember to get going. Move forward. Aim High. Plan a takeoff. Don't just sit on the runway and hope someone will come along and push the airplane. It simply won't happen. Change your attitude and gain some altitude. Believe me, you'll love it up here. And here's $200 so you can go do some hoodrat shit with your friends.

Emoji: Fuck you Donald Trump. You be easy nigga.

The Donald: Twenty-one!

Chapter 53: BITCH BETTER HAVE MY MONEY!

Dear Diary,

RANDOM THOUGHTS:

1.   I'm just gonna be Black like Rachel Dolezal. Shit people see a well-crafted Black man who's hung better than Sea Biscuit when they see me anyway. I get racially profiled like a Black man does. I get followed in department stores all the time. I mean I do be shopliftin' and should probably apologize to the Black race for addin' to the bullshit stereotypes they have to live wit, but fuck it. From now on, I'm Black.

2.   Why come bad built hoes always walk like they pussy got flu symptoms?

3.   That awkward moment when you look at yo life and realize you ain't got no friends and it makes you a lil sad, then you remember you ain't got no fuck niggas tryna fuck yo bitches. You ain't got no fuck niggas always tryna smoke witchu, but ain't never got no weed to smoke witchu. You ain't got no fuck niggas treatin' you like a mufuckin' uber driver cuz they done made a blood sacrifice for every mufuckin' pair of Jordans ever made when they coulda been stackin' that cheese for a whip. You ain't got no bum ass niggas puttin' yo shoes on, leavin' they ol runover, boy you got knocked the fuck out lookin' ass shoes in ya closet, and leavin yo house without lettin' you know they rockin' yo shit. Fuck them niggas.

4.   I wish they made pussy flavored Kool-Aid.

5.   I need to figure out how to stick some Silly Putty in the hose on my vacuum so I can stick it on my dick and make it give me a blowjob.

6.   Sine I'm a male stripper and I still kinda look like a Wii from the back a lil bit, am I supposed to get ass shots on GP? I'm not above it. It'll just be like a lil speed bump booty. Not a whole pachyderm ass.

7.   One day imma tell that bitch I caught stealin' my petty cash from under my bed that I made her pancakes with the Pepsi bottle full of nut I keep on my coffee table as the liquid base to undergird the eggs.

8.   People really be out here breathin' in people's faces when they breath smell like one of them creatures from Slither got lodged in they throat, died and decomposed. Ol foot fungus breath havin' ass people.

9.   I went to church last Sunday cuz like fifty people told me I needed prayer that week, but I got kicked out for body rollin' on this woman's booty who was praise dancin'. Shit, I'm a sinner and that ass was fat. A snake gon be a snake. Shit, grab a Ouija board and ask Eve.

10.   I'm thinkin' about joinin' a fight club, but I grew up in a trailer park wit disenfranchised ass White kids and crackheads, so if a muthafucka chip one of my teeth, I'm sprayin' everybody in that bitch and burnin' my fingerprints off.

11.   I typed up all of the words from all of the Matrix movies and printed em out and now I read from it every night like my granny used to do her Bible. A nigga woke wit no caffeine and I ain't sleepy.

12.   This bitch I'm fuckin' got like a narcoleptic pussy. No, for real. Like when I be beatin' that shit up, it go to snorin' and shit. I told her to go get that shit looked at and she gon tell me it was just purrin' cuz it like me. Naw bitch, that mufucka was callin' Wilbur and every last hog in a ten mile radius, hoe.

13.   Am I the only one who be rubbin' his dick against his iPhone cuz Siri got a sexy ass voice? I wanna fuck the shit outta Siri...lowkey.

14.   I think butt chuggin' all this lean is fuckin' wit my magical powers. I tried to conjure me up a dark-skin, Malaysian bitch and wound up wit a bitch that look like Margaret Cho. I did windmills in that Crab Rangoon pussy tho.

15.   Modern day niggas be confusin' me. A nigga would rather sit up and play Call of Duty and make Whip/Nae Nae videos wit a group of his homeboys and they all saggin' wit

they booty half out and no shirts on instead of spendin' time wit his bitch. Y'all need to quit lettin' these niggas use y'all as porta pussies.

16. Jesus was the first OG gang leader and Peter was a goon. Real talk.

17. Note to Self: Don't be blinded by self-righteousness.

18. Why won't the circle of death let me be great?

19. The dainty weave pat WITH the pinky flexed by the gainfully employed Black woman.

20. It's cuffing season. Tuck those fupas away. They require beauty rest of the fourth kind.

21. Every statement she makes has a side order of query accompanying it and it makes me want to thump her in her adenoids!!!!!

22. Why do people allow their fucking pets to be all over guests in their home? I'm not interested in smelling of or being covered in pet dander. That shit ain't my ministry!

23. I can only fit within a certain mold for so long before I outgrow and warp it.

24. When something is good, the attempt to make it better often desecrates what was good about it in the first place. Lil Kim's face for instance.

25. BET is no longer FUBU.

26. Weave that needs resuscitation ✔. Black burnt toast, unretouched knees and elbows ✔. No makeup✔. A clearance rack Halloween costume from 1993✔. Females doing prison poses tryna be sexy✔.

27. I'm harboring a fugitive, anger, and it's robbing me of my sleep.

28. Loving me isn't complicated. You're just in your feelings.

29.   I'm so sick of coon ass niggas tryna get followers! Proselytizing bullshit doctrine tryna be scholars. Hoe cake niggas fuck demons for petty profits then have ass babies.

30.   Debates/Conversations begin with a question. Arguments begin with an accusation. Don't jump out the gate with what you were told and what you had heard before showing me the common decency of asking me what I said/did. Bad Example: Her: I'm on my way over there right now to bust you in yo muthafuckin face cuz Asia told me you was finger fuckin some mixed bitch at the strip club last night and when I find out who the bitch is I'm fuckin her shit up too!!! Me: BITCH!!!!! Swerve. Good Ex.: Her: So bae, I heard you were at the strip club last night and things got pretty wild and out of hand and I just wanted to give you the opportunity to tell me your side of the story before I present you with what Asia shared with me. Is there anything you need to tell me? Me: Asia had popped four bars and took about six shots on top of tootin' powder every thirty-five minutes so I'm sure whatever she told you is hilarious. Yes, I was there and the night was pretty standard other than Marcus finger fuckin one of Asia's homegirls in the VIP. His fingers smelled like Vienna sausages for the rest of the night! See how that works?

31.   So I read something today that really challenged my position on the Bill Cosby rape allegations. Essentially the post challenged me by stating something to the effect that you can't vilify Daniel Holtzclaw while venerating Bill Cosby. This truly made me go hmmmmm, but then again Daniel Holtzclaw's victims weren't professing to have been drugged prior to having been accosted either, which, in my mind, muddies the certainty of their adamant accusations. Moreover, does the statute of limitations not come into play? Thusly, the pendulum swung back to center for me and I've decided not to concern myself with the matter either way anymore because Bill Cosby nor Cliff Huxtable were ever childhood heroes of mine. I loved The Cosby Show though. It was the cat's pajamas. If those ladies were indeed victimized, then I hope they find both peace and justice. If Bill Cosby is indeed innocent, I hope he finds the same. #HandsWashed #ImMufuckinTired

32.   I must strongly suggest that some of you increase your water intake...because you're aging like milk. #100

33.	I hate when I go to piss and my pisshole is partially pinched off, so the piss shoots outta my tip at a right angle!!!!!!

34.	ATTENTION: White girls are not evolving. Their standards of beauty have just changed. Thick is in. And y'all have the nerve to question the impact of Kim Kardashian with your contoured faces, airbrushed eyebrows and pencil skirts. HA.

35.	I swear niggas with man boobs be lettin' bitches suckle them hoes.

36.	Y'all ain't gon be blessed walkin' around with all those extra teeth and there are people lookin' like jack-o'-lanterns by the mouth.

37.	If you don't get yo partially aborted Darkwing Duck lookin' ass on somewhere witcho uncircumcised dick loogie face ass. Nigga you look like a hemorrhoid come to life, nigga. You look like a gangrenous anal spore, nigga. Nigga you look like an epileptic mole rat. You look like a herniated belly button in the face, nigga. You look like Porky Pig with melanoma and plaque psoriasis, ho ass boy. You look like the before picture for a chubby transgender woman, nigga. You look like the first dike to experiment with hormone therapy and join a monocycle club. Nigga, you look like Countess Vaughan without a wig and fake eyelashes. Nigga, you look like a sweat stain left by a mongoloid. Nigga, you look like the poor man's Goodwill version of Magic Johnson's son EJ. You look like Queen Latifah after six months of chemo, nigga. Nigga, you look like a hermaphrodite with hypothyroidism. Nigga, you look like the lovechild of Lilo & Stitch. Yo ol Care Bear with alopecia face ass. Nigga you look like a shaved Ewok. Ol keloid face ass boy!

38.	Y'all gon be spittin' loogies from Heaven if they present your body at your funeral with no weave, eyelashes, contoured makeup or waist trainer.

39.	Let's talk about cornrows in 2015 and why God is withholding blessings if you're still rockin' them dwarf ass hoes that dangle their feet above your neckline.

40.	Apparently pinching the bottom lip of a booty cheek in your sleep is not classified as cuddling? Well suck my dick and call me hookah! Who knew?

41.   For every group of attractive siblings, there's always an ugly one. Shout out to y'all for taking one for the team. The ugly one usually gets married before everyone else while y'all laughing. Sincerely, an only child.

42.   How do you go from a blob to shapely and then become the very same bitch that once terrorized you for your patty cakes build?

43.   You've got three cars sitting in your driveway that you've given the Extreme Home Makeover treatment, but won't buy your daughter a bag of barrettes, but OK.

44.   #TeamNatural vs. #TeamWeave is the new #TeamDarkskin vs. #TeamLightskin (think about it). And if there's a meme out there that says this, let me live dammit! I ain't seen it!!!!!

45.   The world is filled with far too many people who believe they have the right to disrespect fast food workers. You can't expect him/her to treat you with a modicum of respect and your Fraggle Rock face ass tryna puff up like you're King Jaffe Joffer or Queen Aoleon! On the other side of that coin, fast food workers WASH YOUR DAMN UNIFORM REGULARLY!!! Stop finishing texts while I have my arm out the window to give you change. And don't you dare drag out the "ed" in "I said" when I don't hear you the first time. I will hit you in the face with a Frosty bih!

46.   Sadly, far too many women have been raped "a little bit".

47.   But do you wash your wig though? Because it kinda smells like inner thigh sweat or like you dry off with it after you take a hoe bath.

49.   The New World Order should be the people (99%) usurping power from the masters (1%)...and please don't consider yourself a master because you share their skin color. You're just as much a slave as the rest of us. You're just in the house.

Chapter 54: Travel Log: Somewhere in Some Desert with Sunburn and Chapped Lips

I don't always make my ass clap, but when I do, I'm standing on the side of the highway trying to hitch a ride as close to my destination as possible. They say judgment and vengeance are best left to God, but that sucks for impatient folks like me. TO BE CONTINUED....BY SOMEONE OTHER THAN THIS AUTHOR...

Chapter 55: Destiny's Sasha

So the videalbum is gallivanting along its merry way then out of the blue Malcolm intones: "The most disrespected person in America is the Black woman. The most unprotected person in America is the Black woman. The most neglected person in America is the Black woman."

It's trendy to be hypercritical. I get it. I also understand that having a differing opinion isn't really hating, although it's overly postured as such nowadays.

Shame on you. You who watched Beyoncé's LEMONADE and walked away only concerned with who "Becky with the good hair" is...especially if you're a Black woman. Who am I to admonish you? Just a man. A Black man. A Black who watched and listened intently as Beyoncé gave a shout out for the ages and I think I'll just to take it upon myself to believe that shit like the Oshun reference in "Hold Up" went over your head.

How dare you? How dare you melt your bad bitch/basic bitch superficiality and drizzle it all over this body of work intended to put the elephant in the room in a chokehold until the collective attention of the world took pause to lend an ear to the heart of the matter? Or you, with your seated upon a false pedestal you've erected on a foundation of I'm Pro-Blacker than she could ever be face ass? At some point you just gotta let people live. I'm of the mind that we should be drawing as many people interested in contributing to the improved collective consciousness of Black people as possible. And if that requires that we meet them where they're at and guide them through more "gilded corridors of Blackness" as opposed to picking them apart with our disdain, then so be it. I'm not asking you to join her Beehive. I'm not even asking you to like her. I'm just asking that you at least respect the effort. Because it seems that being more than halfway to being a billionaire is a kind of late to be trying to exploit issues that plague your racial community for monetary gain.

Not Beyoncé. Not Miss Bootylicious. Miss 7/11. Miss Sasha Fierce. Mrs. Knowles-Carter. But yes. I, a man guilty of many of the offenses lullabied in "Pray You Catch",

"Hold Up", "Don't Hurt Yourself" and "Sorry" sat as a student...learning and reconnecting with the Black woman in a manner that transcends sexual gratification and visual stimulation. I sat in a puddle of my guilt. I sat in acknowledgement of truth. The truth that the assault on the Black woman has gone, not unnoticed, but unattended.

Tattered brushes lying within the mouths of those who seek to see her immortalized as angry, aggressive, unsmiling, hardened, unfeminine, unsightly, unlovable (and a laundry list of unflattering and dehumanizing characteristics) paint muted portraits of the Black woman in inept acrylics. She is denied her grace. She is denied her fragility. She is denied her beauty. She is denied her femininity. She is denied her womanhood. The legacy of suffering stitched into the fabric of her being. She has become the denial. She can't be tears. She can't be unapologetically Black in whatever version of Black she represents and retain softness. She has to be tough and scarred. She has to be boisterous. She has to be loud.

I only speak of LEMONADE because it is timely. And I'm not suggesting that she's blazing new trails. People keep citing this great awakening, but Black women have always been conscious of the subclass status within which they've been sequestered. Nina Simone. Maya Angelou. Queen Latifah. MC Lyte. Sista Souljah. Erykah Badu. Lauryn Hill. Jill Scott. India Arie. Worse than that, being the most caricatured human specimen there is. The tragedy of being visibly invisible. The agony of being overlooked, erased and abandoned. The triumph of remaining cerebral and spiritual. I call Beyoncé's project timely because we are seeing the plight of the Black woman catapulted to the epicenter of the social injustice conversation with tragedies such as Sandra Bland and, even closer to home, the survivors of Daniel Holtclaw. For those of you who have no idea who they are, they were daughters, sisters, cousins, aunts, mothers and even grandmothers...just like you they were prey.

Chapter 56: Homogeny

The Naienyrecs have an objective reality within a state of fascination with the unremitting, meticulous chronicling and exploration of antediluvian happenings as relating to the Homogeneighian race so frequent as to seem endless and uninterrupted...perpetual or incessant if you will. The Naienyrec Clan explores, investigates, studies and writes about the past, with Srekal being regarded as the unequivocal authority on it. Nicknamed the Walking Time Capsule, Srekal is able to elucidate on every major event that has taken place on Homogeneigh for the last 100 years. Led by the aforementioned Srekal Selegna Sol, this clan can often be found transcribing the itineraries of events and cataloging photographic images from them. The Naienyrec Clan was the third perfected bloodline of Homogeneigh and holds the honor of being its historians.

Given to a well-developed obsession with debauchery, he often imbibes and consumes hallucinogens for the purpose of broadening the landscape of his tastes. A virtuoso of the fine arts, Ardyh curates all of the artistic expression from the members of his clan. Led by Enohpi Andromedeus, a fiercely flamboyant and enigmatic chieftain of the indigenous strain. The Ardyh Clan was the second perfected bloodline of Homogeneigh. Their function is to forever venerate, revere and champion our cultural tapestry.

Revered among all the clans, Ocat remained largely remanded to solitude, so as not to be poisoned by the banalities of social functioning. Homogeneighian folklore teaches us the Ocat was once an octuplet, but he devoured all seven of his siblings in the womb when his mother, Yungrineh, became stricken with Disturbia, a genetic disorder with the propensity to cause for the production of offspring with genetic defects not encoded in our original DNA synthesis. Ocat Osapoldle has ruled as the leader of this clan for over seventy years. He is both wise and sociopathic, which gifts him with the unique ability to govern without emotion or sentimentality. Their sole purpose is to protect the legacy of the supremacists and ensure that their vision for our world is upheld at all costs. The Naemen Clan was the first perfected bloodline of Homogeneigh.

Over the course of 300 years, 13 bloodlines were bred and perfected. It would be from these bloodlines that all Homogeneighian life would evolve. After several attempts had been made to achieve homeostasis failed organically, the Foreparents decided that genetic engineering would be the best way for our people to flourish. Homogeneighian history teaches us that many battles had to be waged and millions of lives expended in order to achieve the homeostatic society in which we live today. The Supremacists, fought to eradicate genetic outliers and anomalies, so that Homogeny could enjoy a pure race. Life on our planet is governed by peace, order and uniformity.

Below, I and the other Crimson-tressed and cream-filling fleshed inhabitants enjoy a peaceful existence, shielded from Horusatan's tyrannical gaze by the cocoon, a solar-panel that enshrouds the entirety of Homogeneigh and protects us from Horusatan's sinister kiss. The Spherule of Horusatan assault rifles menacing beams of cancerous death from its celestial thrown above Homogeneigh's surface.

Due to the fact that utopia had been a proverbial dick tease time and time again, the Foreparents decided that becoming ethnically homogenous globally was the only way to achieve it. We'd seen experiments blow ass so badly that the idea of the Purges from a time that predated them started to seem like a grand idea again to many. This wasn't the factions of the Divergent series or the districts of the Hunger Games.

Genesis

This is what we had become...sin-stained caricatures of humanity. Imagine, if you will, droves of heartless narcissists clamoring for the fulfillment of their every whim with no thought of another. It was as though our final speck of innocence had been flicked as unto ash. Something broke and descended into an irreparable state within us all. The streets erupted in riotous pandemonium. On the day that her petite, princess gown clad body washed ashore the coast of Waikiki, The American Academy of Arts and Letters had just announced it would be hosting a toure de force of a gala in honor of her being the youngest person in history to ever receive top honors in literature, film, music, theater and fashion all within a calendar year. The year was 2035 and all anyone could think or speak about was the gruesome rape, torture and murder Aauleahia Aurielle, the Disney darling with eyes of emerald and skin of onyx.

Uncleanliness, orgies, theft, godlessness, perversion, socially acceptable substance abuse...these were the trimmings of our life's feast and we couldn't have been happier to wade in the cesspool of our banality. The universal concept of morality was so far removed from our collective consciousness that exploitation, conning and a host of other expressions of lower self had become our modus operandi. Many of us had taken to lying, scheming and all manner of manipulation to get what we wanted. And I wasn't the only one. I've always found it rather 1+1 to get people to pay your tab at Questo Ristorante Ricco Buffet Straordinario Che Chiamiamo Vita. As such, I was waxing vampiric on the amusements of The High Society Wax museum of Photoshop Fails. My memory of a considerate society was figuratively cracked out. We had become debauchery 2.0. Morally ransacked, we tried to Erector Set our humanity into an esoteric architectural anomaly of sorts. It was though the most abstract figments of our imaginations surfaced to purge.

I had always been the type to moonwalk on the cutting edge, so it only made sense that when the shackles were removed from our collective feet, I began to dance the dance electric. My drug of choice was of the available variety. It was nothing for someone to whip a small baggie of sensory orgasm from out of his or her pocket and indulge as though popping a piece of gum in his or her mouth. The state of relying on or being controlled by someone or something else was seen through our beer-goggled mental decrepitude as passion. Addiction was no longer viewed as an illness or a health issue. Drugs were, as they'd always been, an absolute favorite.

The will to be the worst brought out the finest sadism from within us. People have talked about the competitive spirit so much that it's pretty much like become a fucking cliché. The tidal wave of façade homicide enshrouded us so swiftly that we became its cheerleaders. Hollywood had allowed us to convince ourselves that the stuff of human imagination is a scripted exaggeration of actuality. The Real World foretold a time when people stopped being polite and started being real. Who knew that reality was not only stranger than fiction, but more shockingly far grimmer?

Not that commercials and movies and magazines have really ever reflected what real life resembles, but I find it odd that so many people were lulled into this false sense of connectedness. More surprising than anything was the unfettered acceptance of the rather melodramatic erasures of diversity. Sure there were mass hissy-fits when it became apparent that the number and frequency were accelerating, but all it took was a little razzle-dazzle, slight of tongue shaken, not stirred with media inundation and soon meh was the case that they gave us. No one really made a fuss about the disappearances once they became common. It all began with real-world evidence.

To achieve this utopia, centuries of well-planned and carefully executed subterfuge, subliminal messaging and genocide had been waged against all people bearing the most primitive and universal pigment in living organisms, melanin. Homogeneigh, formerly known as Earth, was now transmogrified and home to a pure race of humans called The Xenophobes. Miscellanies of what the planet used to be only to be found in historical texts kept within catacombs within Homogeneigh's core.

Look Back At It.

Now read it in reverse.

TO BE CONTINUED...BY SOMEONE OTHER THAN THIS AUTHOR...

Chapter 57: <u>More Bloviating Please</u>

Crying and it's not as simple as making eye contact with the pain with which you've been playing Hide & Seek. Having to take an unreasonable amount of piss breaks while circling greatness, these are the phantasms from a purgatory of delusion. They say nobody roots for Goliath, but the people of Gath did. The key is not to talk too much, but when you do make sure that you're impressive and amazing.

<u>22Apr2018 0912AM:</u> Beyoncé may want to consider transforming into blue-Black dark skinned a la Alek Wek if she truly wants to achieve the stratospheric fame Michael Jackson did. I suggest dark skinned to rival his albinism transmogrification.

<u>1129AM:</u> I was slipped a handful of breath mints during a Sunday morning service I visited today. Clearly the coffee I consumed prior to entry was doing me no fellowship favors, but there was a balm at New Zion...a balm donning a synthetic wig.

<u>0258PM:</u> Have you ever sat and watched someone who is missing teeth chew gum? If not, try it. It's both ghastly and comedic.

<u>23Apr2018 0709AM:</u> A sweet sunrise terrorizes sound sleeping, but people tend to romanticize them and ignore the bloodshot.

The Fuck It List: The story about a young man who endeavors to chronicle his fulfillment of every bizarre and colloquial stereotype about Black people before he graduates from high school.

<u>25Apr2018 1217PM:</u> Bitch, go play in high volume traffic where the true value of your life will be made manifest to you in an instant.

<u>0350PM:</u> One Upper: The story of a porn addict who becomes a viral sensation when he films himself talking dirty to the porn participants in adult films.

<u>0359PM:</u> I'm still shook from that lady covertly giving a handful of breath mints to me. I will never be foiled by sweltering coffee breath again!

<u>26Apr2018 0326PM:</u> Lil momma, learn how to maintain your pussy's pH balance without the assistance of a YouTube tutorial and then holla at me.

<u>0059PM:</u> Kanye West fan pages have to be in a tailspin right now.

28Apr2018 1137AM: You look like God forgot the wash the recipe for Parkinson's Disease off his hands before he started designing your face.

0943PM: Nigga go duct tape a pocket pussy between yo legs and play wit it cuz you a whole synthetic vagina.

30Apr2018 1202PM: The schizophrenia on steroids weather we've been experiencing lately is communicating to me that planet earth is sick of our shit and is trying to rid herself of us. I'm driving with both windows down and the wind is so strong that it blew all of the trash from under my seats.

1209PM: The Mona Lisa and Benjamin Franklin share a face. I can't be the only one who has noticed this. Let me google.

1212PM: I'm the ultimate hater when it comes to people complaining, moaning and whining on social media about finding love. Like bitch I hope it continues to hide and seek the fuck outta yo ass.

1231PM: Baby, if your boots start swashbuckling around your thighs like Jack Sparrow's, you're clearly losing your wrestling match with meth, but having the urge to wear thigh high boots during tornado season should've told you that already.

1May2018 1114PM: Seeing Kanye's new Snuffalufagus body makes it clear why Chicago West was brought to us via surrogate.

0436PM: Hey Ms. White Lady, I'm not staring at you because I want to Boonk Gang your purse. I'm staring at you because who the fuck carries a purse while they work out?

2May2018 1151AM: People kill me with that "She's trying so hard" bullshit like effort is a bad thing. Then again y'all love these sloppy, thrown together, manufactured puppets, so I get it.

1202PM: At the Lawton Police Department

Me: I'm here to pick up the dispatch records I faxed a request for on Monday.

Lady: Did you bring a copy of the fax?

Me: Why would I bring a copy of something I faxed to you? Does that not defeat the purpose of faxing?

Lady: Well, I think everybody at DHS knows that we're behind.

Me: Well, clearly I don't as evidenced by me standing here having this fruitless exchange with you right now.

1216PM: Only adults who read at a third grade level will actually believe that Kanye lacks the wherewithal to comprehend the impact that proclaiming his love for someone who has denigrated everyone except White men is having on both his career and reputation. Recognize apathy for what it is and keep pushing. NEXT CASE!!!!

1219PM: You don't have to be perfect to not be offensive and absurd.

3May2018: THE RACHEL DIVIDE: **NIGGAAAAAAAA HAHAHAHAHAHA**...this was my immediate reaction upon laying eyes on the opening shot of Rachel Dolezal in her Netflix documentary. **IF SHE DON'T GET HER GOTDAMN!!!!!** Okay, let me try to be objective. **0517PM:** But let me keep it a whole rectangular Benjamin Franklin, regardless of the depths of her racial delusion, I'd trade her for Kanye West in a heartbeat at this point. I mean at least she's actually been in the fuckin' trenches as opposed to trying to synthesize the trenches in the studio. **0534 PM:** One has to beg the question of whether or not she staged these fucking hate crimes not only for sympathy, but also to feel more connected to the hovering overcast of plight that real Blacks are haunted by at every tick of the clock's second hand. **0538 PM:** Okay, I take it back. Hearing about the detriment her deception caused has forced me to withdraw my suggestion of a trade. We'll just leave that seat at the table vacant. **0550 PM:** Well, fuck! Cut to the next scene and you have someone heralding the tremendous social impact she had prior to the scandal and you begin to question if the harm and help balanced or canceled one another out!!!! **0554 PM:** Dear Rachel, you know your fucking parents are White, so a few great first steps in giving your public image the feisty hoe bath it needs in the wake of this scandal is acknowledging that, apologizing for the deception, then stating either that you are choosing to live as Black because that's how you identify or you feel like a Black woman trapped in a White woman's body because this claiming to be Black in the face of clear evidence to the contrary is not working in your favor. We can't argue with facts nor can we argue with how you feel. **0602 PM:** Okay, you acknowledge that you were biologically born as White during your appearance on THE REAL, so either you started to comprehend or you're savvy than a muthafucka. **0605 PM:** Your voice has the quiver of a victim, but if you're a victim, you're a victim of your own imagination. Sometimes saying "I fucked up" goes a long way to heal wounds. And don't say we spun how you identify into our internal dialogue about race. You failed to say you **IDENTIFY** as Black for years. You claimed to **BE** Black. That's your fuck up. Own that truth completely without minimization and perhaps people's ability to use it against you will spring a leak. **0612 PM:** Pause for a brief shoutout to Dr. Boyce Watkins and Minister Louis Farrakhan for hopping on the pendulum and swinging it in the direction of those who shy away from their

Blackness. Say what you will, as hard to digest as her reasoning why may be, you can't deny that she willingly belly flopped into the raging river of bullshit this country has forced Black people to set sail upon. **0616 PM**: I honestly get both sides of the argument. I'm honestly torn on how closely this relates to transgenderism. How can transgenders declare being transgender to be their identity and her claiming to be a performance? Is that not a double-standard and lowkey bigoted? **0702PM:** I ain't reading no damn book now though, Rachel. Not too fuckin' much now dammit! **0708PM:** So the interest in "Black Culture" stemmed from trying to give the adoptive siblings a sense of identity as juxtaposition to the whitewashed existence into which they had been thrust? Interesting. Now let's see how that transmogrifies into your personal identity crisis. **0711PM:** Correction, they were your excuse aka you hid behind them in order to deflect from your true intentions in a way, but you also saw the need to protect them. This shit is indeed a rollercoaster!!! **0715 PM:** In the field of psychology, cognitive dissonance is the mental discomfort (psychological stress) experienced by a person who simultaneously holds two or more contradictory beliefs, ideas, or values. #CopingMechanism **0717PM:** Not gonna lie. She's talented as fuck. She should've sold those paintings because she definitely does great work. **0720PM:** Ritualistic physical abuse and sexual assault!!!!! The heavens spilled that tea like melodies and manna equally. Or maybe not because the counter was not at all flimsy and unbelievable. **0722PM:** I was fully prepared to ridicule. I did not anticipate being this enthralled. **0752PM:** There are 48 minutes remaining in this documentary and at this point, it is hard for me to not have a soft spot for 'ol Rachel. It's not like she's out here representing the worst stereotypes associated with being Black in America (Cough Cough CARDI B). By all intents and purposes, she endeavored to be a representative of Black excellence: Professor, Artist, Activist, Surrogate Mother. I mean it's not like she's been out here thottin', boppin', and ratchetin' like a Whoalts Vicky from Instagram. **0811PM:** I also get the offense, especially in the sense of White privilege and fraudulence and it not being possible in the reverse, especially because she was only committed to this experience of portraying a Black woman for five years. Stepping into the shoes of a people who have been burdened with dehumanization and second class citizenship based solely on the construct of race because of how you feel is extremely treacherous and dismissive of that experience. She could've simply said "I'm White, but I inherently connect far more with Black culture." I get why people are offended. If race is a social construct then why the fuck would you even identify as any race and not simply say "I'm Rachel"? All that being said, I don't think Rachel endeavored to cause damage, but the road to hell is paved with good intentions. **0825PM:** Her children are seemingly in crisis and I see their anger mounting to the point that it gives the impression of morphing into unhinged resentment. **0829PM:** Could it be that she has dove face first into the backlash that is essentially the byproduct of her own doing simply to level the playing field espoused by her absence of true oppression? The absence of struggle is a cornerstone for the stern and scathing side-eye she's consistently receiving. **0840PM:** The quest for redemption can be a heavy bag. Can't be mad at the anger and dismissive. Black women have been in the thick of this thing in full force. There is no question that Black people govern Blackness. You should've petitioned for an invitation as opposed to trying to bumrush your way in. Yes, you should've asked for our permission. We can't allow you to adorn yourself in a costume that makes you feel connected to our experience. I personally have no anger, but the name change was nothing short of a loogie hurled at our protest against your demand to stake this claim to Blackness. You've painted yourself into a corner because you concede, you admit to perpetrating the fraud of which you've been accused. Rachel...where for art thou Rachel?

Cinco de Mayo 1122AM: So for the past two days, people have literally been in an uproar about what DJ Khaled chooses to not do with his mouth. Um, that nigga is married and I'm pretty sure the lap of luxury his HipHop Tourette's affords his wife trumps him placing his tongue in her lap. I mean it ain't your mouth nor is it your pussy being deprived of a motorboat, so Google a hobby on which to focus. Smh

0632 PM: I'm sorry, but if every time I see a picture or video of your baby and there's a SnapChat filter standing in between us then he/she is either ugly or funny-looking, you know it, and don't want us to know it.

6May2018 0252AM: Let me just say that Childish Gambino dropping "This Is America" in the midst of an onslaught of Kanye West coonery and buffoonery just fortified my decision to quit fuckin' with the latter with unabashed reassurance that I can continue to focus on the former without missing an artistic genius beat. It was like creative slithered inside the womb of clever, knocked it up, and birthed a set of twins called brilliantly breathtaking and poignantly paradigm-shifting. Thank you Mr. Glover for holding up that mirror. You are in an elite class of special and I am truly honored to be alive to witness you create within each of your unprecedented threats. May the melanin be with you. And no I don't give a fuck that you fancy nerdy Asian chicas.

1159AM: If I've learned one thing from the show "Once Upon a Time", it's that good guys never listen to reason when it's the most obvious choice to solve the problem...and they can be fucking annoying almost every second of their existence.

1251 PM: I just vacuumed my garage and while that may sound odd to some, it was far more therapeutic than spilling my guts while balled up in the fetal position on some stranger's loveseat from Ikea while he/she secretly sneaks swigs from a flask hidden from eyes wide shut because writing notes is far more important than truly tapping into my frenzy. Plus, I'm of the sort that finds it hard to feel clean after stepping out of the shower knowing there's a graveyard of dead bugs on the other side of the wall.

1255PM: My armpits smell like day-old McDonald's cheeseburgers.

1005PM: The confidence of men and women who shoplift yarn from arts & crafts stores for makeshift crochet braids is buffering in 2018, but greatness awaits. Just you wait and see.

0716AM: When the orgasm is more of a {pregnant pause} than a soul-stirring, mind-frenzy, out of body fantastic voyage, but you don't trip because these are the breaks...and you only have your hand to blame. #WordOfTheDay

***9May2018*1137AM:** I can do all things through YouTube tutorials which educateth me.

0946AM: She was built like a loogie, but somebody was secretly pummeling that pussy into submission. He was built like a clubbed foot, but somebody was swag surfing his face, so she could steal out of his wallet when he finally fell asleep.

***10May2018*1031AM:** Leaving text messages on read for days because absence makes the heart grow fonder is my love language.

***11May2018*0813AM:** What these keyboard critics fail to realize is that the reason people have such staggering reactions to statements made by celebrities like Kanye West And Sabrina Claudio, for example, than the reactions to certain governmental policies and practices is because it seemingly is far easier to control what music you consume than it is to uproot an entire system of oppression. So we withdraw our support to impress upon and put pressure upon these celebrities, who are undoubtedly in greater positions of influence and power, with the hope that they will catch on and lend an ear to our issues and apply that same pressure within their sphere of peer influence to bring about change. It is easy to tell people who and what they should be focused on, but not everyone has the spirit of David. Not everyone has what it takes to tackle giants. Some people are just better suited at combating snarling and vicious dwarves. Isn't the end goal to bring all enemies of equity to heel?

1017AM: I wish people would stop trying to deprive people of a certain age the right to defend themselves. I don't give a fuck if you're 75, if a muthafucka pushes your buttons in the absolute wrong way and you still have a remnant of pow in your punch, lay that muthafucka the fuck out...just don't lose your balance and shatter a hip. And if you're still quick-witted and a muthafucka tries to say something slick, light that muthafucka up until their soul shrivels. Just because a muthafucka has lived on this earth longer than most, that doesn't mean they don't have time nor does it mean they're immature, bitch!

1037AM: Keeping money on my books is not comparable to my freedom. You don't allow someone you love to suffer the consequences of your mistakes and, conversely, you hold those you love accountable for their mistakes. Those things are what make you a standup person. We have to stop glorifying pure ignorance. The streets have absolutely no one's best interest at heart, so please stop using that as the barometer for being real because you've been bullied by your upbringing into ascribing to a modus operandi that essentially makes you prey to a code that demonizes self-preservation if it at all involves the very system all of us are abused by. The truth is what makes you real. Muthafuckas get on my nerves with this ass backwards code of conduct that continues to trap us in a mentality that takes advantage of those who lack the courage to speak out against it.

1048AM: For years I've been wrestling with a strong desire to become a teacher because I know Black males are underrepresented in classrooms, but I enjoy going out and being drunk amongst the people far too much right now. Add to that, the American Education System is a Comedy of Errors and should be dismantled and restructured from top to bottom.

1058AM: Primary Care Physicians have the audacity to ask their patients to arrive fifteen minutes early only to see them thirty to forty-five minutes after their scheduled appointment. I'm sitting here stewing in copious amounts of suck my dick and office chair discomfort induced rage.

1138AM: Logic is only problematic when you're ignorant, uneducated, and boastful in the midst of both.

1238PM: Life is much too short to spend your time trying to avoid being the victim of your coworker's unintentional bigotry.

0137PM: Mixed race women using the race of the women Black men date/marry as a reason to minimize and attack in the attempt of said Black men to participate in conversations about the Black struggle is laughable.

0251PM: I am not anti-makeup by any stretch of the imagination, but the phrase "pretty on purpose" sounds like the motto of women who require no less than 35 products just to avoid looking like an episode of Botched.

0246PM: I guess women have to start wearing body cameras for people to believe them when they say they've been sexually assaulted #FacePalm

0842AM: Azealia Banks has waged an intellectually fueled war against the machine, which includes the latest casualty of modern day coonery disguised as wokeness, Charlemagne the Fraud, and it's going to take the entire platoon of stans who routinely go to bat for her in the comments of the ShadeRoom to serve as ghostwriters on her behalf in this battle of wits because she could easily get outwitted and outmatched if she gets emotionally charged, in my personal opinion.

0412PM: SPEAKING OF THE MILLI VANILLI EFFECT: Damn, Cardi B needed a ghostwriter to articulate her thoughts regarding a social media beef? Azealia Banks is speaking on an issue pertinent to all Black women with regard to how the industry is trying to typecast them according to one particular set of characteristics by using said characteristics to bolster Cardi B's popularity and success and y'all are trying to use isolated incidents in which she (AZEALIA BANKS) has disparaged individuals to poke holes in the truth of her sentiments. Show me where she has made a mockery of all Black women in the same way that pushing this caricatured bundle of stereotypes assigned to Black women is damaging the perception of all Black women and then you'll have a point. I think we've all said some foul shit about certain members of our race, but that's far from reinforcing negative images about the entirety of our race in the media. She was forthcoming about bleaching her skin to even it out because of dark blotches. She owned her truth, so y'all really can't use that against her. She openly said she supported Trump for the tax break and because Hilary's campaign seemed rooted in pushing forward a White feminist agenda, because her and her husband are responsible for thousands of Black people being incarcerated, because she called Black youth superpredators, and because she lampooned the Black experience by saying shit like she has hot sauce in her bag. She also said she withdrew her support of Trump when it became apparent that he supported a white supremacist aka delusions of grandeur agenda, as well as when he began to disrespect every disenfranchised person in the country. What else y'all got?

0542PM: You've got a body made for bingo and the Wobble at family functions.

0543PM: You're built like you're in pursuit of an unaccredited phlebotomy degree from Platt College and your tuition checks keep bouncing.

0544PM: Go check the expiration date on your lacefront please. It's looking like it needs an embalming fluid deep conditioning.

0548PM: I don't speak the language of niggas who were raised by niggas that had to fight over the remote in their cell block's commons area just to watch old reruns of Sally Jessie Raphael and Jenny Jones.

0952PM: Tammy Rivera claimed only women of color tear one another down publicly. Meanwhile Katy Perry and Taylor Swift have been in a public slander-laced feud since before they started appropriating Black culture and slapping a Mickey Mouse Club filter over it.

Mother's Day 2018: Just happened upon a repost from Cardi B's sister, Hennessy, in which she posts some unflattering pictures of Azealia Banks and a video people will run with as "receipts" against her if they aren't in the know. Context: In the video, Azealia was actually responding to Zayn Malik during a minor beef they had when she accused him of copying a lot of her visuals (they were actually quite similar) and she was calling him slurs to both remind him that he's not viewed as white like the other members of One Direction and to ridicule him for trying to escape his true identity. She wasn't bashing Black people here in the least. Full disclosure, I howled internally at the last pic (denim thong and a booty somewhat in need of moisturizer). Talk about me in prayer format ☺ Post Script: She also disparaged some UK rappers and their HipHop ineptitude for coming to Zayn's defense. Post Post Script: Don't confuse context with justification.

0816AM: A mother's love is like the gentle hand of God caressing your soul into a place of sweet and peaceful surrender. It lightens the load of heavy burdens that this sometimes cruel and wicked world tries to place upon us in order to squash our divine light. It sings lullabies to our sadness when we are hurting and in need of repair. It cradles us with tender, loving kindness and calms our fears. It is selfless and life-affirming. So this day, walk proudly while waving the banner of motherhood because you were chosen not only to be a vessel of life, but also a never-ending gift of pure, unadulterated love that can never be matched. Happy Mother's Day!

0939AM: BLACK REPARATIONS: "Black" - This word stands in opposition of pale and will thusly never receive reparations. Reparations are administered to persons "In Propria Persona" (in his or her own person), "In Full Life", "Natural Persons" (in jurisprudence, a natural person is a person (in legal meaning, i.e., one who has its own legal personality) that is an individual human being, as opposed to a legal person, which may be a private (i.e., business entity or non-governmental organization) or public (i.e., government) organization), etc. belonging to nations, Thereby having a "Nationality". "Blacks" Are considered to be chattel (a personal possession) and back the "National Debt" (the total amount of money that a country's government has borrowed, by various means) (see: Pope Francis' Letter to President Barack Obama, 2012). Such "PERSONS" are rendered "Civilited Mortuus" (Civil death is the loss of all or almost all civil rights by a person due to a conviction for a felony or due to an act by the government of a country that results in the loss of civil rights), i.e. "STRAWMAN" (1 - an intentionally misrepresented proposition that is set up because it is easier to defeat than an opponent's real argument. 2 - a person regarded as having no substance or integrity). Such PERSONS have no rights, only privileges stemming from their "DEAD MAN" status. Pertaining to law, the first issue is that STATUS, Which determines the capacity to inherit any estate including rights and privileges, and BLACKS are bound by the BLACK CHRISTIAN SLAVE CODES OF 1724. "The Christian Black Codes of 1724, were initiated during reconstruction after the Civil war to control blacks after they were emancipated. Passed by Southern States, instead of giving blacks the same rights as white people, the codes limited the blacks freedom severely. They included that blacks had to be in service of a white person, that they could not have congregations together, that they could not speak out, and that they could not have weapons. They also included that blacks could not go out without a white 'supervisor', thus blacks had to take on the religions and holidays and gods of their white superiors. These same black codes were said to have been made null and void with the ratification of the 13th Amendment in 1865, although many southern states adopted "Black Codes" to keep former slaves from voting and imposed other restrictions. The 14th and 15th Amendments were to supposedly had eliminated these codes, but as you read them down below, and study the law of the land in conjunction with Religion and Politics, you'll discover these codes have been modernized in a disguise, and many are still in affect." - by Chekesha Roberts for libertyandjusticeforall.org. These codes were adopted by all CORPORATE MUNICIPALITIES (the legal term for a local governing body, including (but not necessarily limited to) cities, counties, towns, townships, charter townships, villages, and boroughs) in the year 1868 to tax all CORPSES (a dead body, especially of a human being rather than an animal) who are listed as STOCK (the goods or merchandise kept on the premises of a business or warehouse and available for sale or distribution), REAL ESTATE, INCOMPETENT, INCOMPETENT HEIR (being unable or legally unqualified to perform specified acts or to be held legally responsible for such acts), and MINORITY (a person who is considered mentally incompetent to handle his/her own affairs, thereby having nothing to do with the population). Such PERSONS are absolute SUBJECTS (likely or prone to be affected by (a particular condition or occurrence, typically an unwelcome or unpleasant one) and are governed by MARTIAL LAW (military government involving the suspension of ordinary law). Such persons operate under "WARDSHIP TENURES" (care and protection of a ward; the right to the custody of an infant heir of a feudal tenant and of the heir's property; the state of being under a guardian). (INSERT: This is why conviction of police brutality and murder, even with video evidence, is virtually impossible. This also means the descendants of SLAVES are still considered the property of descendants of MASTERS, and absolves the descendants of MASTERS from guilt for crimes against descendants of SLAVES). Such PERSONS operate under "NOM DE GUERRE" (an assumed name under which a person engages in combat or some other activity or enterprise), "WARDS" (dependent, charge, protégé), "PSEUDONYMS" (a fictitious name), "WAR TERMS" (a state or period of armed hostility or active military operations), etc. Such PERSONS are absolutely expendable according to the law, as a result of having no affiliation or loyalty to any nation.

Therefore, such PERSONS will be extended no REPARATIONS (the making of amends for a wrong one has done, by paying money to or otherwise helping those who have been wronged), RESTITUTIONS (the restoration of something lost or stolen to its proper owner), TRIBUTES (an act, statement, or gift that is intended to show gratitude, respect, or admiration), etc. because such PERSONS are not recognized anywhere on EARTH because there is no PEOPLES REPUBLIC OF BLACKNESS, which again means there is no NATIONALITY and therefore no REPARATIONS owed. We must first legally ourselves OURSELVES as either true CITIZENS of America, in that he conceptualization of BLACKNESS has its origin, thereby linking us to the full rights and protections of this land. But considering that breaching treaties seems to be this country's hobby, achieving this goal seems excruciatingly far-fetched. I honestly think we're gonna have to FORCE our kids into law enforcement and governmental entities to redirect this country from within!!! We've gotta have more police, lawyers, judges, and policy makers!!!!(Something I found interesting expanded upon from a comment on Instagram made by **Ison.bey7** on a post of Dr. Boyce Watkins).

1125AM: 2018 will go down in my personal history as the year I finally embraced the poverty of my ankles' girth and started rocking shorts in public confidently and without fear of ridicule. Shout out to personal growth and development. Besides, I haven't heard of ankle implants as of yet and it's hot as fuck. #NARF

0305PM: People are growing more and more dimwitted by the day. If you have a personal issue with someone, you're supposed to cuss that muthafucka down to the cellular in private as opposed to running to social media for the purpose of building an army of likes to reinforce what you've said. Anyone who thinks differently is the person with the lopsided and defective character. Not everyone has aspirations of being banal reality TV fodder. Some can rest on the laurels of their God-given talent or hard-earned skills. Additionally, by now their simply can't be someone in the modernized world (who isn't suffering from dementia or some other decrease in mental capacity) that isn't well-aware of screenshots, so if they hit you with the linguistic Kung Fu Louie, surely they didn't give a fuck about you possibly sharing what they've said within your sphere of influence. I say that to say, curb threatening people with screenshots from arguments in an attempt to assassinate their character. It only adds volume to the depths of your weakness and inability to effectively clapback.

0319PM: If you double over laughing at these Instagram comedy sketches and their blatantly obvious punchlines, then you clearly have the comedic intelligence of a one year old. While I can appreciate their usefulness as it pertains to promoting products, let's not pretend they're comedy gold. Random adventures in people watching captured on film are undoubtedly far superior.

0326PM: I've finally reached the age in which I look like an entirely different species when I open my forward facing camera and am leaning forward over it. It doesn't help that my hair looks like Gene Wilder's in this moment either. I'm scary of it.

0438PM: Skylines and beautiful hallways; half-smiles with dimples as she prays for brighter days. Distress in the crease of her blue dress; fear less for loving, body rolling to The Barclays. PowerPoint for a pivotal payday. Cash crop her pussy, trying to break her from mental slave. New tricks for old dick. She loves it. So slick, her body type they covet. And you can say she's a goddess in human flesh, but I call her golden because the sun she reflects. Respect the bustle. Can't knock the hustle. So sick the struggle. Feeling so muddle. Clapback as the whip from a weave track wraps around her neck like a noose and a knapsack. This can't be life. Pipelines, political pathways. Off top she's spitting verbal venom verbatim. And I'm thinking that she's smarter than your average. She writes scripts in little quips, the madness. Hold on tight. You just might forget about your personal plight when she ignites. Powzers! Love life. Bring her into your midnight. Watch for the heavens as they open and shine bright. This must be life. Don't you know that you are golden?

0633PM: Don't Feed the Trolls: What compels us to engage in fruitless arguments with distant strangers whose sole purpose is to get their jollies simply by agitating the peace we claim to so dearly cherish? We know that their goal is to unsettle us, yet we lack the intestinal fortitude to overlook the bait. He who cares the least maintains control in the situation. So when our appearance or personal lives are attacked, we are already at a grave disadvantage because we inherently want to protect that which we hold dear. A simple block is a most effective silencer, but even in doing so, letting shit slide eats away at us and we sit pondering what we should've said. It's time we starve these prickly catfish the attention for which they whore their integrity daily. For if we continually allow them to nibble at our resolve, the sting of their insults will eventually consume our solace.

0705PM: It still cracks me up when people try to call Black people racist. What power and resources do Black people have to oppress the entirety of another group of people based solely on the color of their skin? That's not to say Black people can't be prejudiced, but considering the amount of shit we have to endure globally, cut us some fucking slack. Y'all created our prejudice by way of y'all's racism and it's now a defense mechanism because bigotry has become a sneaky, self-entitled bitch!

0719PM: With all of this body positivity floating around, all of the aspiring models with scrunch booties and cleft kneecaps have unfettered hope. Look at God.

14May2018 0908AM: One thing I've noticed about a large portion of today's HipHop is that there's no subject or central theme. Now when I ask "what the fuck are y'all talking about", I'm not referring to each line in the song because I have the level of comprehension to understand each bar. I'm asking what the overall point of what you're saying is because half the time it has nothing to do with the title of the song unless you're just repeating the title of the song over and over again...ahem "Gucci Gang". Since art, and I'm using that term very loosely, is supposed to be open for interpretation, I suppose I'll interpret the songs to be the abyss of intelligence and creativity.

0918AM: I feel as though many black parents are eager to kick their children out of the nest because raising them has been an ongoing struggle they themselves have survived by the skin of their teeth. While it would undoubtedly make a lot more sense to allow your child/children to remain in the home until a time in which you see fit for them to leave based upon their preparedness, if you yourself are only in possession of base level survival skills, then how much have you really thought them for them to be prepared to face the world alone? On the flipside of that coin, if, as your children have grown older you have gradually made them more and more responsible for the duties of maintaining a home, then kudos to you. I would also encourage you not to neglect educating them about credit cards, bank accounts, paying bills on time, etc. Anyway, as for me and mine, I'm not releasing him into the world until I feel he is prepared...or until he is so sick of my shit that he makes a consorted effort to get his shit together and figure it out for himself.

1220PM: Stop saying someone stole your significant other like these muthafuckas are being smuggled away by a thief in the night when in all actuality your significant other was presented with an option he/she found to be more appealing than you and willingly abandoned your ass.

0229PM: All it takes is an emoji over the nipple and the fuck parts then suddenly the photo is appropriate. My what watered-down standards you have Instagram.

0234PM: Muffin tops are as American as apple pie, baseball, and racism.

16May2018: The feeling of thoroughly enjoying an H-Town song when suddenly the sound of a meat cleaver on a chalkboard radiating from Shazam's throat bitch slaps your aura into a stupor. Imagine being the identical twin of a phenomenal soul singer and you sound like Kibbles & Bits in a rusty food processor. And poor GI just sounds like he used a rescue inhaler filled with expired curl activator smh!

1103AM: Imagine TI attempting to elucidate his thoughts to Cardi B and her resulting facial expression.

0232PM: I can feel my waking up before my alarm clock trying to aggress my focus in this moment.

0339PM: I like that people have taken to repackaging failure as something from which you can learn and grow because it will help people deal with and grow from the disappointment that rides shotgun with failure.

0920PM: The choice to be happy should not be a battle of wits between one's conscience and one's emotional intelligence. Triggers are often well-lubed, but one's cognitive prowess must remain flexed. Bliss is often a voyage that sails upon ebbing and flowing turbulence.

18May2018 1155PM: Falling in love with representatives is the stuff of failed insight. Only time can unmask the monsters that makeup, lust, and expensive, romantic gestures hide. Be patient with the discernment of your side-eye. Many have mastered the art of smoke and mirrors.

0229PM: Adding me to a group text with persons with whom I haven't personally shared my phone number will get you the blocked treatment.

19May2018 0654PM: Said with all the you got me fucked up of a Black woman when shit ain't adding up, I find it funny that the Royal Family of Colonizers welcomed a biracial woman into their ranks on Malcolm X's birthday. Then again my conspiracy theorist senses have been on high alert. And then again still, I could very well be on some bullshit. It's a tossup.

21May2018 0255PM: I'm on the edge of my seat, chomping at the bit, if you will, waiting to see what a fresh crop of rebels and revolutionaries this millennial class of humans produces looks like.

22May2018 0815AM: Mental illness, thug culture, undocumented immigrants, Hollywood, unarmed teachers, video games, not having enough guns, the liberal media, gun free zones, no school prayer, not enough faith, and Ritalin have all been blamed for America's mass shooting issue, but all roads lead to America's #1 terrorist threat...White straight males who feel a sense of entitlement for this country, have unrestricted access to firearms, are diseased by a lack of emotional regulation (Temper Tantrum Syndrome - the name I'm giving the fictional mental health disorder the media loves to label these deviants with), and hatred born of total ignorance. The hidden cowardice within those who use the 2nd Amendment as armor literally begins to boil when any blame is cast in the direction of guns. The mere thought of being unarmed in a world perceived to besiege Whiteness (keyword: perceived) is a phantom menace. I'm tired of the tactic that swings the pendulum so far into the zone of "they're trying to take our guns". The fear-mongers love to use this tizzy to stir a frenzy.

1151AM: I was thoroughly cleansed and healed when I learned to recognize the difference between the things I enjoy spectating versus the things in which I enjoy participating. Ex. I enjoy spectating glamour, but I also enjoy participating in comfort.

0113PM: Sometimes I drive and daydream about what it would be like to receive over 1 million texts from someone I've only went on one date with and at the end of my daydream, I recline to allow my penis to crawl from its hiding place within its foreskin, which must've been difficult to achieve considering that I am circumcised.

0116PM: Cardi B makes music exclusively for women who need Chapstick for their outer labia...figuratively speaking.

0337PM: PornHub could do for a more pompous section of films that feature an assortment of {garrulous} pussies from varying walks of life, thereby broadening the Vagina Monologues audience all the more. #WordOfTheDay #MerriamWebster

0549PM: "Unpacking" and "problematic" are now being used as intellectual rape in order to mindfuck people into thinking that our social consciousness has expanded vastly when they are essentially just buzzwords.

23May2018 1026AM: To where do the windows lead when the body remains transfixed, but the soul is out tripping the life fantastic?

24May2018 0659AM: If your light lacks the power to drive out darkness, then it's undeniably artificial and unquestionably weak. Those who need to be reminded of this from an outside source have deceptive intentions for the deleterious resplendence imposter they bear.

0752AM: It's so disheartening that some are so deficient of communication skills that they respond to open-ended question with the same oratory range required for a close-ended question. The awkward, deafening, and encapsulating silence that fills the room as your brain struggles to expound is quite literally heartbreaking.

0807AM: Celebrities are probably bothered because muthafuckas are bothersome. Who started the lie that fame and wealth make humans less annoying?

0819AM: I'll lose my shit it I feel as though outside air has touched my food that was cooked indoors, but I'll eat food that was cooked outdoors with no problem.

1016AM: It should come as no surprise to anyone and that hundreds of thousands of non-black women actually view riding a bicycle with a basket on the front as a truly spiritual experience.

1108AM: "Freeman went up to women in the circle and would stand maybe within an inch of their face and just look them up and down and not say anything, and then would move on to the next woman...it was really, really strange...he didn't do it to any of the men.'" Now you know what!!!! Slipping a woman a quaalude and ogling women are vastly different things and I may regret feeling this way in the future, but it's going to take a lot more than a group of women saying being looked at by Morgan Freeman made them uncomfortable was enough to destroy his legacy in my mind. This ain't R. Kelly pissing on adolescents on VHS. Now mind you I'm still in the beginning stages of discovery on this story, but if the #MeToo movement is now inclusive of situations that could be remedied by a simple "FUCK IS YOU LOOKIN AT" then all hope is lost and we all better just evolve to a point in which we can jack off and reproduce asexually. If this is what we're doing, muthafuckas with lazy eyes that tend to drift in order to focus are FUCKED!!!! Seriously, who lets a muthafucka stand within an inch of their face, look them up and down, and doesn't step back? And that's not victim-blaming. I'm just wondering if people's kneejerk reactions are out of order because AIN'R NO WAY you're getting that close to my face and I'm just smiling politely inresponse. This shit sounds fabricated and far-fetched. I need more details than this. #MorganFreeman

1125AM: So allegedly there was some inappropriate comments and attempts at lifting skirts. Unfortunate. I don't like to attack what could be actual victims. I'll shift instead and say don't let this distract you from the fact that we have a man in office serving as Commander in Chief who openly admitted to grabbing women by the pussy. I'll keep an eye on this story though.

0145PM: I legit pretended to be receiving an incoming call just now because two chicks whose weave looked like the hole in my sock when my big toe finally bursts through and who had spaces between their teeth wide enough to house a cigar were trying to flirt with me. I'm scary of it. They looked unbathed.

0211PM: Kanye West reportedly spent $85K on a photo of Whitney Houston's paraphernalia-ridden hotel bathroom to use it for Pusha T's next album cover. Three Things: 1. This is America. 2. Please tell me Good Music won't be looking to recoup this amount because, if memory serves me correctly (and I could be totally wrong), Pusha T has never moved large numbers expeditiously. And please don't take that as a jab because I've always been supportive of his work, but was this a gift? 3. How eerie is it that I came across this story at exactly at 2:11 PM? Post Script: Please don't try to tell me this was an expression of freethinking on Kanye's part.

0450PM: So many people confuse being in support of Black people gaining liberty from systematic oppression with being Pro-Black.

0540PM: So basically the pilgrims came to the "New World" to build a nation dedicated to the worship of Satan.

25May2018 0706AM: To surrender is to cease resistance to an enemy or opponent and submit to their authority. It can be argued that surrender is one of the most basic of white privileges. From mass shootings, to sexual misconduct, to expending a profane, shouting soliloquy upon an officer trying to write a citation, having the choice to comply with justice is not a special right, advantage, or immunity granted or available equally to all citizens, and certainly not all residents, of this country. Surrender is a symptom of impunity. Impunity is a luxury consistently made available to the least melanated of our society. Surrender is sometimes accompanied by a Happy Meal. For many, happily enjoying a meal in public is a criminal offense if you're caught wearing the wrong skin at the wrong time in the wrong place in the presence of the wrong people.

0733AM: I'm fresh out of compassion for complacency. I'm fresh out of shoulders to be leaned on by people who keep throwing themselves on swords and grenades and calling it love. I'm fresh out of patience for the poverty mentality. I'm fresh out of faith for religious fiction. I'm fresh out of fake smiles and synthetic forgiveness for "unintentional" racism. I'm fresh out of excuses for dealing with fair-weather friendship. I'm fresh out of fucks to give. I pawned them for peace. #PhraseOfTheDay #EnglishVocabulary

0815AM: Y'all I forgot. I forgot Morgan Freeman said that he finds the concept of Black History Month to be "ridiculous." I forgot Morgan Freeman said race is an excuse for income inequality. I forgot Morgan Freeman said "How are we going to get rid of racism? Stop talking about it!" I forgot that when he decided to speak on issues concerning the Black community he either disparaged or misspoke only to try to clarify later knowing damn well he's old enough to know that you can't be flippant regarding these issues because actual lives are in the balance. I forgot, but now I remember and have withdrawn my outrage from yesterday because there are no refunds when you sell out your race even if it was a misadventure in "freethinking".

0923AM: So I'm back on this Whitney Houston drug paraphernalia-filled hotel room picture being used as the cover art for Pusha T's "Daytona" because sometimes after things settle in my spirit I'm able to look without the lens of my emotions. This shit is still disrespectful, but drug abuse and its accompanying horrors are disrespectful not only to the body, but to the loved ones who have to watch them slowly dismantle the person. I do doubt that Kanye West would consider a photo of his mother's surgery bandages/gauzes or the room in which she died to be art because it's personal to him. However, I also understand that Whitney's battle with drugs is as much a part of her legacy as her golden singing voice and comedic theatrics are. I'm sure there will be an official statement or a press conference addressing exactly why this image was chosen. I'm hoping so. I'm sure peering behind the glamor to see the demons that haunt those we celebrate will be used as a justification. Kanye West and Pusha T have to live with themselves after this decision. We can choose not to be caught up in the wake. We can also choose not to be swept up by the marketing and abstain from endorsing the music. Life is full of choices.

1051AM: A Theory: Those who lack the skills required to fortify friendships go on a quest to accumulate fans even though they're below average and less than mediocre, so they have to resort to antics in order to garner the attention required to build a fan base.

1056AM: I just said "whew chile, the ghetto" when one of my coworkers exited the bathroom without washing his hands. Thanks Nene Leakes.

1113AM: NIGGAAAAAAAAA!!!! So I just watched a clip from the "Going in Style" junket in which Morgan Freeman is being accused of making sexually explicit comments and CLEARLY he was saying he wishes he was present when Michael Caine mistakenly congratulated a non-pregnant woman on her pregnancy not being there to witness this hoe getting dicked down. Now I'm laughing and haven't returned to my previous state of outrage, for the aforementioned reasons, but this bitch tried it with these dandelion soft ass allegations smmfh. CHLOE MELAS MUST BE STOPPED!!!!! There goes one allegation out the window. Let's see how the other seven pan out.

26May2018 1006PM: Wanting something to do, but not wanting to exert the energy to do something is my spirit animal. I wish I could pursue a doctorate in people watching. I hate when people beg me to participate, but that's honestly probably the only way you'll get me to participate. I feel motivated to no longer have to report to a job. This is a defining moment in my life. Remember this.

27May2018 0724AM: In the latest installment of the Drake Wars, on Infrared Pusha T tries to put dents in The Boy's armor by picking at old ghostwriting scabs with the hope of causing impetigo and sepsis to his reign as HipHop's golden boy, but Duppy Freestyle's sigh alone takes the piss out of the attempt by effectively communicating not only Drake's frustration with having to address the shit again, but also his exasperation with having to put yet another rapper shining the glass ceiling that separates moderate success from superstardom in his place. That's not to say that Pusha T is just some slouch ass rapper or that he can't prove to be a formidable opponent...lyrically, but let's not compare pubs to stadiums.

1010PM: Daydreaming about the day when my tightest pair of house shorts no longer becomes relaxed fit after a few hours. #Gains

1015AM: Is <u>The Clapper</u> generally as enjoyable for others as it is for me right now or have I just accepted a lull in fresh ideas for the moment? Haven't heard a film both called groundbreaking and actually living up to it for a while now.

0151PM: He likes collecting things, specifically documentaries, books, and people. He had more college credits than he knew what to do with, but no degree.

0732PM: THIS JUST IN: Drake is upset and surprisingly he still sounds both one degree away from monotone and melodic at the same damn time.

0741PM: The designer of Balenciaga's "T-shirt shirt" Should be hunted like wild pheasant and brought up on criminal charges. No one is paying $1,290 for what looks like a static cling fuck session between Hanes and Faded Glory.

0748PM: This is the story of a gas station clerk who died in small-town America after losing all of her teeth to years of hard-core drug addiction, burning bridges, pissing on the ashes, then getting herself together enough to earn an hourly wage. She had very little impact on the environment and even less impact on society. She will be remembered by those who frequented her store during her shift only for the amount of time it takes for those customers to become familiar with her replacement. She will be mourned by fellow junkies who saw glimpses of her specialness during the many blazes of glory of which she wholeheartedly fed upon. She never saw the importance of being remembered. The end.

0759PM: This is the story of a man who spent his life collecting awards. His home was a shrine to all that he had accomplished. One day, his mind and body caused him to become less active, so he focused all of his attention on having the best yard in his neighborhood.

28May2018 0419PM: The U.S. Government claims it's not responsible for 1,500 missing unaccompanied and undocumented children. Sounds like a bunch of bullshit to me. My parcel doesn't belong to Fedex, but they better safely deliver my shit since they've assumed responsibility for transporting it. You mean to tell me y'all didn't have the forethought to send the poor kids with a fucking packing slip of some sort?

29May2018 0719AM: Ironing a pair of jeans for work and they smell like everything I left in 2017.

0904AM: So Starbucks had to close all of its stores just to discuss racial bias? If your company isn't in support of that type of behavior, simply fire anyone who exhibits it. This seems like you trained your employees to be racially biased and now you're retraining them to do the opposite. No one expects you to be in control of the personal biases your employees carry with them to work each day. We simply expect you to rid your assemblage of employees if racially biased behavior stands in contrast to your way of doing business. I'm sure closing your stores was intended to be an attempt at regaining the faith of some of the customers you may have lost, but I'm almost certain simply separating people who have acted egregiously based upon skin color from your company would've far more been effective. This just seems as though you're trying to reprogram a well-known racially biased Starbucks culture right before our very eyes. #TheyAreOnToUs #HeadAss

1002AM: This year is almost halfway over and I still don't understand the mentality of people who film or take pictures of themselves crying. First of all, you ugly!!!!! It just seems a bit showy and calculated for likes and comments to put your emotions on display in such a voyeur-beckoning way. Like...muthafucka you really sat up there and posed and held that facial expression long enough to snap a picture when you were supposed to be emotionally distraught? Don't cheapen what you're going through by filming yourself or taking selfies. At least let someone else do it for you if you really have to speak on what you're experiencing in the moment that you are supposed to be falling apart.

1125AM: President Emmanuel Macro and Mamoudou Gassama shook the whole damn table that is America's growing nasty attitude toward immigrants and they're way across the pond in France.

0146 PM: I would rather you rock a Caesar fade like Diddy than to rock a perm that looks like a distressed bathmat, weave that looks like swamp moss, or neglected natural hair that looks like the Ghost of Christmas Past's ass crack follicles.

0246PM: SMMFH at the growing number of men who truly believe that the excuses a male-dominated society has come up with to justify rape culture, mishandling women, immaturity well into adulthood, misplaced priorities, leaving children fatherless, and a host of other unforgivable crimes against humanity are remotely acceptable. It's sad, horrible, and sickening.

0250PM: Friends don't let friends dress in summer clothing that will leave their pussy smelling like spam marinated in Worcestershire sauce and front lawn.

0552 PM: As a rule, if you act funny toward me even once and I haven't done anything to you, you're officially cancelled and erased from memory in perpetuity. Don't take your anger toward someone else out on me. I don't play like that.

0848 PM: On this installment of The Drake Wars, the gossip outshines the bars. Pusha T fires back with "The Story of Adidon". I'll be objective. Far better comeback than Meek Mill and exactly the level of clapback I expected from King Push. These jabs below the belt were the equivalent of microwaved lemon juice on paper cuts. Alerting the world to the fact that Drake has a secret child by a porn star is both a pro and a con in this battle. It's a pro because I'm sure it's got Drake verklempt as fuck. It's also a con, however, because if he was indeed trying to give that child the chance at a normal life, Push royally fucked that up. I'm still of the mind that kids should be off limits, but it's out there, so all Drake can do is curb his anger and retaliate in kind. There are no rules to pettiness...even as it pertains to HipHop beefs. Aside from that, the majority of the diss was more about Drake's parents than Drake. Sure Push wove some misadventures in identity crisis in there, but there was undoubtedly an imbalance in the shots fired directly at Drake. The Black face photo was undoubtedly a smear of icing on a solid assault! However, I have to give a point deduction for taking 96 hours or so when Drake responded within the same day.

30May2018 0753AM: Roseanne Barr is just the latest casualty resulting from Donald Trump's White House causing certain White people to speak with the impulsivity of a 14-year-old grappling with puberty. Bitch, you knew your "joke" was both bigoted and xenophobic before you pressed send, so kindly take that weak-ass apology and stuff it in your droopy meat wallet.

0812AM: As if he hadn't already failed his political aptitude test by appointing Dr. Ben Carson to serve as the United States Secretary of Housing and Urban Development, Donald Trump is meeting with Kim Kardashian to discuss prison reform of all things. Correct me if I'm wrong, but I don't think being held hostage and robbed qualifies you as intelligentsia on this matter. That's like comparing a mammogram to breast augmentation. I hope the opening line to this conversation is "I don't have any panties on".

1152AM: If Tinashe's little Brother had defended her album the way he's defending her character as it relates to Ben Simmons dumping her for doing "Kardashian shit" then perhaps she would be getting checks instead of store credit. Nonetheless, kudos to him for coming to her defenses and making rational statements about fidelity, maturity, and the disrespect women suffer at the hands of men who treat them as though they're disposable.

0455PM: I look at Black people doing Black face no differently than many of you view the N word. We've earned the exclusive rights to it.

31May2018 0528AM: In this installment of The Drake Wars, after the people demanded an explanation for the Black face photos, Drake explains that the photos were taken as a part of a project intended to highlight how young Black actors were struggling to get roles, were being stereotyped & typecast; how Black actors have continually been misrepresented in the entertainment industry; and how not much had changed since the time when White people dressed in Black face to mock Black people and reinforce stereotypes. The same people who demand an explanation then said because he's explaining, he's shook and losing the rap battle. I laughed.

0828AM: Dear Kanye West, When you have Bobby Fucking Brown out here commenting on the deterioration of your mental health, it's time to investigate all that free thinking for hidden fees. And for using that picture of Whitney's bathroom for Pusha T's cover art, I hope he succeeds in slapping you so hard your jawline is as cockeyed as his is.

0128 PM: Dear King of Kings and Lord of Lords, why does it only look like Snoop's shoulders are bulking?

0144PM: Aoki Simmons is always trolling her big sister Ming. She's gonna be sick when Ming finally says "You're just mad that I look like Mom and you look like Dad."

0711PM: In the latest installment of The Drake Wars, this man Pusha T is out crip-walking victory laps on the interview circuit while the clock is ticking for Drake's response. Drake has spent the last few days addressing Black Face side-eyes made in "The Story of Adidon", but fuck all these social media press releases. That should've been handled with bars, so either the boy is having to dig deep in the trenches to find some scatching information on his nemesis of the moment or that diss track really did unsettle his spirit. I hate when I know exactly what a celebrity needs to say to win an argument, but don't have access to them. I guess I'll keep it to myself.

0753PM: NIGGA!!! If this isn't a THIS IS AMERICA moment, I don't know what is. So a bunch of slack jaw jurors in Florida awarded the family of Gregory Hill, Jr. FOUR FUCKING DOLLARS for funeral expense and pain & suffering in a lawsuit filed by his mother for wrongful death, negligence and excessive force. Deputy Christopher Newman, responding to a simple NOISE COMPLAINT, thought firing four shots at Hill, who briefly opened and closed his garage, was the appropriate response. Ain't that about a bitch? Apparently Hill's family is heartbroken, which I interpret to mean pissed the fuck off to the highest level of pisstivity. I wouldn't be able to rest until some semblance of true JUSTICE was awarded. Every last one of those raisin stuffed Cornish hen built bitch ass jurors should be brought up on charges. What kind of outhouse education did those muthafuckas receive that caused them to believe Hill was responsible for his own death? That question was rhetorical, but we all know they received a master class in systematic racism...probably the Cliff's Notes by way of PowerPoint, but still. I swear these muthafuckas are trying to summon the spirit of vigilantism, so they can declare Marshall Law. But Jerry Blank warned us when she said "Florida. Beautiful weather — harsh penal system."

The End, the Ender, the Endest: Kill Your Darlings

1 May2018: "Free thinking" is the buzz phrase floating through the air at present as people either attack or defend Kanye West for his seemingly unhinged, off-kilter, White Supremacy sympathizing ways. I watched the interview with Charlamagne with the hopes that sense would be made of statements that caused me to fall out of love with not the man, obviously, but the ideal I thought he represented #BlackPower. The pendulum has swung in a direction that presents itself as a mockery. Love is many things, but let's not feign tearing down walls when in reality we are simply erecting excuses. It is hard for me, someone who has been on a journey of free thought for quite some time, to fathom that this is not a ploy. Soft tones and eye contact do not sincerity make. Were that the case, you would've simply dropped the album or whatever other artistic endeavor upon which you were working on ahead of all the cryptic tweets. I am immortalizing you in this book because you were important to me. Not that I was ever a fan. Fans are purchasers of merchandise who foam at the mouth and abstain from washing hands that were touched by their idols. I was a supporter. I was a member of your tribe....or so I thought. But I will say this, I am no longer disappointed. I am no longer bothered. I have released you into the abyss of whatever stasis you feel necessary to exist within to feel complete and authentic. There are lines drawn in the sand by centuries upon centuries of oppression that you simply can't excuse away because you fancy yourself the greatest of all time. Do I sicken at the sight of ongoing representation in the media and entertainment industry of Black people as slaves and subservient to White culture? You bet. However, to equate being able to link the oppressiveness of the past to its transmogrified present shape is not existing within a state of victimhood. And cozying up to the reigning poster child for a White supremacist ideology does not make you enlightened. It softens the strength upon which you've rested your platform. To err is definitely human and perhaps I would be able to ingest your theories on the current seat-holder in Chief had you given your criticism of the toxin he has become to the sanctity of peace whereas race relations are concerned a head start, but instead you elected to dive head first into chumminess while adorning yourself with a modern day cross burning in the front yard...that

fucking Make America Great Again hat. 2May2018 1007AM: Apathy set in and I am no longer interested. You've now been added to the list of folks I can no longer support because of their egregious character (ahem, R. Kelly), so bye. Post Script: Don't any of y'all try to go adding names to my list. I said no longer support, so anyone y'all add never had my support. FIN!

POST SCRIPT: Please excuse any typos you discover. Hell, let me know personally if you stumble upon one and I'll let you know if it was intentional. I was going to do another round of editing, but I became too anxious to get this work out to the public. As such, I decided against it and am sending this bitch to print!!!!!! #NARF

Triston for Dummies

Tris Ton

Dushane Jackson

Revol Wright Dushane

Thgirw Notsirt

Triston Wright

Made in the USA
Columbia, SC
11 June 2020